A Basic Course in Anthropological Linguistics

A Basic Course in Anthropological Linguistics

Volume 2 in the series
Studies in Linguistic and Cultural Anthropology

**Series Editor:
Marcel Danesi, University of Toronto**

Canadian Scholars' Press Inc.
Toronto

A Basic Course in Anthropological Linguistics
by Marcel Danesi

First published in 2004 by
Canadian Scholars' Press Inc.
180 Bloor Street West, Suite 801
Toronto, Ontario
M5S 2V6

www.cspi.org

CSPI gratefully acknowledges financial support for our publishing activities from the Government of Canada through the Book Publishing Industry Development Program.

National Library of Canada Cataloguing in Publication

Danesi, Marcel, 1946-
      A basic course in anthropological linguistics / Marcel Danesi.

(Studies in cultural and linguistic anthropology)
Includes bibliographical references and index.
ISBN 1-55130-252-7

      1. Anthropological linguistics. I. Title. II. Series.

P35.D35 2004   306.44'089   C2003-907009-3

Cover design by Hothouse Canada
Page design and layout by Brad Horning

04   05   06   07   08   5   4   3   2   1

Printed and bound in Canada by AGMV Marquis Imprimeur Inc.

Canada

Table of Contents

Preface

Language is a truly fascinating and enigmatic phenomenon. The scientific discipline that aims to study it, in all its dimensions, is known as *linguistics*. The particular approach that studies the relation between language, thought, and culture is known as *anthropological linguistics* (AL). Introducing the basics of AL is the subject matter of this textbook. Known variously as *ethnolinguistics, cultural linguistics,* or *linguistic anthropology*, AL is a branch of both anthropology and linguistics. Traditionally, anthropological linguists have aimed to document and study the languages of indigenous cultures, especially North American ones. Today, however, the purview of AL has been extended considerably to encompass the study of language as a general cognitive and cultural phenomenon, and to determine genealogical relations among languages, so as to recreate ancient cultures through them.

As an instructor of courses in anthropological linguistics at the University of Toronto, I have prepared and used my own handouts and materials, tailoring them to meet the needs of students. This textbook constitutes a reworking of those materials into a systematic introduction to the field of AL. I sincerely hope that it will pique the interests of students everywhere to investigate the language-thought-culture nexus on their own. I must warn the users of this book, however, that the topics chosen for presentation, and the ways in which I have treated them, reflects my own views both of the field, and especially of what is of general interest in an introductory format.

There are eight chapters in this book. The first deals with the basic notions, concepts, and techniques of linguistics. The second chapter looks at the origin and evolution of language, focusing on the comparison and reconstruction of language families. The third, fourth, fifth, and sixth chapters look respectively at sound, word-formation, syntactic, and semantic systems from the point of view of linguistic analysis. These chapters introduce the student to what must be known about language, its structure, and its semantics in order to apply it to the study of thought and culture. The final two chapters look at the relation between language, thought, and culture directly, thus bringing the technical apparatus developed in earlier chapters to bear on the central objective of AL. I have also appended a section for activities and topics for study, so as to make the textbook even more pedagogically useful. A glossary of technical terms and a list of cited works and bibliography for general consultation complete the book.

I wish to thank my colleagues in the Department of Anthropology of the University of Toronto for having allowed me the privilege of teaching and coordinating the linguistics component of the department. I am particularly grateful to Sylvia Beilin, Annette Chan, Della Saunders, and Kay Chuckman for all the help they have given me in pedagogical matters. Another debt of gratitude goes to the many students I have taught. Their enthusiasm has made my job as teacher simply wonderful. They are the impetus for this book.

Marcel Danesi
University of Toronto, 2004

Linguistic Method

Without words to objectify and categorize our sensations and place them in relation to one another, we cannot evolve a tradition of what is real in the world.

Ruth Hubbard (1924–)

PRELIMINARY REMARKS

Perhaps no other faculty distinguishes humanity from all other species as language does. The reason for this is because humans use language to encode knowledge and to pass it on to subsequent generations. It is no exaggeration to say that the very survival of civilization depends on the preservation of words. If somehow all memory of language were to be irretrievably lost overnight, the next morning people the world over would have to start anew, literally rebuilding knowledge with new words. In a phrase, language constitutes the overarching memory system of the human species.

There is a deeply rooted feeling within us that if we were ever able to solve the enigma of how language originated in our species, we would then possess a vital clue to the mystery of human existence itself. The Bible starts off with the phrase "In the beginning was the *Word*," acknowledging the close connection that exists between the birth of language and the origin of sentient, sapient life. The ancient Greek philosophers defined it as *logos*, the faculty that, they claimed, had transformed the human animal from an insentient brute into a rational creature. But they also saw language as a dangerous faculty. Their ambivalence towards language continues to this day—language is viewed by people commonly both as a means of gaining and preserving knowledge, and as a barrier bringing about innumerable conflicts between individuals and nations.

Jones

19c

Throughout history people have sought to unravel the riddle of language. The impetus for establishing a "science of language," however, can be traced to 1786. That was the year in which the respected and highly influential English scholar Sir William Jones (1746–1794) suggested that Sanskrit, Persian, Greek, and Latin sprang from the same linguistic source and, thus, belonged to the same "language family." Shortly thereafter, the systematic study of language families started in earnest, leading in the subsequent nineteenth century to the emergence of *linguistics* as a true science. Interest in studying language as a force shaping cultural life also started at about the same time within the emerging science of *anthropology*. Some of this interest was transferred to linguistics as well. However, by the 1930s, the study of the language-culture interface was largely dropped from the agenda of linguistic science, surfacing as a separate enterprise, and becoming a branch of both linguistics and anthropology, by the early 1950s.

The descriptive and theoretical tools used by anthropological linguists are no different from those developed within linguistic science itself. The purpose of this chapter, therefore, is to discuss and illustrate practically what this science is all about.

THE SCIENTIFIC APPROACH TO LANGUAGE

5cBC
Panini

Thrax
170-90BC
Greek

Grimm
Rask
Hp/ H/

The first attempt in history to describe a language scientifically can actually be traced to the fifth century BC, when the Indian scholar Panini compiled a grammar of the Sanskrit language of India. His sophisticated analysis is the first ever to show how words are structures (forms, units) constructed from smaller structures or units. For several centuries after, virtually nothing was written on language that survives, until the Greek scholar Dionysius Thrax, who lived between 170 and 90 BC, wrote a comprehensive grammar of Greek that has remained a basic model to this day, showing how the parts of speech relate to each other in the formation of sentences.

In the sixteenth and seventeenth centuries, the first surveys of the then-known languages were attempted, in order to determine which grammatical facts were universal and which were specific to different languages. In the eighteenth century the surveys became increasingly more precise culminating, as mentioned, in Sir William Jones's assertion that Sanskrit, Greek, and Latin developed from a common source. Shortly thereafter, the German philologist Jacob Grimm (1785–1863) and the Danish philologist Rasmus Christian Rask (1787–1832) started comparing languages systematically, noticing that in some languages the sounds in related words corresponded in regular ways. For example, they found that the initial /p/ sound of Latin PATER ("father") and PEDEM ("foot") corresponded regularly to the initial /f/ sound in the English cognates *father* and *foot*. They concluded that there must be a phylogenetic link between Latin and English. The method of making such linkages came to be called *comparative grammar*—a term coined initially in 1808 by the German scholar Friedrich Schlegel (1772–1829).

The study of sound correspondences between languages such as Latin, Greek, and Sanskrit led the early comparative grammarians to conclude that these languages must have all descended from the same undocumented language, which they called Proto-Indo-European (PIE). The prefix *proto-* was introduced to indicate a hypothetical language that had left no documentation, but which could be reconstructed by the method of comparison. The notion of *protolanguage* thus made it possible to explain the regular differences in sound between certain languages. The /p/-/f/ difference noted by Grimm and Rask above, for instance, was explained as a sound shift in English, whereby the PIE consonant /p/ developed to /f/, or /p/ > /f/ for short (> = "develops to"). It was logical to assume that the Latin /p/ was the original PIE consonant, given that Latin was older than English and thus closer in time to PIE. Likewise, the English word *thaw*, which begins with *th* (= /q/), probably developed from PIE /t/ (/t/ > /q/), since /t/ is found in Greek and Latin versions of the same word—*tekein* and *tabes*.

By the latter part of the nineteenth century extensive research had been conducted on PIE. Differences among the languages descended from PIE were explained as sound shifts of various kinds. In this way, the early comparative grammarians were able to construct the first-ever model of the Indo-European language family, dividing the languages into main branches (the languages closer in time to PIE) and lower branches (the modern day descendants of, for example, Celtic, Germanic, and Latin). The family is charted below:

			Indo-European					
Albanian	Armenian	Balto-Slavic	Celtic	Germanic	Greek	Indo-Iranian		Romance
		Baltic Slavic	Breton	Dutch		Indo-Arayan Iranian	French
			Irish (Gaelic)	English			Italian
		Latvian Belarusian	Scots (Gaelic)	German		Bengali Pashto	Portuguese
		Lithuanian Bulgarian	Welsh	Scandinavian		Gujarati Persian	Romanian
		Czech				Hindi	Spanish
		Macedonian		Danish		Marathi	
		Polish		Faeroese		Urdú	
		Russian		Icelandic		others	
		Serbo-Croatian		Norwegian			
		Slovenian		Swedish			
		Ukranian					

From the research, a movement emerged, based mainly in Germany, called the *neogrammarian school*, which formally introduced the notion of "sound law." The /p/ > /f/ and /t/ > /q/ shifts in English are examples of sound laws. To explain exceptions to these laws, the neogrammarians introduced the notion of *borrowing* (which will be discussed in more detail in chapter 7). For example, according to one sound law, Latin initial /d/ should correspond to English /t/, as it does in DENTALIS vs. *tooth*. The English word *dental*, however, has a /d/ sound instead. The conclusion drawn by the neogrammarians was that English borrowed it directly from Latin without modifying the pronunciation of the initial /d/; whereas *tooth* (which has the expected /t/) was a native English adaptation of the PIE word, showing the /d/ > /t/ sound law.

The work on sound laws made it obvious that a true science of language was crystallizing. Towards the end of the century, the Swiss philologist Ferdinand de Saussure (1857–1913) put the finishing touches on the blueprint for the new science by making a distinction between the comparative study of sounds, which he called *diachronic*, and the systematic study of a language at a specific point in time, which he called *synchronic*. He also proposed that the new science should focus on *langue* ("language"), the system of rules that members of a speech community recognize as their "language," rather than on *parole* ("word"), or the ability to use the rules in conversations, writing, etc. Saussure used an analogy to a chess game to illustrate the difference between the two. Only people who know the rules of the game can play chess. This constitutes knowledge of chess *langue*, which is independent from such variables as the size of the board, the substance the pieces are made of, and so on. The actual use of this knowledge to play a specific game of chess is *parole*. This involves knowing, essentially, how to apply the rules in response to certain moves of the opponent. The goal of *linguistique* ("linguistics"), as he called it, was to understand the nature of *langue*.

Basic to Saussure's plan for the study of *langue* was the notion of *différence* ("difference, opposition"). This is the view that the structures of a language do not take on meaning and function in isolation, but in relation to each other. For example, the linguist can determine the meaning and grammatical function of the word *cat* in English by opposing it to the word *rat*. This opposition will show, among other things, that the initial consonants /k/ and /r/ are important in English for establishing the meaning of both words. From such oppositions we can see, one or two features at a time, what makes the word *cat* unique in English, allowing us to pinpoint what *cat* means by virtue of how it is different from other structures.

Saussure's approach came to be known, logically, as *structuralism*. In America, it was adopted in the early twentieth century by the anthropologist Franz Boas (1858–1942), and a little later by his student Edward Sapir (1884–1939). However, unlike Saussure, Boas did not see the goal of linguistics as a study of *langue* in itself, but rather as the description of how *langue* reflected the cultural emphases of the speech community that used it. Linguists would thus have to explain why, for example, in the Indonesian language the social status of the person addressed is mirrored directly in the vocabulary used; and why in the language spoken by the Nuer, a herding people of eastern Africa, there are so many words for the colors and markings of cattle. In both cases, the structure of the two languages reflects, respectively, the cultural importance of social rank and livestock. In English, on the other hand, there are very few words for describing livestock, but many for describing music (*classical*, *jazz*, *folk*, *rock*, etc.), revealing the importance of music in our daily lives. The study of the relation between language and society is such an obvious one, Boas claimed, that it requires little or no justification.

By the early 1930s, as American structuralists applied and expanded upon the basic Saussurean paradigm, it became obvious that a standard repertoire of notions and techniques was required. This was provided by Leonard Bloomfield (1887–1949) in his 1933 textbook titled *Language*. For two decades after, linguists went about the painstaking work of documenting the structures of different languages and of relating them to different cultural emphases, using a basic Bloomfieldian manual of techniques. The first major break from this tradition came in 1957, when the American linguist Noam Chomsky (1928–) argued that an understanding of language as a universal faculty could never be developed from a piecemeal analysis of the disparate sounds, word forms, etc., of widely divergent languages. Chomsky argued that a true theory of language would have to explain why all languages seem to reveal a similar plan for constructing their sentences. He proposed to do exactly that by shifting the focus in linguistics away from making inventories of isolated facts of language to a study of the "rule-making principles" that went into the construction of sentence types. The basis of Chomsky's approach can be seen in the analysis he put forward of the following two sentences:

(1) John is eager to please
(2) John is easy to please

Both these sentences, Chomsky observed, would seem to be built from the same structural plan on the "surface," each consisting of a proper noun followed by a copula verb and predicate complement:

Structural Plan	Proper Noun	Copula Verb	Predicate	Complement
	↓	↓	↓	↓
Sentence (1)	John	is	eager	to please
Sentence (2)	John	is	easy	to please

Deep v
Surface

However, despite the same structural plan, they mean very different things: the meaning of (1) can be paraphrased as "John is eager to please someone" and of (2) as "It is easy for someone to please John." Chomsky thus concluded that the two sentences had been put together with different "deep structure" rules, and had become merged into one surface structure form as the result of the operation of a transformational rule. Chomsky then suggested something truly radical for linguistics. He claimed that as linguists studied the nature of the deep structure rules of different languages they would eventually come to the conclusion that the rules could be conflated into one universal set of rule-making principles. Chomsky's proposal became immediately attractive for obvious reasons. Above all else, it gave substance to the age-old belief in Western philosophy that the rules of grammar corresponded to universal logical forms. Moreover, it was a very simple and understandable proposal for linguists to pursue. However, since the late 1960s, various schools of linguistics have come forward to challenge the Chomskyan paradigm. It has been pointed out, for instance, that abstract syntactic rule-making principles do not explain the

argument
refuting
deepst

semantic richness of languages, refuting the basic notion of deep structure. Some of the alternatives to studying language universals will be discussed in due course. Suffice it to say for the present purposes that contemporary linguistic theory and methodology have become more eclectic and less partisan

eclectic
partisan

to one school of thought or the other than they ever were at any time in recent history.

Today linguistics is divided into *theoretical* or *applied* subfields. The former is concerned with building language models or theories to describe languages and to explain the similarities of language structures; the latter is concerned

✳

with applying the findings of linguistic research to language teaching, dictionary preparation, speech therapy, computerized machine translation, and automatic speech recognition. There are now also a number of branches that are concerned

Cognate

with the relations between language and the subject matter of cognate academic disciplines, such as *sociolinguistics* (sociology and language), *psycholinguistics* (psychology and language), and *neurolinguistics* (neuropsychology and language). Anthropological linguistics, too, is now considered a branch, rather than a separate approach to language. Recently, a new branch has emerged based on the use of the computer and of artificial intelligence notions. Known as *computational linguistics* it focuses on the design and analysis of natural language processing systems, comparing and contrasting the structure of computer programs to that of "linguistic programs" (phonological, morphological, etc.).

But in all approaches, versions, fields, and subfields there are certain notions and techniques that have withstood the test of time and that now constitute a standard repertoire of procedures for the scientific study of all languages. These include describing a language's sounds (*phonetics* and *phonology*), words (*morphology*), relations among words in a sentence (*syntax*), meaning patterns *syntax* (*semantics*), and variation according to the contexts in which a language is used or applied (*pragmatics*). Each of these will be discussed separately in subsequent chapters.

ANTHROPOLOGICAL LINGUISTICS

The goal of anthropological linguistics (AL) is to study languages by gathering data directly from native speakers. Known as *ethnography* or *participant* vocab *observation*, the central idea behind this approach is that the linguist can get a better understanding of a language and its relation to the overall culture by witnessing the language used in its natural social context.

Chomsky allowed linguists to break from this ethnographic tradition by claiming that the task of the linguist was to describe the "ideal knowledge" of a language, which he called *linguistic competence*. And this, he suggested, was known only to the native speakers of a language and, thus, could never be distilled from the data collected by a non-native observer. So, ideally, linguists native themselves should be native speakers of the languages they aim to investigate, since they can analyze their own intuitions better than anyone else can. Given the importance that Chomskyan linguistics, known as *generative grammar*, gen. grammar had attained in the 1960s and most of the 1970s, many mainstream linguists psr abandoned the ethnographic method. By the 1980s, however, the utility of the method was reestablished by a surge of interest in investigating how language varies according to social situation. Ironically, this revival of interest in AL may have been brought about by the fact that generative grammar research had produced an overload of theorizing, making it virtually useless as a research enterprise in search of a universal set of rule-making principles. Chomsky had forgotten that in every linguist there is a theory!

The ethnographic approach in AL, moreover, was hardly devoid of theorizing. Boas, for example, collected volumes of data on the Kwakiutl, a native society on the northwestern coast of North America, from which he was able to glean overarching principles of grammatical design. Boas showed, in effect, how many of the forms of Kwakiutl and other indigenous languages were reflexes of broader tendencies within the language faculty of humanity for making sense of the world. Boas thus provided a paradigm for investigating both language as a faculty of mind and as a strategy for social living. To this day, anthropological linguistic research remains a comparative and cross-cultural science. It studies the languages of various groups of people in order to determine both their similarities and their differences.

LANGUAGE

Defining language is an impossible task. The best way to formulate a working definition is to consider the origin of the word itself, which comes from the Latin *lingua*, meaning "tongue." As this etymology suggests, language can be defined as the use of the tongue to create meaning-bearing *signs*. A sign is anything that stands for something other than itself. When we use or hear the word *red*, we do not think of the sounds *r-e-d* that comprise it, but rather of a certain kind of color to which these sounds refer in tandem. In other words, we perceive the sound combination *r-e-d* as a single sign—the word *red*. Language can thus be defined more precisely as a mental code whose signs are constructed "with the tongue."

Wherever there are humans, there is language. Languages enable people across the world to classify the things that are relevant and meaningful to them. Without language, there would be no science, religion, commerce, government, literature, philosophy, nor any of the other systems and institutions that characterize human life. There are about 6,000 languages spoken in the world today. This number does not include dialects (local forms of a language). Many languages, however, are spoken only by small groups of a few hundred or a few thousand people. There are barely more than 200 languages with a million or more speakers. Of these, 23 have about 50 million or more speakers each: Arabic, Bengali, Cantonese, English, French, German, Hindi, Italian, Japanese, Javanese, Korean, Malay-Indonesian, Mandarin, Marathi, Portuguese, Punjabi, Russian, Spanish, Tamil, Telugu, Turkish, Vietnamese, and Wu.

All languages have certain things in common. They all have: (1) a system of recognizable sounds, (2) units known as words, (3) grammatical structure, and (4) strategies for using language in various personal and social ways. A sound system constitutes a group of sounds that speakers of a particular language utilize to make up words. Most languages have from 20 to 60 of these sounds. Words are sound units (individual sounds or combinations of sounds) that have a meaning, standing for objects, actions, or ideas. Grammatical structure is the manner in which words are related to each other in forming larger, structural units such as sentences. The strategies for using a language for various purposes, such as communication and representation, are the result of traditions that are deemed important by a speech community.

Before proceeding further, it is obviously essential to differentiate between *language* and *speech*. Language is a mental code, consisting of certain types of signs and of the structural principles for making and using them. Speech, on the other hand, is the use of language to form and transmit messages. Speech can be vocal, involving the use of the vocal organs (tongue, teeth, lungs, etc.), or nonvocal, as in writing or in gesturing. One can have language without speech, but one cannot have speech without language because it is dependent on the categories of the language code. Remarkably, no effort is required to acquire such a powerful sign system. Children quickly gain command of a language simply by being in regular contact with fluent speakers of that language. They listen to older people, gradually mastering the sounds used in the language and associating words with objects, ideas, and actions. In short time, they start making up sentences that other speakers accept as correct, and using them as strategies for regulating interactions with others. By the age of five or six, children control the main structures of their native language, becoming able to communicate most of their needs, desires, and ideas "with the tongue."

Incidentally, the relation between language and speech is not a casual one. Vocal speech is made possible by the lowering of the larynx (the muscle and cartilage at the upper end of the throat containing the vocal cords)—a phenomenon that is unique to the human species. During their first months of life, infants breathe, swallow, and vocalize in ways that are physiologically similar to gorillas and chimpanzees, because they are born with the larynx high in the neck (as are the other primates). Some time around the third month of life, however, the human larynx starts to descend, gradually altering how the child will use the throat, the mouth, and the tongue from then on. The new low position means that the respiratory and digestive tracts will cross above the larynx. This entails a few risks: food can easily lodge in the entrance of the larynx; drinking and breathing simultaneously can lead to choking. In compensation, the lowered larynx permits vocal speech by producing a chamber above the vocal folds that can modify sound. And this, in turn, prepares the child for the acquisition of language as a vocal system of signs.

LINGUISTIC ANALYSIS

Each language is an equal among equals. All languages, no matter what sounds they possess, are constructed on the basis of similar kinds of principles. The science of linguistics aims to study these principles in a systematic fashion. To grasp what this implies, it is instructive to introduce errors into some specific subsystem of a language on purpose. This allows one to focus on "what has gone wrong," fleshing out what structural principle has been breached and, thus, to consciously grasp that principle on its own.

Take, for example, the following English sentence into which an error has been introduced.

(1) Johnny is a pboy who loves pizza

A native speaker of English, or indeed anyone who has studied the language even at an elementary level, can instantly point to the word *pboy* as being decidedly "un-English." The other words, and the sentence itself, are otherwise "well-formed." Now, the question becomes: Why is the word *pboy* un-English? What specific principle of English structure does it violate? Taken separately, each sound in *pboy* is a legitimate one in English:

- the initial *p* is found in words such as *pat, pill, pull*, etc.
- the *b* is found in words such as *ball, bend, bill*, etc.
- the *o* is found in words such as *open, on, over*, etc.
- the *y* is found in words such as *say, bay, pay,* etc.

The violated principle is not to be located in the nature of any one of the sounds in *pboy*, but rather in a specific combination of sounds, namely in the combination /pb/, which violates consonant cluster structure at the beginning of words. To put it more simply, no English words exist, or can exist, with the cluster /pb/ at the beginning.

The study of sounds and how they are structured falls under the rubric of *phonology*. Phonology consists of two main analytical tasks—*phonetic* and *phonemic*. The former is the description of the ways in which the vocal organs can modify the airstream in the mouth, nose, and throat in order to produce sounds; the latter is the identification of the minimal units of sound capable of distinguishing meaning in a language. In English, for example, the /p/ sound is a phoneme because it is the smallest unit of sound that can make a difference of meaning if, for example, it replaces the initial sound of *bill, till,* or *dill,* making the word *pill*. The vowel sound of *pill* is also a phoneme because its distinctiveness in sound makes *pill*, which means one thing, sound different from *pal*, which means another. Phonemes are not letters; they refer to the ~~*True*~~ sounds of a spoken utterance. For example, *flocks* and *phlox* have exactly the same five phonemes, even though they are written differently.

Now, let us return to that same sentence and introduce another kind of error into it:

(2) Johnny is an boy who loves pizza

Once again, to a native speaker of English, it is a simple matter to spot the error in (2). He or she would instantly recognize that the correct form for the indefinite article should be *a*, not *an*. Note that this is not a phonological error, because, taken in isolation, the form *an* is a well-formed English word that occurs in noun phrases such as the following:

an egg
an island
an apple
an opinion

So, what aspect of English structure does the word *an* violate? The answer is to be found by considering the *morphological* subsystem of English, the level at which words are constructed, and made to *agree* in form with one another. In (2), the principle violated is, in fact, one of morphological *agreement*—the indefinite article form *an* is used before nouns or adjectives beginning with a vowel, not a consonant. In the latter case *a* is used. Notice, however, that this principle probably has a basis in articulation. When the indefinite article occurs before a noun beginning with a consonant, the phonetic transition from *a* to the consonant is relatively effortless phonetically: *a boy, a girl, a man, a woman*, etc. However, if the noun begins with a vowel, then the use of *a* would require much more phonetic effort to accomplish the transition—*a egg, a island, a apple, a opinion*, etc. As readers can confirm for themselves, a brief, but effortful, break between the *a* and the subsequent vowel is unavoidable. This break is known technically as a *hiatus*. This analysis suggests *hiatus* two things: (1) that the phonological and morphological levels of language are hardly independent systems; and (2) that the physical effort involved in speaking *(parole)* has an effect on language structure *(langue)*.

PLE

Zipf's
Law

Point (2) implies that a Principle of Least Effort may be operative in determining the actual constitution of linguistic systems. As will become apparent in this book, it manifests itself in many diverse ways in language and discourse. Therefore, it requires a brief initial discussion here. Known more generally as "Zipf's Law," after a communication theorist by that name (Zipf 1949), the Principle suggests that the ways in which human beings organize their linguistic systems and exert themselves in speaking tend towards least effort. Zipf developed his principle on the observation that there is a manifest correlation between the length of a specific word (in number of phonemes) and its rank order in the language (its position in order of its frequency of occurrence). Zipf found that the higher the rank order of a word (the more frequent it was in actual usage), the more it tended to be "shorter" (made up with fewer phonemes). For example, articles *(a, the)*, conjunctions *(and, or)*, and other function words, which have a high rank order in English (and in any other language for that matter), are typically monosyllabic, consisting of one to three phonemes. Zipf's Law can also be seen in the tendency to abbreviate phrases that come into popular use (FYO, UNESCO, NATO, 24/7, etc.). In effect, Zipf's Law proclaims that the more frequent a linguistic form, the more likely it is to be rendered "economical" in physical design.

The study of morphological systems includes determining not only how words are formed, but also what constitutes a word, and how units smaller than words, called *morphemes*, convey meaning. The word *birds*, for instance, can be split into two morphemes—*bird* and the ending -*s*. The former bears dictionary meaning; the latter has a purely grammatical meaning (plural).

As we shall see in chapter 4, the particular characteristics of a language's morphology have been used by linguists as criteria for classifying it as a distinct type. For instance, languages can be classified according to the number of morphemes they use on average for constructing their words. In *analytic* or *isolating* languages, such as Chinese, words tend to be made up of single morphemes (one word = one morpheme); while in *synthetic* or *agglutinating* languages, such as Italian, words may contain several morphemes in combination (one word = combination of separate morphemes). In the case of some Native American languages, a single word may have so many component morphemes that it is the equivalent of an English sentence.

Now, let's go back to our sentence, and introduce into it yet a different type of error:

(3) Johnny is boy a who loves pizza

Although there are no structural errors in this sentence that transgress phonological or morphological structure—indeed, all the words in (3) are well-formed phonologically and morphologically—a native speaker will nevertheless instantly point out that the article is "out of place." The principle violated in this case is, thus, one of *syntax*—English articles must precede nouns and adjectives, not follow them. Note that the "post-positioning" of the article is an acceptable syntactic pattern in other languages, such as Rumanian: *casa* ("house") → *casele* ("the houses"). In syntactic analysis, the primary task is to describe the structure of phrases and sentences in terms of how they are organized into sentences.

So far we have been concerned with infringements of some aspect of the "well-formedness" of consonant clusters, words, and the order of words. Now, let us consider the following two versions of our sentence, both of which are well-formed at all structural levels, but which still present anomalies:

(4) Johnny is a boy who drinks pizza
(5) Johnny is a girl who loves pizza

Because sentence (4) is well-formed, native speakers are inclined to find a meaning for it. But real-world experience tells them that *pizzas* are normally eaten, not drunk. In essence, this sentence has no real-life meaning, although a scenario where a pizza may be ingested with a buccal action that resembles drinking can always be imagined. Sentence (4) thus violates a *semantic* principle. Sentence (5), however, produces a different kind of effect on the native speaker, who might not perceive it as semantically anomalous, but rather as indicating that the name *Johnny* has been assigned to a girl, rather than a boy—a violation of onomastics (naming practices) that is not unusual in English culture, where gender-based onomastic conventions can be modified and changed by individuals, with or without social approval.

Semantics is, clearly, the study of the relation between linguistic forms and the meanings they entail. One overriding fact that has emerged from the research on semantics systems is that meaning is largely a matter of cultural emphasis, need, or tradition. Consider, for instance, the way in which an object which marks the passage of time is named in English and Italian. In the former language it is called *watch* if it is a portable object and worn on the human body, usually on the wrist, but a *clock* if it is to be put somewhere—for example, on a table or on a wall. In Italian no such semantic distinction has been encoded lexically. The word *orologio* refers to any device for keeping track of time, with no regard to its "portability":

Italian		orologio
English	watch *(portable)*	clock *(non-portable)*
Concept	*device for keeping track of time*	

This does not mean that Italian does not have the linguistic resources for making the distinction, if needed. Indeed, the phrase *da + place* allows speakers to provide exactly this kind of information:

orologio da polso	=	wrist watch
orologio da tavolo	=	table clock
orologio da muro	=	wall clock

In effect, Italians do not find it necessary to distinguish between *watches* and *clocks* as a necessary fact of life. They can refer to the portability of the device in other ways, if the situation requires them to do so. Speakers of English, on the other hand, refer to the portability distinction as a necessary fact of life, attending to it on a regular basis, as witnessed by the two words in its lexicon. Historically speaking, the word *watch* originated in the 1850s when people started strapping clocks around their wrists. As the psychologist Robert Levine (1997) argues, this introduced a fixation with watching time pass that has been incorporated into English vocabulary.

The idea that language, thought, and culture are interlinked generally falls under the rubric of the *Whorfian Hypothesis* (WH), after the American anthropological linguist Benjamin Lee Whorf (1897–1941). The WH will be discussed in chapter 8. Suffice it to say here that it posits, basically, that languages predispose speakers to attend to certain concepts as being necessary. But, as Whorf emphasized, this does not mean that understanding between speakers of different language is blocked. On the contrary, through translation people are always attempting to understand each other. Moreover, Whorf claimed, the resources of any language allow its speakers to invent new categories any time they want. For example, if for some reason we decided to refer to "adolescent boys between the ages of 13 and 16 who smoke," then by coining an appropriate word, such as *groon,* we would in effect etch this concept into our minds. When a boy with the stated characteristics came into view, we would immediately recognize him as a *groon*, thinking of him as exemplifying a distinct class of individuals. When we name something, we are classifying. What we are naming belongs to no class until we put it in one.

The WH raises some interesting questions about social inequalities and the structure of the language that encodes them. In English, sexist terms like *chairman, spokesman*, etc., were often cited in the not-too-distant past as examples of how the English language predisposed its users to view certain social roles in gender terms. Feminist critics maintained (correctly) that English grammar was organized from the perspective of those at the center of the society—the men. This is why in the recent past (and even to some extent today) we would say that a woman married into a man's family, and why at wedding ceremonies expressions such as "I pronounce you man and wife" were used. Similarly damaging language was the kind that excluded women, such as "lady atheist" or "lesbian doctor," implying that atheists and doctors were not typically female or lesbian. *matriarchal*

In matriarchal societies the reverse is true. Investigating grammatical gender in the Iroquois language, Alpher (1987) found that in that language the feminine *Alpher 87* gender was the default one, with masculine items being marked by a special prefix. Alpher related this to the fact that Iroquois society is matrilineal. The *matri-lineal* women hold the land, pass it on to their heirs in the female line, are responsible for agricultural production, control the wealth, arrange marriages, and so on. Iroquois grammar is clearly organized from the viewpoint of those at the center of that particular society—the women.

Now, let's return one last time to our illustrative sentence, considering how it might be modified in response to different kinds of questions:

(1)
Question: What is it that Johnny loves?
Answer: Pizza.

(2)
Question: Is it true that Johnny loves pizza?
Answer: Yes, it is.

(3)
Question: Who loves pizza, Johnny or Mary?
Answer: Johnny.

The use of the single word *pizza* in (1) is sufficient to give the required information asked by the question. In this case, it is unnecessary to utter an entire sentence (*Johnny loves pizza*). Incidentally, this is a generally "sentence-abbreviating" tendency that shows the operation of Zipf's Law in the domain *Zipf* of dialogue. The answer in (2) uses a different pattern of response—a pattern intended to provide confirmation of what the questioner asks. And the answer in (3) identifies which of the two alternatives to which the questioner refers is the appropriate one.

The subsystem where such kinds of responses are determined is called the *pragmatic* or *discourse* system. In the early 1970s, the linguist Dell Hymes became fascinated by the fact that we used only bits and pieces of sentences in real discourse. This seemed to impugn the very notion of linguistic competence as based on sentence structure, which, at the time, was considered to be impervious to influences from real-world communication and social interaction. Hymes thus proposed that knowledge of language entailed, in addition to other kinds of structural knowledge, the ability to use it appropriately in specific social and interactive settings. He called this kind of knowledge *communicative competence*, claiming that it had an effect in shaping and even changing linguistic competence. Studies on communication and discourse proliferated shortly thereafter, shedding light on the relation between linguistic and communicative competence or, to use Saussurean terminology, between *langue* and *parole*.

The basic notion in all discourse study is that of *speech act*. It can be defined as knowledge of how to match words to a situation so that some meaning-exchange can be literally "acted out" in a socially appropriate fashion. A simple protocol such as saying hello, for instance, requires a detailed knowledge of the appropriate words, phrases, structures, and nonverbal cues that come together cohesively in a script-like fashion to enable a speaker to make successful social contact with another speaker. It requires, in other words, both *procedural* and *linguistic* knowledge. An infringement of any of the procedural details of this script might lead to a breakdown in communication.

To conclude the analysis of our illustrative sentence, it should be noted that the way in which actual speakers will pronounce it will vary. Speakers in England would tend to pronounce the words in our sentence differently than how people living in New York City would. Within a speech community, there is actually considerable variation in a language. The way people speak will change not only according to where they live, but also according to their age, occupation, socioeconomic status, gender, etc. Variation in language is called *dialectal*. If the variation is due to geography, then the dialects are called *regional* or *geographical*. If, however, the variation is socially based, then the dialects are called *social dialects*—for example, the way teenagers talk among themselves is different than how university professors talk to each other.

An interesting aspect of variation is the fact that all languages have *registers*. These are forms of speech that are used to match the formality of a situation, the medium used (speech or writing), and the topic under discussion. Take, for example, saying good-bye to another person in English. This will vary as follows:

Highly Formal:	Good-bye
Mid Formal:	Bye
Informal:	See ya'

The choice of one or the other is a matter of politeness. In some societies, such as in Java, registers are tied strictly to social groups. At the top of the social hierarchy are the aristocrats; in the middle the townsfolk; and at the bottom the farmers. Each of these classes has a distinct register of speech associated with it. The top register is used by aristocrats who do not know one another very well, but also by a member of the townsfolk if he or she happens to be addressing a high government official. The middle register is used by townsfolk who are not friends, and by peasants when addressing their social superiors. The low register is used by peasants, or by an aristocrat or town person talking to a peasant, and among friends on any level. The latter is also the form of language used to speak to children.

We all use registers unconsciously at different times of the day, as the linguist Martin Joos cleverly argued in his classic 1967 book titled *The Five Clocks of English*. To grasp what Joos contended, consider the different kinds of registers you would use during a typical day. Consider, for instance, how you would speak in the morning when you get up with family members; how you would speak at your place of work with co-workers; how you would speak at your place of work with superiors; how you would converse with friends at a bar after hours; and how you would communicate late at night with a romantic partner.

LEARNING TO SPEAK

As mentioned above, Chomsky argued for a universal deep structure grammar, or Universal Grammar (UG), not only because it would explain the fundamental blueprint on which all language grammars are built, but because it would also explain why children learn to speak so naturally. The latter fact suggested to Chomsky, moreover, the presence in the brain of a Language Acquisition Device (LAD), which made the rule-making principles of the UG available to all children, hence the universality and rapidity of language acquisition—when the child learns one fact about a language, the child can easily infer other facts without having to learn them one by one. Differences in language grammars are thus explainable as choices of rule types, or "parameters," from the universal set.

The problem with UG theory is that it is restricted to accounting for the development of syntax in the child—if it does even that successfully. As such, it ignores a much more fundamental force in early infancy—the ability to make imitative linguistic models. Moreover, it is legitimate to ask if there is only a UG for language, as Chomsky insists. What about the nonverbal modes of communication and of knowledge-making (gesture, drawing, etc.)? Since these develop in tandem with vocal language during infancy without any training, does the brain also possess "universal nonverbal grammars"? Are there also other kinds of acquisition devices in addition to the LAD—such as a gesture acquisition device, a drawing acquisition device, and so on? If the role of culture is simply to set the parameters that determine the specific verbal grammar that develops in the child, could it not also set, say, the specific gestural and drawing parameters that determine the specific forms of gestural and representational knowledge that develop in the child?

Chomsky is right about one thing, however—language acquisition is regular and predictable across the world. At first, all children emit cooing sounds. Around 20 weeks of age, they start producing consonantal sounds. When they reach six months, they start to emit monosyllabic utterances (*mu, ma, da, di*, etc.), called *holophrastic* (one-word). These have been shown to serve three basic functions: (1) naming an object; (2) expressing an action or a desire for some action; and (3) conveying emotional states. Holophrases are typically imitations of adult words—*da* for *dog*, *ca* for *cat*, etc. Over 60% will develop into nouns; and 20% will become verbs. During the second year children typically double their holophrases—*wowo* "water," *bubu* "bottle," *mama* "mother," etc. They also start to use language more and more during play to accompany their rhythmic movements, to simulate the sounds of their toys, and to refer to what they are doing.

In early language, imitation is therefore rather crucial. As Crystal (1987: 232) aptly remarks:

> It has also been recognized that imitation is a distinct skill in language acquisition—many children spend a great deal of time imitating what their parents have just said. This is most noticeable when new sounds or vocabulary are being learned, but it has been shown that imitation may be important in the development of grammar too. Often, children imitate sentence patterns that

they are unable to produce spontaneously, and they stop imitating these structures when they start to use them in speech— suggesting that imitation is a kind of "bridge" between comprehension and spontaneous production.

Early sentence structure reflects the general word order of the language to which the child is exposed. It too is a result of imitation. Typically, early sentences consist of two main classes of words, called the *pivot* class and an *open* class. The former has a few members, and the latter many more. A sample of typical pivot and open words in childhood English are the following:

Pivot Class (A)	Open Class (B)
all-gone	doggie
bye-bye	milk
big	sock
more	mommy
pretty	daddy
my	bro-bro (brother)
hi	hot
see	poon (spoon)

Thus, in an utterance such as "All-gone milk" and "See bro-bro" the structure of the sentence is **A + B**. In other languages, of course, the opposite order may apply (**B + A**). As the child's learning of vocabulary increases, he or she adds more classes to this basic pivot structure: "Alexander make tower," "Pop go weasel," and so on. Only later do function words such as prepositions and conjunctions emerge, allowing the child to connect the pivot and open words in the same way that adults do.

It is interesting to note that children apply the words they learn at first in general ways. For instance, if a child learns the word *kitty*, applying it to small animals, and *doggie* to larger animals, the child tends to call all animals either *kitty* or *doggie* depending on their relative sizes. Narrowing down the meanings or referents of words develops with usage and through correction (social conditioning). Studies show that such narrowing takes place around the age of one to two years. By 36 months, children control around 1,000 words functionally, with which they construct sentences of various types.

In summary, research has found that learning to speak in the human species is a regular process marked by uniform milestones or stages, which are intertwined with the course of cognitive growth and motor development. The main stages are given below:

Age	Stage
12 weeks *3 mos*	Cooing stage marked by vocalizations and pitch modulations
20 weeks *5 mos*	Consonantal sounds emerge
6 months	Cooing changes into babbling; holophrases emerge
12 months	Holophrases are typically replicated (*ma-ma, da-da,* etc.); a pivot grammar surfaces as children start using words to refer to things in general ways
24 months	The pivot grammar expands; function words appear; a narrowing of meaning emerges
36 months	The child possesses a vocabulary of around 1,000 words and starts to create adult-like sentences

What is missing from such an account is the creative nature of childhood language. My grandson was barely 15 months of age when I observed him starting to use language creatively on a regular basis. For example, one day he pointed to our household cat (which had orange hair) with the word "juice"— a word he had been using to refer to the orange juice he drank at breakfast. What he had done, in effect, was to transfer the meaning he had associated with the word *juice* to the designation of another referent ("cat" or "cat's color"). Since no one had ever made such a reference, it was something that he came up with himself. He had bridged a knowledge gap creatively. Examples such as this abound, revealing the presence of a "creative impulse" in children in the ways they use language.

Lennenberg   In 1967, the linguist Eric Lenneberg claimed that the acquisition of language came to an end at the end of childhood. He called childhood, therefore, the *critical period* for language acquisition. Lenneberg came to this conclusion after reviewing an extensive corpus of aphasiology data—data on individuals who had suffered language impairments, called *aphasias*, caused by damage to specific language areas in their brains. From his review, Lenneberg noted a pattern. It was statistically more likely for those who incurred aphasias during childhood to develop language abilities nonetheless, despite their impairments. However, aphasias incurred after puberty tended to cause permanent impairments.

Lenneberg's hypothesis appeared to receive support in the early 1970s from a widely reported case of a child, named Genie, whose abusive father had isolated and physically restrained her day and night in a small bedroom with little light and virtually no stimulation from the age of 20 months (Curtiss 1977). When found at almost the age of 14, and thus after the critical period, Genie could not speak, nor was she ever able (as far as I know) to learn how to speak like someone who had had the benefit of a normal upbringing. However, many doubts have been cast on the case. First, Genie was not an ideal subject for testing Lenneberg's hypothesis, because there was some question as to whether she was mentally retarded from birth. Her father, it is thus claimed, locked her up in cruel response to her abnormality. The extreme deprivation that Genie suffered also may have had biological influences on her brain, making it difficult for her to acquire language after she was found.

Critical period theory suggests that human biology puts limits on our ability to learn a language. But this is not necessarily the case. There are many examples of people learning a new language fluently after puberty. There are simply too *facile = easy* many factors involved in human development and learning that defy facile theories such as UG theory, LAD theory, or a critical period theory. There is some element of truth in all such theories, of course, for learning is subject to some biological constraints. But the unique power of the human mind is that it can transcend these constraints on willpower alone.

CONCLUDING REMARKS

In this opening chapter we looked at a few general aspects of language and of linguistic method. The approach defined as AL—which is now considered a branch of general linguistics—inheres in seeing the various subsystems of language not as autonomous phenomena, to be studied only as physical objects in and of themselves, but in relation to cognition, culture, and the social systems that they undergird. Boas and his student Sapir are the founders of AL. Sapir's own brilliant student, Benjamin Lee Whorf, expanded the purview of AL by elaborating substantively upon his mentor's views and giving them a more

Boas
Sapir
AL
Whorf
purview

Hopi
posited

empirical foundation. Through his in-depth study of the Hopi language of the southwestern US, Whorf posited, in essence, that the categories of one's particular language are much more than simple mediators of thought. He saw them as being the "shapers" of the very thought patterns they embodied: "The world is presented in a kaleidoscopic flux of impressions which has to be organized by our minds—and this means largely by the linguistic systems in our minds" (Whorf 1956: 153). The main objective of AL remains, to this day, to study the "linguistic systems in our mind," as Whorf so eloquently put it.

The Origin and Evolution of Language

Language is a part of our organism and no less complicated than it.

Ludwig Wittgenstein (1889–1951)

PRELIMINARY REMARKS

In 1866 the Linguistic Society of Paris imposed a ban on all discussions related to the question of the origin of language. A similar prohibition was put into place by the Philological Society of London a half century later in 1911. Such drastic actions were motivated by the endless speculations, conjectures, and unfounded theories that were being bandied about by members of the two societies. For most of the latter part of the nineteenth century, and for the greater part of the twentieth century, language scientists tended, in fact, to shy away from engaging in any kind of debate or research related to the seemingly insoluble enigma of the phylogenesis of speech.

In the early 1970s, however, interest in this conundrum was rekindled, probably because of the intriguing and suggestive research that was being conducted in such interrelated fields of inquiry as archeology, paleography, ethology, psychology, neurology, anthropology, semiotics, and linguistics. Anthropological linguists in particular came to see the interrelated findings as tantalizing bits and pieces to the puzzle of language origins. Today, one of the aims of AL is to do exactly what the Linguistic Society of Paris and the Philological Society of London had dismissed as impracticable; namely, to conduct meaningful inquiry into the origin (or origins) of language and to formulate theories on the emergence of speech in the human species.

The aim of this chapter is to take a schematic look at the question of language origins, together with an overview of how languages change over time and how they can be compared historically and genetically. Finally, the experiments of teaching language to primates will be discussed briefly, since these have implications for the study of language origins.

THEORIES

Since the dawn of recorded history, human beings have had an abiding fascination with the origins of things—the universe, life, themselves, and language. The lengths to which some have gone to unravel how language might have originated in our species are quite extraordinary. The fifth-century BC Greek historian Herodotus wrote in his *Historia* that the Egyptian king Psamtik (663–610 BC) purportedly devised the first-ever "experiment" to determine the mother tongue of humanity (Crystal 1987: 288). According to Herodotus, Psamtik gave two newborn babies of ordinary people to a shepherd to nurture among his flocks. The shepherd was commanded not to utter any speech before them. The children were to live by themselves in a solitary habitation. At the due hours the shepherd was instructed to bring goats to them, give them their fill of milk, and perform the necessary things that ensured their survival. After two years the shepherd brought the babies raised in the prescribed manner before Psamtik. The first word uttered by the two sounded like *becos*—the ancient Phrygian word for "bread." Amazed and excited, Psamtik immediately declared Phrygian to be the mother tongue of humanity.

Whether or not Psamtik's experiment ever took place at all is an open historical question. But even if it had, it certainly would not have proven anything. The babbling sounds made by the children—in probable imitation of each other—were interpreted, or more accurately misinterpreted, as constituting the word *becos* by Psamtik, probably in much the same way as parents commonly misinterpret the first sounds made by their children as genuine words. But although the method employed by Psamtik to pursue his objective was clearly bizarre, the premise that was inherent in it was not—namely, that language ontogenesis (the development of language in infancy) reenacts language phylogenesis (the development of language in the species) in a chronologically condensed way. This view has, in fact, informed many of the theories of language origins across the ages.

The revival of interest in the origins question can probably be traced to the work of the Danish linguist, Otto Jespersen (1922). After reviewing previous approaches to the question, Jespersen identified five theoretical frameworks that had been used in the past to explain language origins. He designated them as follows:

- *Bow-Wow Theory.* This posits that speech originated as a result of attempts to imitate the sounds made animals. This theory finds some corroboration in the fact that in the core vocabularies of the world's languages (in vocabularies that refer to the most common things), onomatopoeic words abound (*bow-wow, meow*).

- *Pooh-Pooh Theory.* This claims that speech originated out of the instinctive sounds and grunts our hominid ancestors made in response to pain, anger, love, and other affective states. The main evidence used in support of this theory is the universal presence of interjections—*Ah! Ouch! Yikes! Wow!* etc.—in the world's languages.

- *Ding-Dong Theory.* This postulates that speech resulted from vocal osmosis. For example, a word such as *mama* is postulated as resulting from the sounds made by infants as they suck on the mother's breast. Similarly, forms such as *ding-dong, bing-bang, flip-flop,* suggest an osmotic origin, revealing an attempt to reproduce sounds of various kinds through vocalization.

- *Yo-He-Ho Theory.* This posits that language crystallized from the chants made by early peoples as they worked and played together. The main evidence for this theory is the presence of prosodic features (tone, modulation, rhythm, etc.) in childhood, as children attempt to communicate early needs or to express early concepts. These features are said to be remnants of chanting.

- *La-La Theory.* This claims that language emerged as a consequence of the sounds our human ancestors made in response to lovemaking, play, and other social activities. Essentially, it claims that "poetic forms" were the original words of humanity.

These theories can be called *echoic* and can, generally, be traced to the fertile imagination of the ancient Greeks (Stam 1976). The basic idea in echoism is that of imitation. Echoism is supported by two undeniable facts: (1) as we saw in the previous chapter, imitation is a basic tendency in language ontogenesis; (2) as mentioned above, onomatopoeic words, interjections, and the like make up large portions of the world's basic core vocabularies. Stross (1976: 21) encapsulates the idea behind echoism in the following way:

Humans and birds especially seem to have rather well developed abilities to imitate many environmental sounds, especially sounds made by other animals, and this ability could well have been very useful to protohominids for luring game. Could sounds used by protohominids to lure game or mimic sounds of nature come to represent the game or other objects in nature in the minds of these prelinguistic humans?

Residues of echoism can be seen in various manifestations. Loudness, for example, is used across the world to convey a state of anger. Similarly, speakers of different languages typically increase their rate of speech to express urgency. Whispering seems universally to add "conspiratorial" connotations to verbal messages.

Echoism reveals its most serious shortcomings in its inability to account for: (1) the development of nonvocal language in human beings who lack the anatomy for articulate speech; (2) the presence of non-echoic forms in basic vocabularies; and (3) the presence of gesture as a subsystem of human communication. Nevertheless, it cannot be dismissed entirely. After all, there really is no way to determine whether or not vocal echoism played a much more pivotal creative role in prehistoric times than it does today.

The question of gesture in human communication is of special significance in any consideration of the origins question, since it can easily substitute vocal language in any situation. And, in fact, gesture theories are as old as echoic ones. These posit that the use of the body, and especially the hands, was the protoform of human communication. As Stross (1976: 22) explains:

It is easy to imagine bipedal animals gesturing to attract attention or pointing out a particular object with a wave of the hand. Perhaps you can even visualize a group of prelinguistic humans imitating the shapes of things with hand gestures or pointing to parts of the body. Association of the gesture with the thing indicated would then have to be extended to situations in which the object was not present.

As Brown (1986: 463) remarks, the shift from manual communication to vocal speech probably occurred because it brought along with it several advantages: "vocal language works at night; it gets around obstacles in the line of sight; it does not interrupt useful manual work."

The version of gesture theory that has become a point of reference for all subsequent ones was formulated by the philosopher Jean Jacques Rousseau (1712–1778) in the middle part of the eighteenth century. Rousseau became intrigued by the question of the origins of language while seeking to understand what he called the "noble savage." Rousseau proposed that the cries of nature that early humans must have shared with the animals, and the gestures that they must have used in tandem, led to the invention of vocal language. He explained the evolutionary transition in this way: When the gestures proved to be too cumbersome, their corresponding cries replaced them. Rousseau also proposed what certainly must have been a radical idea for his era—that metaphor was not a mere stylistic variant for a more basic literal mode of expression, but rather, a cognitive remnant of a previous, and hence more fundamental, stage in the evolution of the rational, or logical, mind. Rousseau considered the first metaphorical utterances to be the mental counterparts of physical gestures (Rousseau 1966: 12): *tropes n, "a figure of speech using words in non-literal ways, eg a metaphor"*

> As man's first motions for speaking were of the passions, his first expressions were tropes. Figurative language was the first to be born. Proper meaning was discovered last. One calls things by their true name only when one sees them in their true form. At first only poetry was spoken; there was no hint of reasoning until much later.

In the early part of the twentieth century, Richard Paget (1931) attempted to fill in the gap that previous gesture theories had left by relating gesture to vocalism. His explanation has come to be known as *mouth-gesture* theory. It claims that manual gestures were copied unconsciously by positions and movements of the lips and tongue. The continual apposition of gestures and imitative vocal movements led eventually to the replacement of the former by the latter (Paget 1930: 24):

> Human speech arose out of a generalized unconscious pantomimic gesture language—made by the limbs as a whole (including the tongue and lips)—which became specialized in gestures of the organs of articulation, owing to the hands becoming continually occupied with the use of tools. The gestures of the organs of articulation were recognized by the hearer because the hearer unconsciously reproduced in his mind the actual gesture which had produced the sound.

But, even though Paget's theory does indeed plausibly explain how gestures may have been transformed into sounds, and although it has more recently been shown to be compatible with brain and vocal tract evolution (Hewes 1973), it ignores a whole range of rudimentary questions: What feature of the brain made the transition from gesture to vocalism possible? Why has gesture survived as a communicative subsystem? How did syntax develop out of the oral substitutes for gestures? Nevertheless, mouth-gesture theory has an intuitive appeal. Moreover, it could well be that the transition from gesture to vocalism was triggered during work activities. As the Russian neurologist Luria (1970: 80) explains: "There is every reason to believe that speech originated in productive activity and arose in the form of abbreviated activities which represented work activities." Many grunts too could have become words during such activities, as Stross (1976: 22) explains:

Hewes 1973

Luria 1970-80

> Groups of early humans, straining with the intense and common effort necessary to move a fallen log or other such occupation, came to emit spontaneous grunts which were partly consonantal and which would eventually be used to signal common exertion in much the same way that today we use "heave" or "pull" in group lifting or pulling efforts. Eventually the grunts used for coordinating the efforts of many persons in a rhythmic way came to be associated with the work performed and then to stand for the work itself in symbolic communication.

grunts work

In 1959, Diamond argued that language originated from the primitive verb roots that our early ancestors must have used to request assistance from their group members. The first commands referring to common bodily actions like breaking, killing, cutting, etc., were the first "protoverbs" of humanity. As evolutionary changes took place, Diamond suggested, nouns and adjectives were added to this verbal base to generate language as we know it today. Although Diamond did indeed present a well-argued case, his theory can hardly explain why nouns seem to emerge first in infancy and why verbs constitute only a minor part of the vocabularies of languages in comparison to nouns—in European languages, statistical studies show that from 75%–80% off all words are nouns; and that the total number of verbs rarely exceeds 20%.

Diamond 1959

proto verbs

Europ nouns 75-80% verbs 20%

Diamond's work became widely discussed within AL because he used a large database to support his theory. But perhaps the first true scientific approach to the origins question can be found in the work of the American structuralist Morris Swadesh (see especially his posthumous 1971 volume, *The Origin and*

Swadesh 1971

posthumous

Diversification of Language). Swadesh divided the origin and evolution of language into four primary periods, in synchrony with the major ages: (1) the Eolithic (the dawn stone age), (2) the Paleolithic (the Old Stone Age), (3) the Neolithic (the New Stone Age), and (4) the Historical, spanning the last 10,000 years. Within these time frames Swadesh located corresponding stages of linguistic evolution, and suggested that all languages in the world today derived from one source during the Paleolithic period. Swadesh's scenario was challenged on several counts. But his method showed, once and for all, that a scientific approach to the age-old question of language origins was conceivable. Using data from archeology and anthropology, together with a detailed knowledge of language reconstruction, Swadesh demonstrated how a plausible primal scene could be drafted, and how the transition to contemporary language behavior could be envisaged. Crucial to his framework are the notions of *core vocabulary* and *sound symbolism*, both of which will be discussed below.

Contemporary work on the origins question has produced a list of "facts on file." For example, the plaster casts of skulls found at archeological sites that have been used to reconstruct hominid brains have revealed that both our Neanderthal and Cro-Magnon ancestors (pre-30,000 BC) had brains of similar size to ours and structurally similar vocal tracts (Lieberman 1972). The Neanderthals had the requisite brain structure and anatomy for speech, but to a limited extent. Crystal (1987: 290) offers the following comment on this type of finding:

> Linguists and anatomists have compared the reconstructed vocal tract of a Neanderthal skull with those of a newborn and an adult modern man. The newborn and the Neanderthal vocal tracts are remarkably similar. Neanderthal man would have been able to utter only a few front consonant-like sounds and centralized vowel-like sounds, and may have been unable to make a contrast between nasal and oral sounds.

The speech of the Neanderthals, therefore, may have been similar to that of children. On the other hand, the Cro-Magnons, who had a skeletal structure and vocal tract that were very close to those of the modern adult human, were probably capable of full speech.

A second major finding is the fact that speech was seemingly developed at the expense of an anatomical system intended primarily for breathing and eating. As Laitman and his associates (1983, 1990) have shown, at birth the position of the larynx in human infants is high in the neck, like it is in that of other

? homo erectus
homo habilis [handwritten top margin]

primates (as mentioned in chapter 1). Infants breathe, swallow, and vocalize in ways that are similar to how other primates carry out these functions. But, some time around the first year of life, the infant's larynx descends down the neck, changing the ways in which the child will carry out such physiological functions from then on. Nobody knows why this descent occurs. It is a phenomenon that is unique to humans, producing a pharyngeal chamber above the vocal cords that can modify sound.

yr 1 [margin]
larynx descends below voc cords [margin]

By examining fossil skulls, Laitman found that the australopithecines of southern and eastern Africa of 1.5 to 4 million years ago had the skull-larynx configuration of a monkey or ape, with the larynx high in the vocal tract. Those hominids, therefore, could not have had speech, although they may have had some type of communication system (probably gestural). Laitman documented the same skull-larynx pattern in *Homo erectus* (1.5 million to 300,000 or 400,000 years ago). It was not until the arrival of *Homo sapiens* that Laitman found evidence for the formation of a lowered vocal tract that had the capacity to produce articulate speech.

vocab [margin]
hominids [margin]
? [margin]
homo erectus [margin]
homo sapiens [margin]
lowered voc tract ∴ speech [margin]
modern humans [interlinear above "Homo sapiens"]

The lowering of the larynx is probably a consequence of bipedalism. In standing up straight, the early humans put themselves in an orientation that is, obviously, conducive to organs lowering under the force of gravity. According to Lieberman (1972, 1984) this started 100,000 years ago. Using endocranial casting—the method of reconstructing the brain in a skull by comparing the characteristics of the skull to what is known about brain anatomy—Lieberman found that in reconstructed adult skulls (endocasts) that are older than 100,000 years the anatomical and neural characteristics for language are lacking. They are present, however, in those that are less than 100,000 years old. Lieberman thus concluded that a fully developed capacity for articulate speech was in place 100,000 years ago, not before.

bipedalism [margin]
Lieberman 1972 [margin]
2-foot [interlinear]
speech [margin]
speech devel'd 100,000 yrs ago & not before. [margin]

This does not mean, as mentioned, that the ability to communicate in other ways, especially through gesture, did not exist before *Homo sapiens (sapiens)* (Cartmill, Pilbeam, and Isaac 1986). Endocranial analyses of *Homo habilis*—discovered in 1964—show that this hominid had an enlarged brain (600–800 cm^3) with a developed left hemisphere (which is the seat of language). Language could thus have existed in *Homo habilis* without speech, as it did in *Homo erectus* (1–1.5 million years ago), which had an even larger brain (800–1300 cm^3).

homo habilis [margin]

RECONSTRUCTION TECHNIQUES

As we saw in the previous chapter, starting in the eighteenth century language *18c* scientists began to compare related languages in order to make hypotheses about their common ancestor or protolanguage. By the middle part of the *19c* nineteenth century, they had amassed sufficient evidence to suggest that there was once a single language from which most of the modern Eurasian languages had evolved, which they called <u>Proto-Indo-European (PIE)</u>, hypothesizing that *PIE* it was spoken long before the first civilizations, and that it had split up into different languages in the subsequent millennium through *diversification*, that is, through <u>sound shifts</u>.

The sound shifts were established by means of the <u>comparative analysis</u> *cognates* of *cognates*—words that have a common origin. Moreover, if the source language was not documented, then it could be reconstructed by examining the cognates. The older the language, the more likely it was to have the original sound. Below, Sanskrit, Greek, Latin, and English cognates are compared in order to reconstruct PIE consonants (from Pearson 1977). The oldest of these is Sanskrit, explaining the reason why its sounds were thought to be generally the PIE sounds:

Sanskrit	Greek	Latin	English	Reconstructed Sound
pitar	*pater*	*pater*	*father*	*p
trajah	*trejs*	*tres*	*three*	*t
kravih	*kreas*	*cruor*	raw (from *hreaw*)	*k
pa*d*	po*da*	pe*dem*	foo*t*	*d
yu*ga*	zu*gon*	iu*gum*	yo*ke*	*g
—	kanna*bis*	—	hem*p*	*b
*bh*ratar	*ph*rater	*f*rater	brother	*bh
vi*dh*ava	ei*th*eos	divi*do*	wi*d*ow	*dh
*h*ari	*kh*olos	*h*elvus	gold	*gh

Marginal notes:
- p > f
- tr > th
- k > c → raw shortened
- h ?

Note: The asterisk is used in linguistic practice to identify a reconstructed form (a sound, a word, etc.)

The validity of the above method was tested extensively by applying it to the Romance languages—the languages derived from Latin. The reason for this was a simple one—in this case the source language was documented and could thus be consulted directly. The comparative analysis of the Romance language family was thus used as a litmus test to evaluate the accuracy of the reconstruction technique itself. As a case in point, consider the following cognates in three Romance languages—Italian, French, and Spanish. The Latin words from which they derived are provided as well:

/ˈlɪt mʊs/

Latin		Italian	French	Spanish
NOCTE(M)	*night*	notte	nuit	noche
OCTO	*eight*	otto	huit	ocho
TECTU(M)	*roof*	tetto	toit	techo

Now, a comparison of the sounds derived from Latin *ct* (pronounced /kt/) indicates that it developed to *tt* (= /tt/) in Italian, to *it* (ǐt/) in French, and to *ch* (= /č/) in Spanish. The /ǐ/ is a sound similar to the *y* in English *say*; it is no longer pronounced in Modern French. The /č/ is a sound similar to the *ch* sound in *church*. These are, in effect, the sound shifts that occurred in Italian, French, and Spanish:

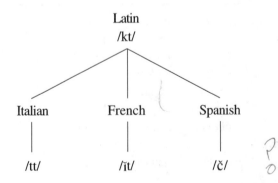

Having established the sound shifts, one can now guess what the words for "milk" and "fact" should be in the source language, given the Italian, French, and Spanish cognates for them. Since the two source words are, in actual fact, documented, they can be simply examined to see if our guesses—based on the reconstruction technique above—yields the correct results (which of course they do):

Latin		Italian	French	Spanish
LACTE(M)	*milk*	latte	lait	leche
FACTU(M)	*fact*	fatto	fait	hecho (Old Spanish, fecho)

Given the type of consistent results it produced, comparative analysis was used not only to reconstruct undocumented protolanguages, but also to understand the nature of <u>sound shifts</u>. Consider how the Latin cluster /kt/ diversified in the case of the three languages examined above (> = "develops to"):

- /kt/ > /tt/ in Italian;
- /kt/ > /ĭt/ in Old French;   *palatal ization*
- /kt/ > /č/ in Spanish.   *f palati.ation*

In Italian, it can be seen that the first consonant /k/ *assimilated* completely in pronunciation to the second one, /t/. Assimilation is the process whereby <u>one sound takes on the characteristic sound properties of another</u>, either partially or totally. In Old French, the assimilation process was only partial, since the zone of articulation of the semivowel sound (a sound that is partially a vowel and partially a consonant, as the "y" in "payment") /ĭ/ in the mouth is close, but not identical, to that of /t/. This particular type of assimilation is called *vocalization*. In Spanish, the /k/ and /t/ merged, so to speak, to produce a *palatal* sound, /č/, which is articulated midway between /k/ and /t/. The process is known logically as *palatalization*. As a factor in sound shift, assimilation can easily be seen as a <u>manifestation of Zipf's Law</u> (chapter 1)—that is to say, in all three Romance languages, the outcome of the cluster /kt/ reflects an attempt to mitigate the gap between the /k/ sound, which is articulated in the back of the throat, and the /t/ sound, which is articulated at the front end of the mouth. Phonetically, the distance between these two sounds makes it effortful to articulate the cluster /kt/ (as readers can confirm for themselves by pronouncing the Latin words slowly). Assimilation makes the articulation much more effortless by either gapping the distance between /k/ and /t/ or <u>eliminating it altogether</u>.

The predictive power of the reconstruction technique was established beyond any shadow of a doubt after a remarkable discovery in the first part of the twentieth century. In his work on Hittite—an ancient Indo-European language of Asia Minor spoken in the second millennium BC—Ferdinand de Saussure had proposed to resolve various anomalies in the reconstructed PIE vowel system by postulating the existence of a laryngeal sound /h/ (similar to the English *h* in *house)* that, he claimed, must have caused the changes in the length and quality of adjacent vowels to occur in PIE's linguistic descendants. Saussure's suggestion was based purely on reconstructive reasoning. It was considered clever, but dismissed as improbable because it could not be substantiated. However, in 1927 when cuneiform tablets of Hittite were dug up by archeologists in Turkey, they revealed, upon close scrutiny, the presence of an /h/ sound in that language that occurred in places within words where Saussure had predicted it should be!

Linguists have reconstructed various language families. By going further and further down the trunk to the "roots" of the protolinguistic tree, the idea has been to reconstruct one of the original tongues of humanity—which has been designated recently as "Nostratic" (from Latin *noster* "ours"). The linguist Shevoroshkin (1990: 22) explains the importance of work on Nostratic as follows:

> Spoken 14,000 years ago, it [Nostratic] links the Indo-European protolanguage with language families encompassing the Near East and northern Asia. But now a group of scholars believe they have taken the final step. By painstaking comparison of Nostratic with the ancestral languages of Africa, Southeast Asia, Australia and the Americas, they believe they have partially reconstructed human language as it was first uttered 100,000 years ago.

Several thousand words of Nostratic have been reconstructed so far (Ross 1991; Bomhard 1992). The words are mainly concrete ones referring to body parts and natural objects. They suggest that our ancestors were mainly hunters and gatherers, that they dwelled in villages in times of bounty, that they used twigs covered with mud to build their abodes, but that they had virtually no knowledge of agriculture. Remarkably, archeologists have been discovering many of the things—bones, remnants of dwellings, etc.—that linguists have indicated should exist! Aided by computer technology, linguists can now scan thousands of words. Almost instantaneously, they can establish lexical relations among many languages and generate precise algorithms for mapping phonetic correspondences among them. As Gamkrelidze and Ivanov (1990: 110) have put it, it is quite remarkable to note that linguistics "can reach more deeply into the human past than the most ancient records."

CORE VOCABULARIES

As we have seen, reconstructing the basic vocabularies of protolanguages affords crucial information about early cultures. Known as *core vocabularies*, they provide anthropologists with a database for inferring what social and kinship systems were like in a specific people, what kinds of activities they engaged in, what values they espoused, and so on and so forth. The work on PIE has remained the most useful one for checking the usefulness of the core vocabulary notion, for the simple reason that knowledge about this protolanguage is detailed and extensive (Renfrew 1987; Mallory 1989). Already in the nineteenth century, linguists had a pretty good idea both of what PIE sounded like, and of what kind of core vocabulary it had. Speakers of PIE lived around 5,000 to 10,000 years ago in southeastern Europe, north of the Black Sea. Their culture was named *Kurgan*, meaning "barrow," from the practice of placing mounds of dirt over individual graves. PIE had words for animals, plants, parts of the body, tools, weapons, and various abstract notions.

The core vocabulary notion has been used to reconstruct other language families and to compare languages within them. On the following page is an example of a core vocabulary of 11 items used to compare languages within the Bantu family (Werner 1919).

This core vocabulary allows linguists to accomplish several things at once. It allows them to reconstruct proto-Bantu and to determine various sound shifts that occurred in the languages of the Bantu family. It also provides a database for comparing certain grammatical patterns, and for understanding cultural differences among the speakers of Bantu languages in terms of the presence or absence of certain words.

Core vocabularies, as Swadesh (1951, 1959) showed, can also be used to estimate the relative length of time that might have elapsed—known as *time depth*—since two languages in a family began to diverge into independent codes. His method of calculating time depth is known as *glottochronology*. It consists of the following three general procedures:

(1) First, a core vocabulary appropriate to the language family is established. Swadesh claimed that the list should generally contain

English Gloss	Zulu	Chwana	Herero	Nyanja	Swahili	Ganda	Giau	Kongo
human	umuntu	motho	omundu	muntu	mtu	omuntu	umundu	muntu
humans	abantu	vatho	ovandu	antu	watu	abantu	babandu	antu
tree	umuti	more	omuti	mtengo	mti	omuti	—	—
trees	imiti	mere	omiti	mitengo	miti	emiti	—	—
tooth	ilizinyo	leino	eyo	dzino	jino	erinyo	lisino	dinu
teeth	amazinyo	maino	omayo	mano	meno	amanyo	kamasino	menu
chest	isifuba	sehuba	—	chifua	kifua	ekifuba	—	—
chests	izifuba	lihuba	—	zifua	vifua	ebifuba	—	—
elephant	indhlovu	tlou	ondyou	njobvu	ndovu	enjovu	itsofu	nzau
elephants	izindhlovu	litlou	ozondyou	njonvu	ndovu	enjovu	tsitsofu	nzau
wand	uluti	lore	oruti	—	uti	—	—	—

words such as *bird, dog, skin, blood, bone, drink, eat*, etc., which referred to concepts that probably exist in all languages.

(2) Culturally biased words, such as the names of specific kinds of plants or animals, are to be included in the core vocabulary only if relevant in the analysis of a specific language family. *2) cult words*

(3) The core vocabulary is then assessed as to the number of cognates it reveals between the languages being compared, allowing for sound shifts and variation. The lower the number of cognates, the longer the languages are deemed to have been separated. Two languages that can be shown to have 60% of the cognates in common are said to have diverged before two that had, instead, 80% in common. *3) cognates*

In 1953, the linguist Robert Lees came up with a more precise mathematical way for estimating time depth. Lees assumed the rate of loss in basic core vocabularies to be constant. He estimated that the time depth, **t**, was equal to the logarithm of the percentage of cognates, **c**, divided by twice the logarithm of the percentage of cognates retained after a millennium of separation, **r**: *Lees 1953 logarithm*

$$t = \frac{\log \mathbf{c}}{2 \log \mathbf{r}}$$

The reader is reminded that in mathematics a *logarithm* is the power to which a base, usually 10, must be raised to produce a given number. If $n^x = a$, the logarithm of *a*, with *n* as the base, is *x*; symbolically, $\log_n a = x$. For example, $10^3 = 1,000$; therefore, $\log_{10} 1,000 = 3$. Logarithms were devised originally to facilitate computation. To get a sense of what Lees's formula allows the linguist to accomplish, an analogy is perhaps useful. Suppose you wanted to calculate the number of ancestors you have in any previous generation. You have two parents, so you have two ancestors in the first generation. This calculation can be expressed as $2^1 = 2$. Each of your parents has two parents, so you have $2 \times 2 = 2^2 = 4$ ancestors in the second generation. Each of your four grandparents has two parents, so you have $4 \times 2 = 2 \times 2 \times 2 = 2^3 = 8$ ancestors in the third generation. The calculation continues according to this pattern. In which generation do you have 1,024 ancestors? That is, for which exponent *x* is it true that $2^x = 1,024$? You can find the answer by multiplying 2 by itself until you reach 1,024. But if you know that $\log_2 1,024 = 10$, you can estimate the answer much more quickly.

It is not possible to go here into the mathematical reasoning used by Lees. Suffice it to say that it is very similar to that used above to calculate the

lees
cognates

number of ancestors in any previous generation. Instead of generations, Lees dealt with cognates. Remarkably, his formula has produced fairly accurate estimates of time depth for the Romance languages. However, it has also produced ambiguous estimates for other languages (one of these being the Bantu languages). Known more specifically as *lexicostatistics* (rather than

lexico-
statistics

glottochronology), the accuracy of the time depth formula will depend on the accuracy of the core vocabularies used. Moreover, since logarithms are exponents, the slightest computational error will lead to a high degree of inaccuracy. But despite such drawbacks, the value of lexicostatistics for contemporary work on language evolution is undeniable. It is an approach that stresses the use of precise methods for the reconstruction of protolanguages and for estimating when these languages might have diversified from the source language.

sound
symbolism

The work on core vocabularies has also been useful in helping establish a relation between the nature of the sounds built into core words and the meanings they encode. The relation is called *sound symbolism*. For instance, the reconstructed PIE word for "ox," *$k^w ou$* (Gamkrelidze and Ivanov 1990: 113) can be easily seen to be imitative of the sound that an ox might make. Here are a few other examples of sound symbolic proto-words in both PIE and Nostratic (Wescott 1980: 14–16; Gamkrelidze and Ivanov 1990: 114–115; Shevoroshkin 1990: 23–27):

- PIE *yotor* "water" (= sound made by liquid in motion);
- PIE *$ek^h os$* "horse" (= expiratory sounds emitted by a horse);
- PIE *woi-no* "grape" (= sound made when a grape is squeezed);
- PIE *klak-* "laugh" (= sound made when laughing);
- Nostratic *kküyna* "wolf, dog" (= sounds uttered by wolves and dogs);
- Nostratic *lapa* "leaf" (= sound made when touching a leaf);
- Nostratic *chunga* "odor" (= responsive sound to odor made when air is expelled through the nasal canal);
- PIE *pek-* "to fleece" (= sound suggestive of the action of fleecing);
- PIE *$b^h eg^u$-* "to flee" (= sound suggestive of the action of fleeing);
- PIE *keu-* "to hear" (= expiration sounds that accompany the emphatic articulation of words);
- PIE *$b^h reg$-* "to break" (= sounds suggestive of the action of breaking things);
- PIE *$g^h ed$-* "to take" (= sounds suggestive of the action of taking things swiftly from others).

Sound symbolism is an "originating force" in language. It explains why certain phonic features are built into words in a regular way. For example, the use of nasals to designate negation, as Swadesh (1971: 193) explains, is due to the nasal character of grunting:

grunting – nasal negation

> The use of nasal phonemes in the negative in so many languages of the world must in some way be related to the prevailing nasal character of the grunt. In English, the vocable of denial is almost always nasal; but it can vary from a nasalized vowel to any of the nasal consonants: *ã!ã, õ!õ, m!m, n!n* …Why is nasality so common? Surely because it results from the relaxation of the velum; the most usual position of the velum is down, and the most relaxed form of grunt is nasal. The prevalence of nasals in the negative…may therefore be due to the fact that they are based on grunts.

negatives based on grunts.

LANGUAGE CHANGE

Why/how lang change

Reconstruction and the establishment of sound shift laws are based on the presupposition that languages constantly undergo change. For example, a sound law that characterizes some Romance languages, setting them apart from others, is the *voicing* of the Latin consonants /p/, /t/, and /k/ between vowels—a *voiced* consonant is produced by vibrating the vocal cords in the larynx; a *voiceless* one by keeping them taut. The difference between the voiceless /s/ of *sip* and the voiced /z/ of *zip* can be easily detected by putting a finger on the larynx while pronouncing each word. In the case of *sip* no vibration will be felt, while in the case of *zip* a distinct vibration will be noticeable. The /t/ in the Latin word LATU(M) ("side"), for instance, has remained in the Italian word *lato,* but has developed into the voiced counterpart /d/ in the Spanish version of the word, *lado*; the /k/ in URTICA(M) ("nettle grass") has remained in the Italian form *ortica,* but has become voiced /g/ in the Spanish form, *ortiga*.

lang + change

Various theories have been put forward to explain why languages change. One of the most interesting ones was articulated in the 1950s by the French linguist André Martinet (1955), who claimed that languages change as a result of the operation of Zipf's Law in human affairs. Calling it the Principle of Economic Change, Martinet posited that complex language forms tend towards reduction, abbreviation, compression, leveling, or elimination over time. For example, the opposition between short and long vowels in Latin, which produced

Zipf's

martinet 1955
lang chang
Zipf's Law in hum affairs.
P of EC

a relatively large inventory of distinct words in that language, was "leveled" in the emerging sound systems of the Romance languages and later eliminated. Latin had ten distinct vowel sounds, equivalent approximately to *a, e, i, o, u.* In addition, each vowel sound was pronounced as either long or short—for example, the pronunciation of the word spelled os could mean either "mouth" or "bone," depending on whether the vowel was long or short (respectively). The ten-vowel phoneme system was, to a large extent, reduced or leveled in the Romance languages, in line with the Principle of Economic Change.

The loss of the distinction between the nominative, or subject, form *who* and the accusative, or object, form *whom* in English is another obvious example of economic change. Grammatical change is usually a consequence of previous phonetic change. A classic example of this is the loss of the Latin declension system in the Romance languages. Take, for instance, the declension of the feminine noun PUELLA ("girl"):

Nominative	puella	puellae
	girl	*girls*
Genitive	puellae	puellarum
	of the girl	*of the girls*
Dative	puellae	puellis
	to the girl	*to the girls*
Accusative	puellam	puellas
	the girl	*the girls*
Ablative	puella	puellis
	from the girl	*from the girls*
Vocative	puella	puellae
	Oh girl!	*Oh girls!*

As a result of phonetic changes, the suffixes shown above were eliminated, and this, in turn, led to the elimination of the entire declension system. Grammatical devices were developed by the Romance languages to maintain case distinctions—the preposition *a,* for example, became necessary to distinguish dative from accusative functions in Italian:

Ho parlato a Maria   (= dative = indirect object)
("I talked to Mary")

Ho chiamato la ragazza   (= accusative = direct object)
("I called the girl")

Although the interaction between sound and grammatical change comes under various names in the linguistic literature, it can be called the Principle of the Historical Cycle to emphasize the fact that change in grammar is connected cyclically to change in sound. This principle is thus a corollary of the Principle of Least Effort.

P of HC

change grammar ↕ sound

result / proposition

P of LE

Borrowing, as it is called, is further evidence supporting the plausibility of the latter principle. Simply put, it takes much less cognitive effort to borrow something from another language to fill a conceptual gap than to create a new form. The English suffix /-er/, which is added to verbs to form corresponding nouns, as in the formation of *baker* (noun) from *bake* (verb), is a borrowing from the Latin suffix /-arius/. The suffix reduces the effort that would otherwise be needed to come up with, and then remember, different lexical items for separate verb and noun forms. It has been a very productive suffix indeed in reducing such effort, as the following chart shows:

Borrow

bake v > bakeer n

1   2

Verb Form ⟶	Noun Form Derived by Adding /-er/
take	taker
hike	hiker
give	giver
send	sender
receive	receiver
build	builder
ask	asker

er borrowed from Latin /-arius/

PRIMATE LANGUAGE EXPERIMENTS

Since human beings are basically primates, the question of language origins can be approached from a different angle: Can the evolutionary processes underlying the birth of language in the human primate be set in motion by teaching language to other primates? If so, this would then lead to a better understanding of those very processes by observing them in a "test primate," so to speak. Starting in the 1950s, the "primate language experiments" have, in fact, been conducted in large part to answer this very question.

1950s primate lang experiments

Since gorillas and chimpanzees are incapable of oral speech because they lack the requisite vocal tract, the first experimenters chose American Sign

ASL

Washoe
Gardner
1969, 75

Language (ASL) as the code for imparting human language to them. One of the first subjects was a female chimpanzee named Washoe, whose training by the Gardner husband and wife team (Gardner and Gardner 1969, 1975) began in 1966 when she was almost one year of age. Remarkably, Washoe learned to use 132 ASL signs in just over four years. What is even more remarkable is the fact that Washoe learned to put signs together to express a small set of syntactic relations.

Premack
Sarah
1954
plastic

"Yerk-
ish"

The Premack husband and wife team (Premack and Premack 1983), whose work with a five-year-old chimpanzee named Sarah began in 1954, used a different method. They taught their subject a form of written language, training Sarah to arrange and respond to vertical sequences of plastic tokens on a magnetic board, which represented individual words: e.g., a small pink square = "banana"; a small blue triangle = "apple"; and so on. Sarah eventually developed the ability to respond to combinations of such symbols, which included references to abstract notions.

✗

Hockett
1960
Properties
13

Although there is much enthusiasm over such results, with the media reporting on them on a regular basis, there really has emerged no solid evidence to suggest that chimpanzees and gorillas are capable of language *in the same way* that humans are, nor of having the ability or desire to pass on to their offspring what they have learned from their human mentors. Aware of the importance of such experiments, in 1960 the linguist Charles Hockett proposed a typology of 13 design features that he suggested would allow the researchers to establish what true language behavior was:

Design Feature	Properties and Manifestations in Language
1. Auditory-vocal	vocal language and communication involves mainly mouth and ear work, as opposed to visual, tactile, or other modes of communication.
2. Broadcast transmission and directional reception	a verbal signal can be heard by any auditory system within ear range, and by which the source can be located using the ears' direction-finding capacity.
3. Rapid fading	auditory signals are transitory and do not await the hearer's convenience.

Non-directional   Picked up by anyone who is listening

disappears instantly

4. Interchangeability *communication*   speakers of a language can reproduce any linguistic message they can understand.

5. Total feedback   speakers of a language hear and can reflect upon everything that they say (unlike the visual displays often used in animal courtship signaling).

6. Specialization   speech sound waves have no function other than to signal meaning. *1 function*

7. Semanticity   the elements of the linguistic signal convey meaning through their stable reference to real-world situations.

8. Arbitrariness   there is no necessary dependence of the element of a verbal signal on the nature of the referent. *sign for table has no conn to referent*

9. Discreteness   *we can separate sounds bane pane* speech uses a small set of sound elements (phonemes) that form meaningful oppositions with each other.

10. Displacement *Bees*   language has the capacity to refer to situations remote in space and time from their occurrence. *past present future space → distance.*

11. Productivity   language users have the infinite capacity to express and understand meaning by using old elements to produce new ones. *new words*

12. Traditional transmission *Cultural trans*   language is transmitted from one generation to the next primarily by a process of teaching and learning (not only by genetic inheritance). *Born abil. to acq any lang.*

13. Duality of patterning *Sound + meaning*   vocal sounds have no intrinsic meaning in themselves but combine in different ways to form elements (e.g., words) that convey meanings.

Hockett himself applied the typology to study such behavior as bee dancing in order to show in what specific ways animal communication systems differed from language. Worker honey bees returning to the hive from foraging trips have the extraordinary capacity to inform the other bees in the hive about the direction, distance, and quality of the food with amazing accuracy through movement sequences that biologists call a "dance." The remarkable thing about the dance is that it appears to share with human language the feature of displacement, i.e., of conveying information about something even though it is not present.

vocab

Entomologists have documented several kinds of dance patterns. In the "round" dance, the bee moves in circles alternately to the left and to the right. This dance form is apparently deployed when the cache of food is nearby:

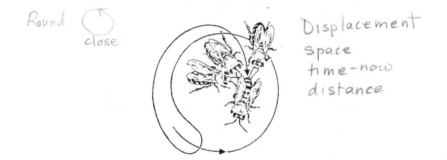

Round
close

Displacement
space
time-now
distance

When the food source is further away, then the bee dances in a "wagging" fashion, moving in a straight line while wagging its abdomen from side to side and then returning to its starting point:

direction
Tail wagg
20'

The straight line in the dance form points in the direction of the food source, the energy level of the dance indicates how rich the food source is, and the tempo provides information about its distance. Although this is indeed a remarkable communication system, it is still vastly different from language, as Hockett showed by comparing the two as follows:

Feature	Bee Dancing	Language
Auditory-vocal channel	no *no mouthear*	yes
Broadcast transmission and directional reception	*Signal picked up by any bee listening/watching* yes	yes
Rapid fading	?	yes
Interchangeability	limited	yes
Total feedback	?	yes
Specialization	?	yes
Semanticity *— conveys food source*	yes	yes
Arbitrariness	no	yes
Discreteness	no *can't sep sounds*	yes
Displacement *— 5' vs 20'*	yes *distance, not time*	yes
Productivity	*NO* yes ? *no, only 3 dances*	yes
Traditional transmission	probably not	yes
Duality of patterning	no	yes

see notes

Although many more features apply to the communicative behaviors observed in primates who have been taught a version of human language, in no primate other than the human one do all these operate in tandem. The primate experiments have revealed, nevertheless, a series of truly fascinating and important things: (1) human language is unique; (2) nevertheless, aspects of language can be imparted to primates, who have shown many of the intellectual and emotional qualities that were once thought to be exclusively human; (3) as models of early language in the human species, primate speech behaviors are indeed fascinating in themselves; and (4) there is an awful lot we do not know both about ourselves and about animals.

Primate Exper.
1) unique
2) aspects / primate ltd
3) prim sp. fasc
4) unkn own

CONCLUDING REMARKS

The question of language origins is a fascinating one on many counts. Using mainly reconstruction concepts such as core vocabularies, sound symbolism,

Recon. struction techniq

and time depth, the current work on language origins is shedding some valuable light on how language and culture might have originated in tandem.

Often, the linguist must delve into the history and evolution of cognate forms in order to establish what they mean. Historical change can affect all components of language. Consider, as one last example, how some Latin words have changed in meaning after they developed into Italian forms:

Word	Original Meaning	Italian Form	New Meaning
DOMU(S)	"house"	duomo	"dome"
CASA(M)	"shack"	casa	"house"
CABALLU(S)	"work horse"	cavallo	"horse (in general)"

Incorporating the diachronic dimension into the description of a language has, in fact, always distinguished anthropological method from other linguistic approaches.

Sounds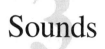

A linguistic system is a series of differences of sound combined with a series of differences of ideas.

Ferdinand de Saussure (1857–1913)

PRELIMINARY REMARKS

As the comparative grammarians of the nineteenth century went about the task of examining cognates, it became obvious to them early on that they could not rely on alphabet symbols to establish sound correspondences accurately and, thus, to derive true "sound laws" from the method of comparison. Alphabet characters, they discovered, did not always provide a consistent guide to the actual pronunciation of the sounds in words. For example, how would the linguist represent the "f" sound in English, given that it is written in one of three ways?

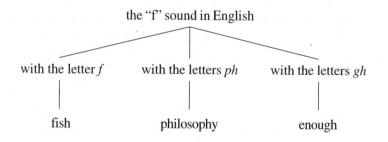

The presence of such inconsistencies in alphabet systems is what led the nineteenth-century linguists to devise a special and standardized system of notation, known as the International Phonetic Alphabet (IPA), in which one symbol, usually an alphabet character incidentally, will always be understood to represent one and only one sound. For example, the symbol [f], put between square brackets to distinguish it from the corresponding alphabet character, is the one used by the IPA to indicate the "f" sound represented vicariously by the letters *f, ph,* and *gh* in the above words.

The scientific study of sounds has ever since constituted the point of departure for the linguistic analysis of a language. This now involves: (1) the actual physical description of the sounds used by a language, known as *phonetic description*; (2) the analysis of how these relate to each other structurally, known as *phonemic analysis*; (3) the description of syllable structure; (4) the description of intonation features, stress patterns, etc., known as *prosodic analysis*; and (5) an investigation of the relation between sounds and writing symbols, known as *orthographic analysis*. Topic (5) will be dealt with in chapter 7. In this one, the focus will be on the other four.

PHONETIC DESCRIPTION

Phonetics is concerned with describing how linguistic sounds are produced. The symbols most commonly used to represent sounds are those established by the International Phonetic Association (IPA) in 1886. For example, the [f] sound above can be described as a sound produced by: (1) making the lower lip touch the upper teeth; (2) expelling the airstream emanating from the lungs in a constricted fashion; and (3) keeping the vocal cords (in the larynx) taut (non-vibrating). To render this phonetic description efficient, the three articulatory activities are designated as follows: feature (1) is termed *interdental*, (2) *fricative*, and (3) *voiceless*. Thus, the phonetic symbol [f], known more technically as a *phone*, stands for a *voiceless interdental fricative*.

The organs used in articulating sounds are either movable or stationary. Movable organs are the lips, jaws, tongue, and vocal cords. These modify the flow of air from the lungs. Stationary organs include the teeth, the alveolar arch behind them, the hard palate, the softer palate (known as the velum) behind it, the uvula (back of the throat), and the pharynx. The airstream can pass through the oral or nasal cavity. In general, only sounds produced through the latter cavity are named explicitly *(nasal)*. In the larynx there are two vocal cords, which (as we have seen already) can be either vibrating or taut—if the cords are close together when air passes through, they vibrate producing *voiced* sounds; if they are apart and stationary, the resulting sounds are *voiceless*.

Sounds made by touching two moveable organs—for example, the [p] of *pill*, which requires both lips—or those made with a moveable and a stationary part of the vocal apparatus, such as the [f] above, are named in terms of the organs that make the juncture, which is called the *point of articulation*. Reference to the tongue, when it is an articulator in the production of consonants, is not expressed—for example, the English [t] sound, which is produced with the tongue touching the alveolar arch, is called simply *alveolar*. However, in the production of vowels the various parts of the tongue may be named. These are: (1) the apex (tip), (2) the lamina (or blade), and (3) the dorsum (back).

The relevant parts of the vocal apparatus, and their names, are shown below:

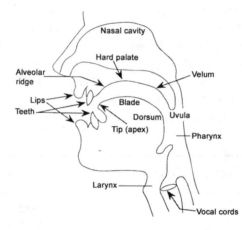

The ways in which the airstream is modified by the movable organs is called the *manner of articulation*. Sounds can be articulated by:

- expelling the airstream through the oral cavity without any significant blockage or friction (e.g., the [a] in *cane*);
- completely blocking the airstream and then expelling it abruptly (e.g., the [p] in *pill*);
- partially directing the airstream through the nasal cavity (e.g., the [n] in *nose*);
- expelling the airstream on either side of the tongue as it makes contact with the teeth, alveolar ridge, or palate (e.g., the [l] in *live*);
- expelling the airstream as a light vibrating contact is made with the tongue against the soft palate (e.g., the [r] in *rare*);

- expelling the airstream through a constriction in the front of the mouth (e.g., the [f] in *fact*).

There are two basic kinds of phones—*vowels* and *consonants*. The former are produced when the airstream is allowed to pass through the mouth without significant blockage; the latter are produced instead by means of some modifying blockage (partial or complete) of the airstream.

Vowels can be described in terms of the position of the tongue on its vertical (*high, mid, low*) or horizontal axis (*front, central, back*). For example, the front of the tongue is moved from low to high in pronouncing the vowel in the word *beet*, and the back of the tongue is raised in pronouncing the vowel in *boot*. The quality of a vowel depends on whether the lips are *rounded* or *unrounded*, the jaws *close* together or *open*, or the tip of the tongue *flat* or curled up (*retroflex*). In some languages, vowels can take on the quality of any nasal consonant that surrounds them in words. For instance, in French the vowel [a] becomes nasalized, shown with the symbol [ã], before a nasal consonant—e.g., the word *gant* ("glove") is pronounced [gã].

The English vowel system has twelve main phones. The phonetic symbols used to represent them are given below:

Tongue in Front		Tongue in Center		Tongue in Back	
				High	
i	(b*ee*t)	ɨ	(b*u*st)	u	(b*oo*t)
I	(b*i*t)	ə	(b*u*t)	ʊ	(b*oo*k)
e	(b*ai*t)	a	(b*o*t)	**Mid**	
ɛ	(b*e*t)			o	(b*oa*t)
æ	(b*a*t)			**Low**	
				ɔ	(b*ou*ght)

+ schwa
butter ʌ

If unusual detail is required for representing the vowels of a language or dialect, then the linguist can refer to the IPA, which contains a large inventory of symbols and diacritics for such a purpose. Otherwise, the linguist may have to come up with a new symbol to represent a sound previously unknown—constituting thus a veritable phonetic discovery.

Consonants can be described, as mentioned, in terms of the point and the manner or mode of articulation involved in their production:

place

Main Points of Articulation:

- *bilabial* (produced with the upper and lower lips touching); e.g., the [b] in *bin*, and the [m] in *man*;
- *labiodental* (produced with the lower lip touching the upper teeth); e.g., the [f] in *fun* and the [v] in *vine*;
- ? *dental* (produced with the tongue touching the upper teeth or with the upper and lower teeth close to each other); e.g., the [t] in *toy*, the [d] in *did*, the [n] in *nose*, the [s] is *sip*, the [z] in *zip*, and the [l] in *love*;

  discrepancy shd be / alveolar

- *interdental* (produced by putting the tongue between the teeth); e.g., the [θ] in *thing* and the [δ] in *that*;
- *alveolar* (produced with the tongue touching the gum ridge); e.g. the [ṭ] in *train* and the [ḍ] in *drain*;
- *alveopalatal* (produced with the tongue touching the soft palate); e.g., the [č] in *chin*, the [j] of *jar*, and the [ʃ] in *shin*;
- *velar* (produced with the back of the tongue touching the soft palate); e.g., the [k] in *king* and the [g] in *game*;
- *uvular* (produced at or near the uvula); e.g., the [x] in German *ich*;
- *glottal* (produced at or near throat); e.g., the [h] in *house*.

manner

Main Modes of Articulation:

- *plosive* (produced by means of a complete stoppage of the airstream), also known as *stop* or *occlusive*; e.g., the [p] in *pull* and the [b] in *bull*;
- *fricative* (produced by means of a constriction of the airstream); e.g., the [f] in *four*, the [v] in *vet*, the [s] in *sun*, and the [ʃ] in *shop*;
- *affricate* (produced by means of a combination of plosive and fricative articulations); e.g., the [ts] in *cats* and the [dz] in *fads*;
- *flap* (produced by means of a flapping action of the tongue), also known as *vibrant*; e.g., the [r] in *right*; *butter*
- *lateral* (produced by means of a narrowing of the tongue as the airstream escapes from the sides of the tongue); e.g., the [l] in *love*;
- *nasal* (produced by directing the airstream partially through the nasal passage); e.g., the [m] in *mom* and the [n] in *nine*.

Flaps and laterals are classified together as *liquids*. Some phoneticians prefer to use the term *sibilant* in place of *fricative* to describe consonants that are produced by hissing—as, for example, the [s] in *sing* or the [ʃ] in *shin*.

sibilant fricative

Some consonants can be produced with or without the vibration of the vocal cords in the larynx, known respectively as *voiced* and *voiceless*. For example, the articulatory difference between the initial sounds of *sip* and *zip*, as mentioned in the previous chapter, can be easily identified by putting a finger over the throat as they are pronounced: in the pronunciation of [s] no vibration can be felt, while in the pronunciation of [z] a distinct vibration can be felt. Nasals, flaps, and laterals are, by their very nature, always voiced (as are the vowels). It is thus the practice not to mark the voiced feature in the case of vowels, nasals, flaps, and laterals. Here are a few examples of how consonants are named phonetically:

[p] (as in *part*) = voiceless bilabial plosive (stop)
[b] (as in *bust*) = voiced bilabial plosive (stop)
[v] (as in *vine*) = voiced labiodental fricative
[θ] (as in *thing*) = voiceless interdental sibilant
[k] (as in *king*) = voiceless velar plosive (stop)

Phoneticians also employ more general descriptors in order to indicate how sounds relate to each other. Two of the more commonly used ones are the following:

- *Noncontinuants vs. Continuants:* The plosive consonants are classified as *noncontinuants*, because they are produced with a total obstruction of the airstream; all other consonants (fricatives, liquids, and nasals) are classified instead as *continuants*, because they are produced by allowing the airstream to flow continuously.
- *Obstruents vs. Sonorants:* The plosives, fricatives, and affricates are classified as *obstruents* because the airstream cannot escape through the nose when they are produced and because the airstream is either totally or partially obstructed in its flow through the oral cavity. The *sonorants* are sounds produced with a relatively free flow of air through the vocal or nasal cavities, and thus have greater sonority than obstruents. The vowels and the liquids ([l], [r]), for example, are sonorants, since they can only be produced with a strong vibration of the vocal cords.

There are several things to note with regard to the above classificatory schemes. First, the actual pronunciation of a sound can vary from speaker to speaker, which may be due to either geographic or social factors. Speakers of

English living in Alabama, for instance, pronounce vowel sounds slightly differently from those living in Newfoundland. In some societies, men and women are expected to pronounce words differently. In others, aristocrats and common folk are identified in part by how they pronounce words. In all societies, certain types of pronunciation are perceived as "more refined" than others, and some as "crude" or "vulgar."

PHONOLOGICAL ANALYSIS

Certain phones can take on slightly different articulations in certain positions within words. For example, in English the voiceless bilabial plosive [p] is aspirated—that is, pronounced with a slight puff of air (represented as [p^h])—when it occurs in word-initial position followed by a vowel, as readers can confirm for themselves by pronouncing the following words while keeping the palm of one hand near the mouth. Note that if [s] is put before, the aspiration is blocked.

[p^h]	[p]
pill	spill
pin	spin
pit	spit
punk	spunk
pat	spat

The use of [p^h] is a predictable feature of English pronunciation. If we represent the voiceless bilabial plosive sound within slant lines as /p/ to distinguish it from the aspirated variant [p^h], we can now make a general statement about English *phonology*—when /p/ occurs in word-initial position followed by a vowel it is aspirated as [p^h].

The /p/ symbol is called, more technically, a *phoneme*. This is defined as a minimal unit of sound that can distinguish the meaning of different words in a language. This implies, basically, that /p/ can replace other consonants, such as /w/ and /b/, to make English words—e.g., *pin* vs. *win* vs. *bin*. The pronunciation of the phoneme /p/ as either unaspirated ([p]) or aspirated ([p^h]) is due to the fact that it is influenced by its position within words. Note,

the pʰ

however, that this is not a universal feature of human pronunciation—in some North American indigenous languages the [pʰ] is a phoneme (/pʰ/) because it signals differences in meaning between words (Chafe 1963). Moreover, the aspirated pronunciation is totally absent from languages such as Italian, French, and Spanish.

A common technique used to identify the phonemes of a language is called the *commutation test*. It consists in comparing two words that are alike in all respects except one, in order to see if a difference in meaning results (*sip* vs. *zip*, *sing* vs. *zing*, etc.). The differential phone must occur in the same position within the word pair, which is called a *minimal pair*. If the commutation of the different phones produces a difference in meaning, the two sounds are said to be *contrastive* or *phonemic*. In the commutation test the "~" symbol is shorthand for "is commuted with." Here are some minimal pairs in English that identify the consonants /s/, /z/, /l/, and /r/ as having phonemic (contrastive) status:

/s/ ~ /z/

sip ~ zip
fuss ~ fuzz
sing ~ zing

/s/ ~ /l/

sip ~ lip
sight ~ light
song ~ long

/s/ ~ /r/

sip ~ rip
sat ~ rat
sing ~ ring

/l/ ~ /r/

lip ~ rip
lice ~ rice
lack ~ rack

Variant = allophone

If a phoneme has variants, such as /p/, then the variants are called *allophones*. Thus, the unaspirated [p] and the aspirated [pʰ] are classified as allophonic variants of /p/ in English.

Sometimes two phonemes, which can be shown to be in contrast in certain minimal pairs, will not always be contrastive in words. In English, for example, the vowels /i/ and /ɛ/ are phonemic in pairs such as: *beet ~ bet* = /bit/ ~ /bɛt/. However, some speakers pronounce the word *economics* with an initial [i], others with an initial [ɛ]. When this happens, the two sounds are said to be in *free variation*. This is a rare phenomenon, however, and is usually a consequence of regionally based pronunciation. It is, in other words, part of what Saussure called *parole* (chapter 1), or the actual use of a language in specific speech communities.

parole

The allophones of a phoneme are said to *complement* each other—where one occurs the other does not. The rule that specifies the way in which allophones complement each other is called a rule of *complementary distribution*. In the case of English /p/ the appropriate rule is, as we have, seen: [pʰ] occurs in word-initial position followed by a vowel, whereas [p] occurs in all other positions (or elsewhere). For linguists, such a verbal statement is too cumbersome. So, they prefer to condense it into a schematic rule such as the following one:

$$/p/ \rightarrow \begin{Bmatrix} [pʰ] \,/\, \# \_ V \\ [p] \,/\, \text{elsewhere} \end{Bmatrix}$$

pick #__V
spick /elsewhere

The arrow (→) stands for "is realized as"; the slash (/) for "in the environment"; # for "initial position"; V for "vowel"; and __ for "in this position." This is called a *phonological rule*, showing in a precise outline form how the allophones of /p/ are distributed.

As another example of complementary distribution, consider the /l/ phoneme in English. First, it can be seen to have phonemic status by means of the commutation test:

/l/ ~ /r/

led ~ red
lip ~ rip
lead ~ read

/l/ ~ /k/

lit ~ kit
last ~ cast
lap ~ cap

/l/ ~ /d/

love ~ dove
line ~ dine
late ~ date

Now, in word-final or syllable-final position, the /l/ takes on a velar quality (represented with the symbol [ɫ]). It is pronounced by raising the back part of the tongue slightly towards the velum, as readers can confirm for themselves by articulating the words in the chart below:

velar tongue arched @ bk [ɫ] at end of syllable	dental [l]
pill	lip
will	belt
bull	laugh
apple	silicone
ankle	slight

The complementary distribution of this phoneme can now be put into rule form as follows (# = "syllable-final or word-final position"):

l becomes velar at end of syll
otherwise use dental l

$$[l] \rightarrow \begin{cases} [ɫ] \ / \ \_\ \# \\ [l] \ / \ elsewhere \end{cases}$$

As the foregoing discussion illustrates, phonological analysis involves several basic tasks, such as: (1) determining which sounds are phonemic by means of the commutation test; (2) establishing how allophones relate to each other by means of a complementary distribution rule; and (3) determining which features of sound are critical in both setting up phonemic status and predictable allophonic variation. With respect to the third task, linguists have devised a technique for referring to minimal sound differences, known as *distinctive feature analysis*. For instance, the difference between the two allophones of /l/ is the fact that the [ɫ] is pronounced with a raising of the back part of the tongue towards the velum. If we represent this feature with the symbol [+velar], we can now specify the difference between the two allophones more precisely—[ɫ] is marked as [+velar] and [l], which does not have this feature, as [-velar]. The [±velar] symbol is a *distinctive feature*—it is the critical feature that keeps the two allophones distinct.

In effect, all sounds, whether they have phonemic or allophonic status, can be described in terms of such features. Take, for instance, the English phonemes /p/, /b/, /t/, /d/, /m/, and /n/. What features keep them distinct?

- First, since they are all consonants, they share the feature [+consonantal]. Vowels and glides (semiconsonants and semivowels), on the other hand, share the feature [+vocalic]. Obviously, consonants can be marked (if need be) as [-vocalic], and vowels and glides as [-consonantal].

- The consonants /b/, /d/, /m/, and /n/ are different from the consonants /p/ and /t/ by virtue of the fact that they are voiced. So, they can be marked as [+voiced]. The voiceless consonants can be marked instead as [-voiced].

- The phonemes /p/, /b/, and /m/ are different from /t/, /d/, and /n/ by virtue of the fact that they are pronounced with the lips and, thus, share the feature [+labial]. The consonants /t/, /d/, and /n/ are not and, therefore, are marked as [-labial].

- And the phonemes /m/ and /n/ share the feature [+nasal], since they are pronounced by expelling the airstream partially through the nose. All the others are oral consonants and are thus marked as [-nasal].

We can now draw up a chart to show which features are possessed by each phoneme as follows:

	/p/	/t/	/b/	/d/	/m/	/n/
consonantal	+	+	+	+	+	+
vocalic	-	-	-	-	-	-
voiced	-	-	+	+	+	+
labial	+	-	+	-	+	-
nasal	-	-	-	-	+	+

This chart makes it possible to pinpoint with precision what feature or features trigger a contrast in the commutation test:

/p/ ~ /b/

pin ~ bin
[-voiced] ~ [+voiced]

/p/ ~ /t/

pop ~ top
[+labial] ~ [-labial]

/p/ ~ /d/

puck ~ duck
[+labial] ~ [-labial]
[-voiced] ~ [+voiced]

/b/ ~ /m/

ball ~ mall
[-nasal] ~ [+nasal]

/d/ ~ /m/

dare ~ mare
[-nasal] ~ [+nasal]
[-labial] ~ [+labial]

Distinctive features also make it possible to write the phonological rules of a language in a more exact way. Take, for instance, the distribution rule for /p/ formulated above. This can now be reformulated as follows (C = consonant):

C [-voiced, + labial]   →   [+ aspirated] / # _ [+ vocalic]

The rule states that a voiceless labial consonant (/p/ in this case) will take on the feature [+ aspirated] in word-initial position followed by a vowel. The feature [+aspirated] is said therefore to be *noncontrastive* because it is predictable. When a feature is predictable it is called *redundant*. Certain features of sounds are, *de facto,* redundant. For instance, all nasal consonants are [+voiced]. Specifying which features are redundant for which phonemes and which features are contrastive constitutes the sum and substance of a detailed phonological analysis.

Know for test

The relevant distinctive features of some English consonant phonemes are given in the table on the following page (a *coronal* is a sound articulated by raising the tongue blade towards the hard palate).

coronal

SYLLABLE STRUCTURE

Consonant and vowel phones are physical *segments* of sound. When used to make up words they cluster in predictable ways. The clusters are known as *syllables*. A syllable is a word, or a part of a word, uttered in a single vocal impulse. It can also be defined as a breath group, because it consists of a sound or group of sounds that, after they have been uttered, allow the speaker to take in breath if required.

The segment that forms the *nucleus* of a syllable is a vowel, although in some languages certain consonants can be used. The nucleus is always pronounced with a certain degree of *stress* (or accent). If it is the main stress, it is called *primary*; otherwise it is called *secondary* or *tertiary* when the syllable in question is part of a polysyllabic word (a word with many syllables). The diacritic used typically to indicate primary stress is ['], put on the syllable (*meter* = *mé-ter* = [mí- tər]). Stress is called a *suprasegmental* feature, because it occurs in a "superimposed" fashion with a vocalic segment (i.e., concomitantly with a vowel). The table on page 61 shows how syllables can have both primary and secondary stress according to the words in which they occur:

	p	b	t	d	è	j	k	g	f	v	s	ʃ	ts	dz	r	l	m	n
consonantal	+	+	+	+	+	+	+	+	+	+	+	+	+	+	+	+	+	+
sonorant	–	–	–	–	–	–	–	–	–	–	–	–	–	–	+	+	+	+
nasal	–	–	–	–	–	–	–	–	–	–	–	–	–	–	–	–	+	+
voiced	–	+	–	+	–	+	–	+	–	+	–	–	–	+	+	+	+	+
continuant	–	–	–	–	–	–	–	–	+	+	+	+	–	–	+	+	+	+
labial	+	+	–	–	–	–	–	–	+	+	–	–	–	–	–	–	+	–
dental	–	–	+	+	–	–	–	–	–	–	+	–	+	+	–	+	–	+
palatal	–	–	–	–	+	+	–	–	–	–	–	+	–	–	+	–	–	–
anterior	+	+	+	+	+	–	–	–	+	+	+	+	+	+	–	–	+	+
velar	–	–	–	–	–	–	+	+	–	–	–	–	–	–	–	–	–	–
coronal	–	–	+	+	+	+	–	–	–	–	+	+	+	+	+	+	–	+
sibilant	–	–	–	–	–	–	–	–	–	–	+	+	–	–	–	–	–	–

Syllables with Primary Stress *main stress*	Same Syllables with Secondary Stress
locus = *ló*-cus	location = *lo*-cá-tion
caption = *cáp*-tion	capsizing = *cap*-síz-ing
recommend = re-com-*ménd*	recommendation = re-com-*mend*-á-tion
company = *cóm*-pa-ny	companion = *com*-pá-nion

The sounds that can come before or after a nucleus are known as *contours*. If another vowel comes before, then it is called a *semiconsonant glide* and the syllable is called a *rising diphthong*, because the stress pattern of the syllable starts with the glide and peaks at the vocalic nucleus: for example, the first syllable of *yesterday* is a rising diphthong because the voice pitch is raised as it moves from the glide [y] to the vowel [e]. A *falling diphthong* is a syllable consisting of a glide after the vowel nucleus, which is less tense than a semiconsonant glide and is thus called a *semivowel* glide. The *y* in *say* is such a glide and the syllable in this case is a falling diphthong. A diphthong is, in effect, a blend of two vowel sounds in one syllable.

Contours that come before the vowel nucleus are classified under the rubric of *onset*, and those that come after under *coda*. The *nucleus + coda* sequence constitutes a more general category known as a *rhyme*. For example, the word *special* has the following syllabic structure:

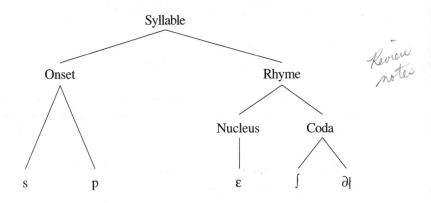

Using a similar type of tree diagram, it can be shown how, for instance, the word *discover* retains the rhythmic pattern of its two parts *dis + cover*, with *cover* bearing the primary stress (S = strong or primary stress, W = weak or secondary stress):

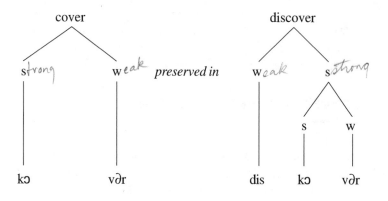

In addition to syllable and word stress, phoneticians also study sentence stress patterns, because these affect how meanings are extracted from an utterance. In simple English statements and questions, the main stress is normally placed on the last word:

Sarah is Itálian.
Alex is arriving tomórrow.
What's your náme?
Where did you gó?

Simple sentences such as these can, of course, be spoken with a different stress pattern to highlight different intentions or meanings:

Sárah is Italian (not Mary).
Aléx is arriving tomorrow (not Fred).

If words of the same kind (all nouns, all adjectives, etc.) occur in a series, then each one is stressed, showing in effect that they have equal importance in the sentence:

Sárah, Aléx, and Dánny are Italian.
Would you like cóffee or téa?

Another important aspect of pronunciation is *tone*. Tone is defined as the relative pitch with which a syllable, a word, phrase, or sentence is pronounced.

In some languages, such as North Mandarin Chinese, tone is a critical phonemic feature, since it is used contrastively. The single syllable [ma], for example, can have various meanings according to whether the tone is level (—), rising (↑), dipping (↕) or falling (↓):

[ma —]	=	*mother*
[ma ↑]	=	*hemp*
[ma ↕]	=	*horse*
[ma ↓]	=	*scold*

In English, tone is used typically to signal differences in the intent or function of sentences. This use of tone is known more specifically as *intonation*. English statements, for instance, end with a falling intonation pattern:

Marie is French. (↓)
He's coming tomorrow. (↓)

The same intonation pattern applies to questions that start with interrogative words:

What's your name? (↓)
Where do you live? (↓)

On the other hand, English questions that require a *yes* or a *no* response end with a rising intonation pattern:

Do you speak Italian? (↑)
Do you know her? (↑)

This intonation pattern applies as well to *tag* questions, which are questions with phrases and words such as *isn't he, don't you*, etc., tagged on to the end:

John is Italian, isn't he? (↑)
You know her, don't you? (↑)

Raising or lowering the tone often changes the meaning of words. Take, for example, the word *Yes*. If uttered with a level tone it indicates affirmation. If uttered with a rising tone *(Yes?)* it indicates "Can I help you?" If uttered with an emphatic tone *(Yes!)* it indicates assertion and satisfaction.

SLIPS OF THE TONGUE

As we saw in chapter 1, phonological structure can be examined indirectly by introducing phonetic errors artificially into the make-up of words. Actually, the study of real errors in speech production is just as revealing, if not more so. Such errors are called "slips of the tongue," since they involve a discrepancy between what is actually said and what the speaker intended to say. For example, in the slip "I need to show (sew) up my shirt," the speaker anticipated the initial sound of *shirt* as he or she was about to say *sew*. Here are other examples of anticipation slips (Fromkin 1973):

" metaphony " '

anticipation (1) Send the letter ail (air) mail.
(2) Puck (pick) up your book.
(3) This is the lust (last) of the rust.
(4) Jack (Jerry) is back from vacation.
(5) Flow (throw) out the flour.
(6) Where's the leading list (reading list)?
(7) It's a meal (real) mystery.

repetition   Another type of slip is the repetition of one or more sounds that have already been uttered as part of an earlier word. In the sentence "This is a new gain (game)," the initial sound of *new* is repeated in the final sound of *game*. Such an error is called a sound preservation slip. Here are a few other examples of such slips:

both stops

(1) Fetch the tan (pan).
(2) You really gave me a bowl foll (full).
(3) He pulled a pantrum (tantrum).
(4) It appeared at the beginning of the burn (turn).

Other types of slips are called reversals—"a two-sen pet" for "a two-pen set" and "preach seduction" instead of "speech production." In sum, slips of the tongue reveal how *langue* and *parole* intermingle in actual speech.

SOUND SYMBOLISM

Sound symbolism

As discussed in the previous chapter, sound symbolism is the tendency to use sounds to reflect some aspect of reality. Sound symbolism is so deeply rooted that we hardly ever notice that it guides our interpretation of the meaning of words.

In one relevant study, the psycholinguist Roger Brown (1970: 258–273) asked native speakers of English to listen to pairs of antonyms from a language unrelated to English and then to try to guess, given the English equivalents, which foreign word translated which English word. The subjects were asked to guess the meaning of the foreign words by attending to their sounds. When he asked them, for example, to match the words *ch'ing* and *chung* to the English equivalents *light* and *heavy*, not necessarily in that order, Brown found that about 90% of English speakers correctly matched *ch'ing* to *light* and *chung* to *heavy*. He concluded that the degree of translation accuracy could only be explained "as indicative of a primitive phonetic symbolism deriving from the origin of speech in some kind of imitative or physiognomic linkage of sounds and meanings" (Brown 1970: 272). Put more specifically, words constructed with the vowel /i/ have a perceptible "lightness" quality to them and those constructed with /ʊ/ a 'heaviness" quality. This perceptual differentiation shows up in the kinds of meanings assigned to the words themselves.

Sound symbolism theory in linguistics was pioneered by Morris Swadesh throughout his professional career (Swadesh 1951, 1959, 1971). Swadesh drew attention to such suggestive features as the fact that many of the world's languages used front vowels (/i/-type and /e/-type vowels) to construct words in which "nearness" was implied, in contrast to back vowels (/a/-type, /o/-type, and /u/-type vowels) to construct words in which the opposite concept of "distance" was implied. Here are some manifestations of this front vs. back opposition in English:

Nearness Concepts	Distance Concepts
here = [hir] *front*	there = [ðær]
near = [nir] *vowels*	far = [far] *back*
this = [ðɪs]	that = [ðæt] *shd be front*
in = [ɪn] *front*	out = [awt]
these –	*those – back*

a raw – back

The same kind of opposition is found across languages to distinguish between *this* (implying nearness) and *that/you* (implying distance), suggesting that it might be a universal tendency:

Language	"This" = [i]	"That/You" = [a]/[u]
Chinook	-i-	-u-
Klamath	ke- *Key*	ho-, ha-
Tsimshian	gwii-	gwa-
Guaraní	tyé	tuvicha
Maya	li'	la', lo'
Binga	ti	ta
Fur	in	illa
Didinga	ici	ica
Tamil	idi	adi
Thai	nii	nan
Burmese	dii	thoo

Rarely do we realize how productive sound symbolism is in our own language. Here are some of the ways it manifests itself in English:

- in the *alliteration* or repetition of sounds for various effects: *sing-song*; *no-no*, etc.; *tic tac ding dong* / *gesture!*
- in the *lengthening* of sounds for emphasis: *Yessssss!, Noooooo!*, etc.;
- in the use of *intonation* to express emotional states, to emphasize something, to shock someone, etc.: *Are you absolutely sure? Noooooo way!* etc.;
- in *sound modeling*, as in the language used in cartoons and comic books: *Zap!, Boom!, Pow!*, etc.; *Batman create words to model sounds*
- in *onomatopoeic* words: *bang, boom, swish, plop*, etc.;
- in the use of *loudness* to convey a state of anger, urgency, etc.; and in its opposite, *whispering*, to convey secrecy, conspiracy, etc.

Body lang accompanies sound also (gesture!) lectured this

Sound symbolism is a basic and largely unconscious tendency in the construction and interpretation of words. For example, continuants are found typically in words that refer to things that are perceived to have "continuity." Take, for example, the /fl/ cluster, which is found commonly in the make-up of English words that refer to things that move or run smoothly with unbroken continuity, in the manner that is characteristic of a fluid:

construction interpretation

flow   *fl common sound*
flake   *suggests continuity ⇒ not interrupted*

flee
float
fly

On the other hand, the cluster /bl/, which consists of an obstruent, is found in words that refer typically to actions that involve blocking, impeding, or some other form of occlusion:

bl → stop combination

block
blitz
blunt
blow

In effect, stop phonemes are found in words that refer to objects or actions perceived to involve "stoppage," continuants in words that refer to objects or actions that are perceived to involve "flow." Here are other examples of this dichotomy in word construction (Crystal 1987: 174):

/p/: dip, rip, sip,…
/k/: crack, click, creak,… *stops*
/b/: rub, jab, blob,…
/l/: rustle, bustle, trickle,…
/z/: ooze, wheeze, squeeze,…
/f/: puff, huff, cough,…

The universality and pervasiveness of sound symbolism suggests that it may be a tendency built into the very blueprint for language. The study of sound symbolism thus provides a unique kind of insight into language processes that may have been operative during the original formation of speech.

CONCLUDING REMARKS

The study of sound systems constitutes the initial stage in studying the relation among words, their meanings, and their use in social contexts. Linguistics makes available a standard and comprehensive repertoire of phonetic symbols and of theoretical notions for describing sounds, classifying them, and relating them to each other. On a broader anthropological scale, phonological analysis allows the linguist to differentiate between tendencies and patterns that are universal and those that are culture-specific.

Words

Give the people a new word and they think they have a new fact.

Willa Cather (1873–1947)

PRELIMINARY REMARKS

In the previous chapter, we were concerned with the underlying system that governed the pronunciation of *words*, without ever having defined, however, what a *word* is. As the nineteenth-century linguists soon came to realize by comparing cognates and reconstructing proto-words, defining what a word is is not a simple task—what is a word in one language may be two in another or part of a word in yet another. For most intents and purposes, a word can be defined, simply, as a form that has meaning. A form that conveys a "single piece of meaning" is known more technically as a *minimal free form*. For example, *logic* is a minimal free form because it conveys a single piece of meaning and thus cannot be broken down further. Forms that must occur in tandem with others are known instead as *bound forms*. The word *illogical*, for instance, contains two bound forms in addition to the minimal free form *logic*. These are: (1) the negative prefix *il-*, which conveys the meaning "opposite of"; and (2) the suffix *–al*, which conveys the meaning "act or process of being something." In addition to prefixes and suffixes, bound forms may be roots (as the *rasp-* in *raspberry*), endings (as the *-s* in *boys, -ed* in *played,* and *-ing* in *playing*), or internal alterations indicating such grammatical categories as tense (*sing-sang*) and number (*mouse-mice*).

The study of how words are put together in a language and of what "bits of pieces" of sound can coalesce into the make-up and meaning of words comes under the rubric of *morphology*. For an anthropological linguist, the initial stages of data analysis may be geared towards the phonetic transcription of the data and a phonological analysis of the sounds; but as he or she well knows, the data will not yield its culture-specific insights until the morphology of the words within it, not to mention their meanings, is deciphered.

WORDS

One way to understand how we perceive words as units of meaning is to look at slips of the tongue, such as those involving the erroneous blending of parts or the erroneous use of suffixes:

Error Type	What Was Said	What Was Intended
Blends	symblem	symbol or emblem
	postcarrier	postman or lettercarrier
Suffix Errors	groupment	grouping
	ambigual	ambiguous

The fact that such slips were made at all bears witness to the fact that the speaker knows how words are constructed in English. In forming *symblem* the speaker confused endings with suffixes, exchanging the ending *-ol* of *symbol* with the ending *-em* of *emblem*, as if they were suffixes. In forming *postcarrier* the speaker put forms together erroneously that occur as parts of other words: *post* (in *postman*) and *carrier* (in *lettercarrier*). In *groupment* and *ambigual* the speaker used the legitimate suffixes *-ment* and *-al*, but he or she put them on words that require other kinds of suffixes (*-ing* and *-ous*) to render the intended meaning (*grouping* and *ambiguous*).

Most words can, in fact, be defined by their formal features and by their position in sentences or phrases. However, some words, such as prepositions and conjunctions, have no formal features. They can be defined only by their function and position in a sentence. The traditional taxonomy lists eight classes of words: nouns, pronouns, verbs, adjectives, adverbs, prepositions, conjunctions, and interjections. Some however prefer to distinguish *form classes*—nouns, verbs, adjectives, and adverbs—from *function words*—prepositions, determiners, auxiliaries, and conjunctions. Others distinguish

inflected classes (such as *boy* and *boys*) from all other words, called *particles*
(*to, with*).

The term *vocabulary* is used to indicate the total number of words in a
language. That number is, however, always changing. As life becomes more
complex, people devise or borrow new words to describe new ideas and things,
and they change the meanings of existing words to fit new circumstances.
New words are often constructed by derivation. For example, shortly after
microwave ovens became available, the verb *to microwave* appeared in sentences
such as "John *microwaved* the frozen rolls." The same type of derivational
process can be seen in the coining of the following recent verbs, from the
computer and Internet areas:

derivation used in coining of new words

Noun	Derived Verb
e-mail	e-mailing
Internet	Internetting
word-processor	word-processing
format	formatting

Active vocab = 10,000
Passive vocab = 30,000

People have two kinds of vocabularies. Their *active* vocabulary is made
up of the actual words they tend to use in speaking or writing; their *passive*
vocabulary consists of words they understand when listening or reading, but
which they do not use with regularity. Many people have a passive vocabulary
several times larger than their active vocabulary. For the average American,
the active vocabulary is 10,000 words, but the passive vocabulary is 30,000 to
40,000 words. The range of a person's vocabulary is a clue to the person's
education, experiences, preferences, or interests.

Edward Sapir (1921) was probably the first to point out the presence of a
"vocabulary blueprint" in the human brain that allowed speakers of different
languages to communicate the same ideas with the specific vocabulary resources
at their disposal. To show this, he simply got speakers of several indigenous
languages of the southwestern US to render the English sentence *He will give*
it to you in their respective languages (Sapir and Swadesh 1946):

indigen-ous

Sapir = vocab blueprint

Language	"He will give it to you"	Structure in English Terms
Wishram	a-č-i-m-l-úd-a	will-he-him-you-to-give-will
Takelma	ök-t-xpi-nk	will-give-to-you-he or they
South Paiute	maya-vaania-aka-ana-mi	give-will-visible thing-visible creature-you
Yana	ba-ja-ma-si-wa-numa	round thing-away-to-does-unto-you
Nootka	o-yi-aqλ-at-eik	that-give-will-done unto-you are
Navaho	n-a-yi-diho-a	you-to transitive-will-round thing

The fact that the English sentence was so easily translated by speakers of the above languages gives substance to Sapir's claim of a vocabulary blueprint, despite differences in actual vocabulary items and linguistic structure. A language might include information that may be excluded by others, or else it may eliminate details that others consider relevant to the message. In English, for instance, we must indicate the gender of the actor (masculine *he*) and the object (neuter *it*), as well as the number (singular in this case) and tense of the verb (future in this case *will give*). We do not need to indicate, as speakers of some of the other languages above need to do, the size or shape of the object, whether or not it is visible, or whether the action was observed by the speaker.

Such examples show that words reflect both universal tendencies in language know-how and culture-specific solutions to conceptual problems. In a relevant study, the linguist William Labov (1973) showed how this duality manifested itself in simple naming tasks. He presented drawings of cups and cuplike containers to subjects, asking them to name the items with words such as *cup, mug, bowl, dish,* and *pitcher.* The subjects were then asked to imagine the same series of objects containing coffee, mashed potatoes, or flowers. The subjects were most likely to label untypical objects as "cups" if they contained coffee and least likely to do so if they held flowers. Labov concluded that words are essentially "categorical devices." More will be said about the relation between words and cognition below and in subsequent chapters.

THE MORPHEME

[handwritten: morphemes = basic parts of word-formation]

The bits and pieces that make up the single words in the aboriginal languages above are called, more precisely, *morphemes*. These are the basic units of word formation. The word *cats,* for instance, consists of two morphemes: *[handwritten: cat s 2]* *cat,* whose meaning can be roughly rendered as "feline animal," and *-s,* whose meaning is "more than one." *Antimicrobial,* meaning "capable of destroying microorganisms," consists of three morphemes: (1) *anti-* ("against"), (2) *microbe* ("microorganism"), and (3) *-ial* (a suffix that makes the word an adjective).

A morpheme can be defined, more formally, as the smallest unit of sound or sounds that bears a meaning. If the meaning is lexical (e.g., *cat*), then it is called a *root morpheme* or *lexeme*; if it is purely grammatical (e.g., the *-s* in *cats*) it is called a *grammatical morpheme.* The word *incompletely,* for instance, is made up of three morphemes:

in	complete	ly
↑	↑	↑
grammatical	*lexical*	*grammatical*
morpheme meaning	*morpheme meaning*	*morpheme meaning*
"opposite of"	*"full" or "whole"*	*"in the manner of"*
or "negative"		

[handwritten: segmentation]

The process of identifying morphemes is known as *segmentation*, since it entails breaking up a word into sounds or sound combinations that cannot be split any further. Take, for instance, the following forms in Swahili, a northern Bantu language:

nitasoma	=	"I will read"	*[handwritten: ni I ta soma = read]*
nilisoma	=	"I read (past)"	*[handwritten: li]*
utasoma	=	"you will read"	*[handwritten: u you ta will (future)]*
ulisoma	=	"you read (past)"	*[handwritten: li past]*

By comparing these forms systematically, it is possible to establish the following facts:

(1) Since /-soma/ occurs in all four, we can deduce that it is a root or lexical morpheme, which has a meaning that corresponds to English "read."

(2) Comparing the first two forms against the last two, we can see that the morpheme /ni-/ corresponds to the English pronoun "I" and /u-/ to the pronoun "you."

(3) Comparing the first and second forms in tandem with the third and fourth, we can see that /-ta-/ is a future tense grammatical morpheme and /-li-/ a past tense grammatical morpheme.

Segmentation also allows us to separate morphemes that can stand on their own as separate words and those that cannot. The former, as mentioned at the start of this chapter, are known as *free*, and the latter as *bound*. In the word *incompletely*, only the internal morpheme, *complete*, can occur by itself as an autonomous free morpheme. On the other hand, /in-/ and /-ly/ can only be used as bound morphemes, that is, as morphemes attached to other morphemes. Similarly, in Swahili, only *soma* can occur as a free form; the other morphemes are all bound.

There are two main types of bound morphemes. In the form *learned*, the bound grammatical morpheme /-ed/ is known as an *inflectional morpheme* because it provides further information about /learn/, namely that the action of learning has occurred in the past. Compare this to the grammatical morpheme /-ly/, as used in *completely*, which has a different function. It allows us to create a word with a different grammatical function than the word to which it is bound (the word *complete* is an adjective, while *completely* is an adverb). This kind of morpheme is called *derivational*.

A type of bound morpheme that requires special mention here, given its frequency in the formation of words in languages across the world, is the *affix*. This is defined as a morpheme that is attached to other morphemes in specific positions. The /in-/ and /-ly/ in *incompletely* are examples of affixes. The former is known more specifically as a *prefix* because it is attached before another morpheme; the latter is known instead as a *suffix* because it is attached after another morpheme. The morphological structure of *incompletely* can now be shown more precisely with a tree diagram as follows:

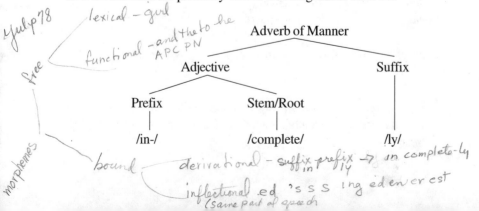

There are two other types of affixes that have been documented by linguists. They are called *infixes* and *circumfixes*. An infix is an affix that is inserted within another morpheme. Take, for example, the following Bantoc words, a language spoken in the Philippines:

um = to be

fikas	= "strong"	→	*fumikas*	= "to be strong"
kilad	= "red"	→	*kumilad*	= "to be red"
fusul	= "enemy"	→	*fumusul*	= "to be an enemy"

As these examples show, inserting the /-um-/ infix after the initial consonant adds the meaning "to be" to the root morpheme. Circumfixes are affixes that come "as a package," so to speak, since they are attached to a root morpheme in tandem. For instance, in Chickasaw, a Native language spoken in Oklahoma, a root morpheme is rendered negative by attaching both the prefix /ik-/ and the suffix /-o/ to it (eliminating the final vowel of the root):

lakna	= "it is yellow"	→	*iklakno*	= "it isn't yellow"
palli	= "it is hot"	→	*ikpallo*	= "it isn't hot"

ik + pall + o

circumfix

Words can be compared to molecules, since they are unit structures that are made up of smaller segments (morphemes), but end up being "holistic structures" that are different than any of their constituent parts. In the physical world, salt consists of the elements sodium and chlorine. Its chemical name is, in fact, *sodium chloride,* and its formula is NaCl. But NaCl is different from any of its two constituent parts. Salt is an edible substance, but neither sodium nor chlorine are when taken separately. In chemistry, as in language, things in combination are not the simple sum of the parts. They form integral wholes.

Sometimes the use of a bound morpheme is intended not to change the meaning but to add nuance, perspective, or a different modality to the meaning of the root. Take, as a case-in-point, the suffix *-ish* added to English morphemes:

child	→	childish
tall	→	tallish
boor	→	boorish

nuance = subtle difference or shade in meaning

This suffix adds the nuance "in the manner of," or "rather, quite" to the root meaning. It can be added almost at will to any word to render this nuance. The same kind of additive "modality function" can be seen in a host of other productive suffixes in English:

-able

like	→	likable
love	→	loveable
reason	→	reasonable

-y

shade	→	shady
chew	→	chewy
goo	→	gooey

-like

story	→	story-like
trial	→	trial-like
adventure	→	adventure-like

MORPHOLOGICAL ANALYSIS

The form that a morpheme takes in actual words or phrases might sometimes vary, depending on certain factors. Take the plural suffix /-s/ in English. In actual fact, this morpheme has three variants, as can be seen in the following chart:

/-s/ /-z/ and /-ɔz/ are allomorphs (plurals)

(1) /-s/	(2) /-z/	(3) /-ɔz/
		x lass + s
pot + /-s/ → pots	load + /-z/ → loads	lass + /-ɔz/ → lasses
top + /-s/ → tops	dog + /-z/ → dogs	church + /-ɔz/ → churches
kick + /-s/ → kicks	bra + /-z/ → bras	judge + /-ɔz/ → judges
-Vₐ -V	*+V +V*	*articulatory difficult*
final sound		*x churchs*

Review sibilant

Column (1) contains root morphemes that end with any voiceless consonant other than a sibilant or affricate; column (2) contains root morphemes that end with a vowel or any voiced consonant other than a sibilant or affricate; and column (3) contains root morphemes that end with any sibilant or affricate.

sibilant - a fricative in which there is a high pitched turbulent noise ie /s/ sip

This suggests, of course, a rule of complementary distribution—the plural morpheme /-s/ in English is voiced (/-z/) when attached to a root ending in a voiced sound, unless that sound is a sibilant or affricate, in which case it is changed to /-ðz/.

The variant forms /-s/, /-z/, and /-ðz/ are known as *allomorphs*. In this *allomorph* case, the allomorphs are phonologically conditioned variants, because they vary according to the phonemic features of the final phoneme of the morpheme to which they are attached. The complementary distribution rule is thus called *morphophonemic*.

The indefinite article in English presents another case of morphophonemic variation:

(1) /a/ *unmarked - typical*   *morphophonemic*
                                                   a vs an.

a boy
a girl
a friend
a mother
a father

(2) /æn/   *marked, conditioned or exceptional*

an egg
an island
an apple
an opera

As can be seen by comparing the forms in (1) and (2), the allomorph /a/ occurs before a morpheme beginning with a consonant and its complementary allomorph /æn/ before a morpheme beginning with a vowel. Incidentally, linguists refer to (1) as the *unmarked* form and (2) as the *marked* one. The former is the most typical representative (nonspecific) of a class; the latter the conditioned or exceptional member. In Italian, the masculine plural form of nouns referring to people is the unmarked one, because it can refer (nonspecifically) to any person, male or female; whereas the feminine plural form is marked, since it refers specifically to females:

Masculine Plural Forms	Feminine Plural Forms
i turisti = all tourists, males and females	*le turiste* = female tourists
gli amici = all friends, males and females	*le amiche* = female friends
i bambini = all children, males and females	*le bambine* = female children
gli studenti = all students, males and females	*le studentesse* = female students

The gender system of a language is said to be marked insofar as it requires male human beings to be named with the masculine gender, and female human beings to be named with the feminine gender. In this way the appropriate morphemes allow speakers to refer to the biological sex of human referents. For inanimate referents, the conventional view is that gender assignment is unpredictable and therefore arbitrary. Markedness is irrelevant in this case. For example, there appears to be no natural link between the grammatical gender of a word like Italian *casa* (which is feminine) and its referent ("house"). But do links between morphological form and meaning exist beyond marked categories? Yes

The linguist Ronald W. Langacker (1987, 1999) has argued persuasively that such links do indeed exist. For instance, Langacker notes that in English nouns refer to things that have or do not have boundaries (edges, margins, finite shape, etc.). For example, the noun *leaf* refers to something [bounded], since leaves have edges, whereas the noun *water* refers to something that is [non-bounded], since water does not have edges or definite shape. Now, it is this difference in type of referent that influences the morphological treatment of each noun. Because [bounded] referents can be counted, the noun *leaf* has a corresponding plural form *leaves*, but *water* does not (unless the word is used metaphorically as in *the waters of Babylon*). Moreover *leaf* can be preceded by an indefinite article (*a leaf*), *water* cannot. Langacker has established linkages of this type throughout the grammar of English, suggesting that grammar and reality are intertwined. This topic will be taken up in more detail in the final chapter.

Abbreviations/acronyms

l.m. acronyms   lol
(innovations)

ZIPF'S LAW AGAIN

Recall Zipf's Law, which states basically that the more frequently a word or expression is used, the more likely it will be replaced by a shorter equivalent. More generally, it claims that language forms are being constantly condensed, abbreviated, reduced, or eliminated in order to minimize the effort expended to produce and use them. Zipf's Law can be seen to manifest itself across languages in similar ways. For example, it can be seen to undergird the following abbreviations and acronyms:

ad = *ad*vertisement
photo = *photo*graph
NATO = *N*orth *A*tlantic *T*reaty *O*rganization
laser = *l*ight *a*mplification by *s*timulated *e*mission of *r*adiation
24/7 = 24 hours a day, seven days a week

Some abbreviations are formed with only the initial letters of a word, as when *Feb.* is used to stand for *February.* Other abbreviations are created with the first and last letters, as when *VT* is used to stand for *Vermont.* Key letters in a word or phrase may also be used—e.g., *VCR* for *videocassette recorder.* Here are some common examples in English:

AA	Alcoholics Anonymous; Associate in Arts
AAA	American Automobile Association
AAU	Amateur Athletic Union
AC	alternating current
AIDS	acquired immunodeficiency syndrome
a.k.a.	also known as
ALA	American Library Association
AM	amplitude modulation
AMA	American Medical Association
anon.	anonymous
AP	Associated Press
assn.	association
assoc.	associate; association
asst.	assistant
ATM	automated teller machine
atty.	attorney
ave.	avenue

blvd.	boulevard
cal.	calorie (heat)
CBC	Canadian Broadcasting Corporation
CD	compact disc
CEO	chief executive officer
CIA	Central Intelligence Agency
c/o	in care of
co.	company; county
COD	cash on delivery; collect on delivery
corp.	corporation
DA	district attorney
DC	direct current
DNA	deoxyribonucleic acid
Dr.	doctor
EPA	Environmental Protection Agency
ERA	Equal Rights Amendment
ESP	extrasensory perception
ETA	estimated time of arrival
EU	European Union
FBI	Federal Bureau of Investigation
GNP	gross national product
hr.	hour
IBM	International Business Machines Corporation
inc.	incorporated; including
IQ	intelligence quotient
Ltd.	Limited
mph	miles per hour
no.	number
p.	page
PBS	Public Broadcasting System
PC	personal computer
PIN	personal identification number
Rev.	Reverend
ROM	read-only memory
St.	Saint; street
UFO	unidentified flying object
US	United States
VIP	very important person
Xmas	Christmas

Abbreviations save effort. They are used in tables, in technical and scientific material, in indexes, in footnotes, and in bibliographies. They are also used in place of long official names, as in AFL-CIO (American Federation of Labor and Congress of Industrial Organizations).

Abbreviations have been found on the earliest known tombs, monuments, and coins; and they have been found in ancient manuscripts written by hand. Many Latin abbreviations are still used in English. Here are some of them:

ad lib	*ad libitum* (as one pleases)
e.g.	*exempli gratia* (for example)
et al.	*et alibi* (and elsewhere, and others)
etc.	*et cetera* (and so forth)
ibid.	*ibidem* (in the same place)
id.	*idem* (the same)
i.e.	*id est* (that is)
loc. cit.	*loco citato* (in the place cited)
N.B.	*nota bene* (note well)
op. cit.	*opere citato* (in the work cited)
P.S.	*post scriptum* (postscript)
Q.E.D.	*quod erat demonstrandum* (which was to be shown or proved)
q.v.	*quod vide* (which see)
v.	*vide* (see)
vs.	*versus* (against)

Innovations in language also seem to be governed by Zipf's Principle of Least Effort. Take, for example, "instant message" (IM) acronyms. Unlike e-mail, IMs are sent in real time, like a phone call, but with text rather than spoken words. To increase the speed at which IMs can be inputted and received, a series of common acronyms have been created that are now part of "computer language." Here are a few of them:

b4	=	before
bf/gf	=	boyfriend/girlfriend
f2f	=	face-to-face
gr8	=	great
h2cus	=	hope to see you soon
idk	=	I don't know
j4f	=	just for fun
lol	=	laughing out loud

cm	=	call me
2dA	=	today
wan2	=	want to
ruok	=	Are you OK?
2moro	=	tomorrow
g2g	=	gotta "got to" go

[handwritten: Classification 1. historical 2. morphological]

LINGUISTIC TYPOLOGY

[handwritten: Indigenous - people born in a region]

The ways in which morphemes are used to construct words provide a rationale for classifying languages. For example, Turkish, Basque, and a number of indigenous American languages use suffixes abundantly in the construction of their words. They are thus characterized as *agglutinative*. Languages using prefixes abundantly are much less numerous. Thai is one example. Infixation is a minor component of English morphology—*mouse* vs. *mice*—but it is a major component of the morphology of many Semitic languages. Most languages employ affixes of various types in word formation to lesser or greater degrees. Affixation, thus, can be used to classify languages in terms of frequency and type of affixes used.

Another morphemic criterion used in classification is the relative number of morphemes employed in word construction and the degree of fusion among them. The theoretical extreme is one morpheme per word. The language that tends to form its words in this way is known as an *isolating* language. Chinese is an isolating language, although it too uses affixes, but less frequently than other languages do. As mentioned above, languages that make up their words frequently with combinations of morphemes, such as Latin, are known as agglutinative.

Edward Sapir (1921) developed one of the first elaborate systems for classifying languages on the basis of morphological criteria. He took into consideration both the number of morphemes used in word formation (*isolating*, *agglutinative*, and *fusional*) and the degree of synthesis in the formation process *(analytic, synthetic,* and *polysynthetic)*. For example, the English words *goodness* and *depth* are similar in that they are composed of a root morpheme (*good* and *deep*) and a suffix (*-ness* and *-th*). The word *depth*, however, shows a greater degree of synthesis, since it shows a fusion of the root and suffix morphemes, whereas *goodness* just shows the suffix added to the root with no phonic changes.

The American linguist Joseph Greenberg (1968) refined Sapir's typological method, making it more precise, introducing the concept of the morphological index. The index is derived by taking a representative and large sample of text, counting the words and the morphemes in it, and then dividing the number of morphemes by the number of words. The index is, obviously, the average number of morphemes per word (I = index, M = number of morphemes, W = number of words):

$$I = M \div W$$

In a perfectly isolating language, the I will be equal to 1, because there is a perfect match between number of words (W) and number of morphemes (M), or M = W. In agglutinating languages, the M will be greater than W. The greater it is, the higher the index, and thus, the higher the degree of agglutination. The highest index Greenberg discovered with his method was 3.72 for Eskimo. Greenberg suggested that:

- languages in the 1.0–2.2 range be classified as analytic;
- languages in the 2.2–3.0 range be classified as synthetic;
- languages in the 3.0 and above range be classified as polysynthetic.

The main weakness in classifying languages in this way lies in the lack of a definitive method for determining what constitutes a word in one language or another. The classification of languages according to morphemic criteria has, nevertheless, gained wide acceptance because of the central role of words in the phenomenon of language.

Assigning languages to different types involves a delicate procedure of balancing one part of the grammar against another and deciding which type of structure predominates and how well the other types are represented. This is why linguists also use historical criteria to group languages together. As discussed in previous chapters, language families can be established on the basis of descent; i.e., on the basis of unbroken development from an earlier common parent language. Though the two types of classification—historical and morphological—may coincide in classifying certain languages consistently, as is the case to a great extent in the case of the languages of the Bantu family, they do not coincide in all cases.

CONCLUDING REMARKS

To conclude the discussion of words it should be mentioned that there are many who believe that words set people apart and may bring about misunderstanding and conflict. For this reason, people have often dreamed of creating an artificial, universal language that all people could speak and understand unambiguously. The reason given for such a language is a simple one—if all people spoke the same tongue, cultural and economic ties might be much closer, and goodwill would increase between countries.

French philosopher and mathematician Rene Descartes (1596–1650) is believed to have originated the idea of a universal language in the 1600s. More than 200 such languages have been invented since he made his proposal. Volapuk—invented by Johann Martin Schleyer, a German priest, in 1879—was the earliest of these languages to gain success. The name of the language comes from two of its words meaning "world" and "speak." Today, only Esperanto is used somewhat. It was devised by L. L. Zamenhof, a Polish physician. The name of the language is derived from the book he published about it, *Lingvo Internacia* (1887), under the pen name Dr. Esperanto. The word *esperanto* means "one who hopes." Esperanto has a simple, uniform morphological structure—adjectives end in *a*, adverbs end in *e*, nouns end in *o*, an *n* is added at the end of a noun used as an object; and plurals end in *j*. The basic core vocabulary of Esperanto consists mainly of root morphemes common to the Indo-European languages. The following sentence is written in Esperanto: *La astronauto, per speciala instrumento, fotografas la lunon* = "The astronaut, with a special instrument, photographs the moon." It is ironic to note, however, that recent research on Esperanto indicates that it is developing dialects, thus impugning its *raison d'être*. It would seem that variation is an inescapable fact of human linguistic life.

Sentences

The words of the world want to make sentences.

Gaston Bachelard (1884–1962)

PRELIMINARY REMARKS

Consider the following seven arrangements of the same words. All, except for one, have been strung together in a random fashion:

(1) boy the is eating pizza a
(2) boy pizza the a is eating
(3) boy pizza a the is eating
(4) pizza boy the a is eating
(5) is eating a boy pizza the
(6) a the is eating boy pizza
(7) the boy is eating a pizza

Clearly, only in arrangement (7) have the words not been put together randomly. It is the only legitimate *sentence*. The other six are meaningless strings because, even though they all consist of valid English words, they lack the appropriate *syntactic structure* that governs word order in English sentences. Like the term *word*, *sentence* refers to a notion that everyone intuitively knows, but which defies precise definition. This is why linguists prefer to characterize a sentence *structurally* as a string of words organized around a *subject* and a *predicate*. Generally speaking, the subject is what or who the sentence is about; and the predicate indicates what the subject does, thinks, says, etc., or else what is said, thought, etc., about the subject. The basic syntactic structure of an English sentence can thus be shown as follows:

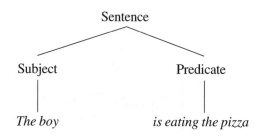

All languages use word order of some sort to make sentences. In some languages, however, it is less crucial than it is in others. As mentioned, Latin, for example, allowed more variation in word order than English does. The Latin sentences *Johannes videt Marcum* and *Marcum videt Johannes* both meant "John sees Mark." Morphological elements in the two sentences indicate the relationship of the words to one another—*Johannes* ("John") is the subject of the sentence, no matter where it occurs in it, because it ends in *-s* (not *-um*); *Marcum* ("Mark") is the object of the sentence, no matter where it is placed in it, because it ends in *-um* (not *-s*). The purpose of this chapter is to discuss the role of syntactic structure in language and its relation to theories of language in general.

SENTENCES

A general characteristic of sentences is that they have a hierarchical or "clustering" structure. This means that the morphemes in them are not organized as singular elements in a line, but rather in terms of how they cluster with each other as manifestations of the subject-predicate relation and, more specifically, as manifestations of certain types of phrases and word classes. The hierarchical relations that conjoin *the boy, is eating*, and *a pizza* as distinct clusters in the above sentence are shown below:

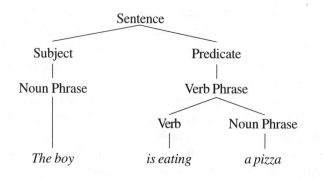

The hierarchical structure of the sentence is what determines which word clusters can be used to replace *The boy is eating a pizza*. So, for instance, *the boy* can be replaced with *a girl, is eating* with *is having*, and so on, because these manifest the same phrase structure:

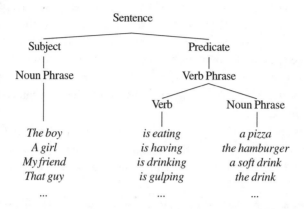

In all sentences there is an interplay between syntax and morphology. This interplay can be seen even in *nonsense* sentences, which have the "feel" of real sentences because the elements in them have appropriate structure. Take, for example, the following string of nonsense words:

The pluming rasinkers kirked the rampix at the minter pintically

We perceive the string to have the structure of an English sentence, even though it has no meaning. This is because the string has the rhythm of an English sentence; the forms in it have the look of English words; and they are felt to relate to each other hierarchically as follows (Adj = Adjective, Adv = Adverb):

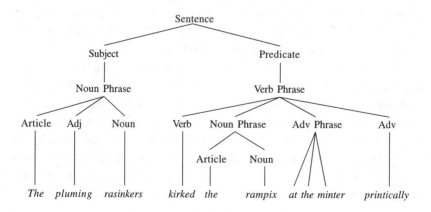

We identify the word *rasinkers* as a noun because it has a plural ending, /-s/ and because it is preceded by the definite article. In the same way, we perceive *rampix* and *minter* as nouns because both are preceded by the article *the*. The two are probably singular because they do not appear to have a plural ending. The word *pluming* is probably an adjective because it appears between an article and a noun. The form *kirked* is probably a verb because /-ed/ is a characteristic past tense ending of verbs. The word also has a position in the sentence typical of where a verb should be. It is a transitive verb because it has an object, *rampix*. The cluster *at the minter* can be identified as a phrase that modifies *kirked*. *Pintically* is probably an adverb because it ends in /-ly/, modifying *kirked*.

It is such morphological and syntactic cues that force us to interpret the string as a legitimate, although meaningless, sentence. By replacing the nonsense words with legitimate ones we can, in fact, construct "real" sentences:

The	pluming	rasinkers	kirked	the	rampix	at	the	minter	pintically
↓	↓	↓	↓	↓	↓	↓	↓	↓	↓
The	…/-ing/	…/-s/	…/-ed/	the	(noun)	at	the	(noun)	…/-ly/
↓	↓	↓	↓	↓	↓	↓	↓	↓	↓
The	loving	sisters	raised	the	banner	at	the	game	proudly
The	rowing	members	started	the	rumor	at	the	club	unintentionally

GRAMMAR

Although the above sentence has no discernible meaning, we still perceive it to be a sentence because it has the formal structure of one. The term *grammar* is used to designate this kind of formal knowledge, which consists, clearly, of knowing: (1) how words cluster in phrases and sentences; (2) how they are inflected; and (3) which words (known as *function words*) can be used to relate the other words in a sentence to each other.

Word order ranks as the most important feature of English grammar. Changing the order of the words in a sentence can change the meaning of the sentence. For example, if the words in the sentence *Alex teased Sarah* are reversed to *Sarah teased Alex*, the meanings are also reversed. The reason why this occurs is because the words in the sentence are governed by an actor-action-goal hierarchical relationship. This expresses the idea that somebody or something does something to someone or something else. The actor functions as the subject of a sentence, the action as its verb, and the goal as its complement (or object). The latter two function together as the predicate of a sentence. This relationship in English is thus why we read the two sentences differently:

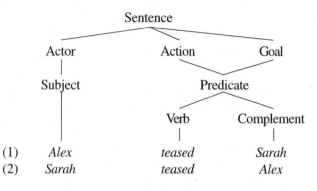

As can be seen, in (1) *Alex* is the actor while in (2) it is *Sarah*. In (1) *Sarah* is the receiver of the *teasing* action, while in (2) the receiver is *Alex*.

Another important grammatical relationship involves the conjoining or coordination of the ideas of two sentences into one sentence that preserves the ideas as equal. For example, we interpret the two parts of the sentence *She had been to Japan and had traveled to Russia* as equal, even though they really belong to two distinct sentences that have been conjoined with the word *and*:

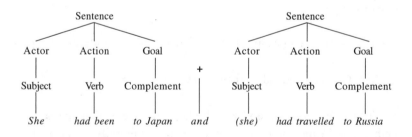

The fact that the subject *She* is not repeated can be explained in several ways. The most traditional explanation is stylistic—repetition is not considered to be "good grammar" in English. Generative grammarians (chapter 1), on the other hand, would see the elimination of the repeated subject as the result of a transformational rule, called a "deletion rule." But the fact that the two *she's* can be used for various reasons to emphasize the subject (*She had been to Japan and she had also traveled to Russia!*) seems to favor the stylistic

Zipf's

interpretation. A third way to explain it is, of course, in terms of Zipf's Law. Repetitions of any kind, but especially those that carry no new information (as in the case of the repeated *she*), tend to be avoided. Indeed, Zipf's Law would also explain why deleting the auxiliary verb as well would not alter the meaning of the sentence, making it simply shorter: *She had been to Japan and traveled to Russia.* deleted she + had.

Subordination is another main type of grammatical relationship, indicating that one thing depends on another. The subordinate parts of most sentences serve as modifiers. They change in some way the meaning of the passage to which they are subordinate. In most English sentences, word order and function words show subordination, as in *After the peaches ripened, the farmer took them to the local market*. The clause *the farmer took them* forms the actor-action-goal core of the sentence. The rest is subordination. The phrase *after the apples ripened* modifies the main action. The phrase *to the local market* is a complement.

GRAMMAR AND USE

X

To use Saussurean terminology once again, grammatical knowledge is part of *langue*, whereas the deployment of this knowledge in actual situations is part of *parole*. But grammar and use are hardly independent of each other. Consider a sentence such as *Old men and women love that program*, which has potentially two meanings:

(1) Old men and women (who are not necessarily old) love that program

(2) Old men and old women love that program

These are elaborations which show, in effect, that the sentence is ambiguous in meaning. The source of the ambiguity is the fact that in coordination, as we saw above, repetition is discouraged. Sequence (2) *old men and old women* has the form $XY + XZ$, where X = old, Y = men, and Z = women. Style dictates that this be reduced to $X(Y + Z)$ = *Old men and women*. But, as the algebraic form shows, we still interpret the X as applying to both Y and Z (as we do in mathematics). Sequence (1), on the other hand, has the different algebraic form $XY + Z$, which leads to a different interpretation of its meaning: *Old men and (not old) women*. Now, communicative competence provides us with the know-how for resolving the ambiguity in real situations.

For example, uttering *old men* followed by a brief pause will render the meaning of XY + Z; on the other hand a brief pause after *old* will render the meaning of X(Y + Z).

As this example shows, the task of the linguist involves not only determining grammatical relationships, but also how these are implemented and modified in communicative situations. Communicative competence involves knowing what devices are available to speakers of a language to resolve ambiguities; what stylistic practices apply in certain situations; and what stylistic features constrain the use of certain forms of grammar.

Take, as an example of the latter, the differential communicative effects produced by active and passive sentences:

(1)
The apple was eaten by Jennie. It was not eaten by me, nor was it my intention to do so. The eating action was accomplished quickly. The apple was devoured by her.

(2)
I put sodium together with chlorine. I knew I was going to get a reaction. I thought I would get salt. But it didn't work out for some reason.

If told that (1) was written by one friend to another and (2) by a scientist in a professional journal, we would immediately perceive both utterances as anomalous. The reason for this is simple—stylistic practices dictate that (1) should be phrased in active sentences and (2) in passive ones. Active sentences are used to emphasize the speaker as the actor in a direct relation with the goal (the person spoken to), whereas passive ones are used to de-emphasize the speaker as actor and highlight the goal as the "object" of interest. The requirement of "objectivity" in scientific writing, in effect, translates into the practice of using passive sentences, where the "goal-object" is highlighted over the "subject-actor." Reformulating both sentences by reversing their voice rectifies their stylistic abnormality:

(1)
Jennie ate the apple. I didn't eat it, nor did I intend to do so. She ate it quickly. She devoured the apple.

(2)
Sodium and chlorine were mixed, in order to attain the expected reaction. The anticipated outcome was salt. However, this outcome was not achieved.

As this example shows, more often than not, <u>rules of syntax turn out to be rules of style</u>. As another case-in-point of this general principle consider the relation between style and humor. In one fascinating study, the psychologist Best (1975) asked a group of college students what they thought about when they saw or heard a well-known comedian. Various students were instructed to name five different adjectival concepts the comedians made them think of. Then, they were told to circle the best one among the five they listed. For example, the name of Phyllis Diller yielded the response *loud* 20 times; Joan Rivers produced the same response 18 times; Bob Hope produced the response 0 times. By analyzing all the responses, Best was able to determine which comedians were most similar to one another. The more responses shared the more similar the comedians; the less responses shared the less similar the comedians. Below are the comedians grouped by shared descriptive adjectives (note that these comedians were well known in the mid-1970s when the study was conducted):

Johnny Carson	*kind*
Danny Thomas	*believable*
Red Skelton	*rich*
Bob Hope	*patriotic*
W. C. Fields	*deadpan*
Alan King	*quick*
Robin Williams	
Don Rickles	*insulting*
John Belushi	
Pat Paulson	*absent-minded*
Bob Newhart	
Don Knotts	*skinny*
Lucille Ball	*wild*
Steve Martin	*loud*
Phyllis Diller	*insane*
Sammy Davis, Jr.	*black*
Flip Wilson	*talented*
Bill Cosby	

As a follow-up study, I instructed a group of my students at the University of Toronto in 2000 to examine the kinds of sentences used typically by each of the above comedians as part of their humorous styles. The students collected tapes of TV programs, movies, and (in some cases) books. Each of the above descriptor categories was given a number: Carson–Thomas–Skelton–Hope = 1, Fields–King–Williams = 2, Rickles–Belushi = 3, Paulson–Newhart = 4, Knotts = 5, Ball–Martin–Diller = 6, Davis, Jr.–Wilson–Cosby = 7. From the audiovisual and written materials, the students selected 100 random sentences for each comedian. The average word lengths of the 100 sentences were then determined. This produced a remarkable pattern of findings, as can be seen in the chart below:

Descriptor category	Typical Sentence Type Used	Average Word Length of 100 Sentences
1: kind, believable, rich, patriotic	Mainly active sentences, with a straightforward actor-action-complement structure	7.2 S V O
2: deadpan, quick	Mainly elliptical sentences (missing parts), with abbreviated phrase structure	5.8
3: insulting	Mainly brief active sentences, with abbreviated phrase structure and much use of emphatic sentences (exclamations, proclamations, etc.)	6.1
4: absent-minded	Many passive sentences, with the use of many questions (usually rhetorical in intent)	9.9
5: skinny	Very brief sentences, usually active	5.9
6: wild, loud, insane	All kinds of sentences, but emphasis normally added through tone, intonation, and exclamation	8.9
7: black, talented	Much use of coordination and subordination, and much use of passive sentences	10.5

The chart is self-explanatory. It shows that the choice of descriptive adjective in the original study was likely influenced in part by type and length of sentence used by the comedians as part of their style: e.g., those comedians labeled as *quick* had an average sentence length of 5.8; those labeled as *talented* an average length of 10.5; those labeled as *insulting* had a comparable sentence length to those labeled as *quick* (6.1), but were differentiated in the fact that they used emphatic sentences. It is interesting to note that those comedians labeled as *talented* had a style that is very similar to "academic speech," with long elaborate sentences.

There is, of course, much more to humor than this. But overall, it is fair to say that the way in which words are put together, the length of sentences, and the mode of sentence construction convey a certain "feel" to the humor that people seem to interpret in specific ways.

THE LEXICON

[handwritten: Lexicon = set of morphemes in a language. Lexicon includes syntactic + morphological knowledge]

Recall the nonsense sentence on page 87 one more time. As discussed, its morphological and syntactic properties are what made us perceive it as a potential sentence in English. In bare outline, these properties can be shown as follows:

The	.../-ing/	.../-s/	.../-ed/	the	(noun)	at	the	(noun)	.../-ly/
↓	↓	↓	↓	↓	↓	↓	↓	↓	↓
The	pluming	rasinkers	kirked	the	rampix	at	the	minter	pintically

Now, as this analysis makes clear, the insertion of real morphemes from the English *lexicon* into the above slots requires knowledge of both the meaning of words and their structural profile. This kind of knowledge is called *lexical insertion*. The *lexicon* is a particular kind of dictionary that contains not only the meaning of items, but also their syntactic specification, known as *subcategorization.* Thus, for example, the verb *put* would be subcategorized with the syntactic specification that it must be followed by a noun phrase and a prepositional phrase (e.g., *I put the book on the table*). Thus, it cannot replace *kirked* above. On the other hand, *played* would fit nicely. But then the other words that precede and follow it must have semantic and syntactic features that make sense in the given slots. Here is one possibility:

[handwritten margin notes: lexical insertion; Subcate-gorization]

The	.../-ing/	.../-s/	.../-ed/	the	(noun)	at	the	(noun)	.../-ly/
↓	↓	↓	↓	↓	↓	↓	↓	↓	↓
The	scheming	minstrels	played	the	flute	at	the	school	beautifully

As the above example makes clear, lexical insertion involves not only knowing the meaning of words in themselves, but also where they are "locatable" in sentence structures. At one level, this involves grasping words in terms of their <u>distinctive features</u>. For example, a verb such as *drink* can be preceded only by a subject that is marked as [+animate] (*the boy, the girl,* etc.). If it is so marked, then it entails further feature-specification in terms of gender ([+male], [+female]), age ([+adult], [-adult]), and other similar notions that keeps it distinct lexically:

distinctive features
animate vs inanimate
m/F
adult/child

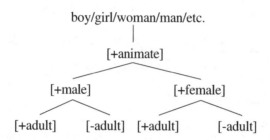

boy/girl/woman/man/etc.

[+animate]

[+male]　　　　[+female]

[+adult]　[-adult]　[+adult]　[-adult]

Any violation of lexical subcategorization (using a subject marked as [-animate] with the verb *drink*) would lead to an <u>anomaly</u>, such as *The house drinks wine*, although metaphorical meaning can always be assigned to such a string (as we shall see in the next chapter). It is beyond the scope of this chapter to deal with subcategorization rules and the nature of the lexicon in detail. Suffice it to say that the lexicon is more than a mere dictionary knowledge of words and their meanings; <u>it includes syntactic and morphological knowledge as well.</u>

GRAMMAR AND CONCEPTS

As we saw above, some linguists claim that the rules of grammar might mirror the structure of concepts. Of course, not all share this view. <u>Noam Chomsky</u>, for instance, has made the claim that <u>grammar is independent of conceptual considerations</u> and that even <u>meaning relations among</u> words are determined by syntactic criteria and processes such as <u>lexical insertion</u> and <u>subcategorization.</u> The goal of linguistics is, according to Chomsky, to unravel

Chomsky

anomaly = irregularity

Chomsky → UG

how the rules of different grammars are derived from an innate set of rule-making principles in the Universal Grammar (UG) of humanity.

Without doubt, Chomsky's notion of a UG is an attractive one, for it would imply that all natural languages are built on the same basic grammatical plan and that differences among languages are explainable as choices of rule types from a fairly small inventory of possibilities. The basic character of the UG is its *recursiveness*—the repeated application of a rule or procedure to successive results. The study of how this feature manifests itself across languages comes under the rubric of *X-Bar Theory*. Take, as an example, the *X-Bar Theory* English sentence *The chair is in the corner*. X-bar Theory would analyze this sentence as follows:

$$x\text{-bar} \to x + y\text{-bar} \to y + x\text{-bar} \to y$$

where:
x-bar = *noun phrase (the chair, the corner)*
y-bar = *prepositional phrase (in the corner)*
x   = *noun*
y   = *preposition*

Supplemented with an appropriate system of rules that determine word order and how some sentences relate to each other—known as transformational rules—Chomsky asserts that X-Bar Theory is sufficient to explain the basic plan of the UG. How so? If Chomsky is right, then the uniqueness of language comes down to a single rule of grammar! Is his rule the "DNA" of the language faculty?

But even if recursiveness can be seen to operate across languages, it would tell us nothing about how grammar and meaning seem to mirror each other. Consider the use of the English prepositions *since* and *for* in sentences such as the following:

(1) I have been living here *since* 1999.
(2) I have known Lucy *since* November.
(3) I have not been able to sleep *since* Monday.
(4) I have been living here *for* twenty years.
(5) I have known Lucy *for* nine months.
(6) I have not been able to sleep *for* seven days.

The complements that follow *since* are conceptually *points in time*, i.e., they are complements that reflect a conceptualization of *time* as *a point on a timeline* on which specific years, months, etc., can be shown: *1980, November, Monday*, etc. Complements that follow *for*, on the other hand, reflect a conceptualization of *time* as *a quantity* and can thus be counted, i.e., *twenty years, nine months, seven days*, etc. This type of analysis suggests that different perceptions of time are built directly into the structure of grammar. Simply put, the choice of *since* or *for* is governed by a conceptual distinction, not by any abstract rule of grammar.

[handwritten margin note: Use of since + for gov'd by conceptual distinction]

Consider, as another example, the selection of certain verbs in Italian that hold the nouns *caldo* ("heat") and *freddo* ("cold") as predicates. The verb *fare* "to make" is used if the sentence subject is the weather—*fa caldo* (literally) "it is hot" (literally: "it makes hot"), *fa freddo* "it is cold" (literally: "it makes cold"). If the subject is an object, the verb *essere* is used instead—*è caldo* "it is hot," *è freddo* "it is cold." And if the subject is a person, *avere* "to have" is used—*ha caldo* "he or she is hot" (literally: "he or she has heat"), *ha freddo* "he or she is cold" (literally: "he or she has cold"). Evidently, the use of one verb or the other—*fare, essere,* or *avere*—is governed by an underlying conceptualization of Nature, things, and people as containers of heat and cold. If the container is Nature, then Nature is said to make the heat and cold *(fa caldo/freddo)*; if the container is the human body, then the body is said to have the heat or cold in it *(ha caldo/freddo)*; and if the container is an object, then the object is the source of heat and cold to human perception *(è caldo/freddo).*

Sapir argued throughout his career that grammar mirrored conceptual structure. Even changing the order of words in a sentence such as *The farmer kills the duckling (Kills the farmer the duckling)*, or omitting any of the words in it *(Farmer, kill the duckling)*, brings about a shift in its "modality," as Sapir called it. Sapir (1921: 87) showed that 13 distinct concepts could be expressed with the words making up this simple sentence, which reveal more about how these words have been used in a culture's past than they do about some innate grammatical rule system: "The sentence is the outgrowth of historical and of unreasoning psychological forces rather than of a logical synthesis of elements that have been clearly grasped in their individuality."

[handwritten margin note: Sapir]

CONCLUDING REMARKS

Stringing words together in rule-based ways to produce sentences is one of the means by which humans across the world generate messages. But in all sentences, the meaning of the constituent words, their relation to each other, and the forms they assume all enter into the picture. This is perhaps why syntax raises important questions about language in general that continue to intrigue linguists to this day: Are there general principles that underlie the grammatical rules of languages? Do these mirror cognitive processes? Do speakers of isolating languages experience reality differently from speakers of agglutinating languages? These questions probably defy answers. The fun, however, lies in investigating them.

Meanings

For a large class of cases—though not for all—in which we employ the word "meaning" it can be defined thus: the meaning of a word is its use in the language.

Ludwig Wittgenstein (1889–1951)

PRELIMINARY REMARKS

The word *meaning* has been used throughout this textbook. But it has never been defined. The reason for this is simply that it cannot be defined. Like *word* or *sentence*, meaning is something that people intuitively understand, but which defies precise definition. So, linguists have devised techniques for fleshing out the meanings of linguistic forms, to get around the question of what meaning is in any absolute sense. The most common one is, as we have seen throughout this book, the technique of comparison. This allows the linguist to relate words in terms of sameness (*big-large*); opposition (*big-little*); taxonomy (*rose-flower*); and part-whole relations (*handle-cup*). Another technique is to look at how words acquire meanings through association and extension.

The purpose of this chapter is to look more closely at how meanings are encoded by words, sentences, and utterances. The study of this aspect of language goes under the rubric of *semantics*. It is impossible to give an in-depth treatment of semantic phenomena in a single chapter. So, the discussion will be limited to illustrating what kinds of topics semantic analysis within an AL framework would embrace.

MEANING

To study meaning, it is necessary to start by noting that every word, phrase, or sentence is a *sign*—it is something that stands for something other than itself. The word *cat*, for instance, is a sign because it does not stand for the phonemes that comprise it, /kæt/, but rather for "a feline mammal." The latter is known, more specifically, as the *referent*. There are two kinds of referents that signs encode, *concrete* and *abstract*:

- a concrete referent, such as the animal designated by the word *cat*, is something existing in reality or in real experience and is normally available to direct perception by the senses (a cat can be seen, touched, etc.);
- an abstract referent, such as the meaning captured by the word *idea*, is something that is formed in the mind and is not normally available to direct perception by the senses (an idea cannot be seen or touched physically).

The sign is a powerful mental tool because it allows its users to conjure up the things to which it refers even though these might not be physically present for the senses to perceive. This feature of signs is known psychologically as *displacement*. By simply uttering the word *cat*, people understand what is being singled out in the world of experience, even though an actual "cat" may not be present for people to observe. Similarly, by simply saying the expression *a bright idea*, people will understand what is being implied, even though no such thing is available for the senses to detect. This remarkable feature of signs has endowed the human species with the ability to refer to anything at will, even to something that is made up completely by human fancy.

The relation that holds between a sign and its referent is what is intended with the word *meaning*. This encompasses all the possible uses of the sign. Take the English word *cat*, again. Some of its referents are as follows:

(1) a small carnivorous mammal domesticated since early times as a catcher of rats and mice and as a pet and existing in several distinctive breeds and varieties;

(2) an attractive and suave person, especially a male player or devotee of jazz music, as in *He's a cool cat;*

(3) a secret, as in *He let the cat out of the bag.*

Connote: = imply, meaning in addition to its literal or primary meaning.

literal = denotative
denote - be a sign of
- indicate
eg the arrow denotes direction
- means/conveys

The three referents together (among others) constitute the meaning of the sign *cat*. The use of *cat* to encode referent (1) constitutes what is commonly known as *literal* or, more accurately, *denotative* meaning. The use of the same sign to encode the meaning illustrated by (2) shows that a sign can be extended to embrace other referents that are seen to have something in common with the basic referent. This type of meaning is known as *connotative*. Use (3) reveals that a word's meaning can be used *figuratively*, that is, by associations with other signs and their meanings. All three types will be discussed in the next section. It is sufficient to note here that deciphering the meaning of words and other structures is hardly a simple "dictionary-type" process. Since the use of the sign is what determines its meaning, the linguist will always have to keep in mind: (1) the pragmatic or contextual conditions that hold between speakers and signs; and (2) the rules of discourse, which govern relations among the elements within utterances.

The pragmatic aspect of a sign's meaning will also be discussed below. However, it requires some initial commentary here. The British philosopher J. L. Austin (1911–1960) claimed in his posthumous 1962 book, *How to Do Things with Words*, that by speaking, a person performs an *act* (such as stating, predicting, or warning), and that the meaning of the act is to be found in what it brings about. The American philosopher John R. Searle extended Austin's ideas in 1969, emphasizing the need to relate the functions of speech acts to their social contexts. Searle observed that speech encompasses at least three kinds of acts:

(1) *locutionary acts*, in which things are said with a certain sense (*The moon is a sphere*);
(2) *illocutionary acts*, in which something has been promised or ordered (*I'll do it, sooner or later; Come here!* etc.);
(3) *perlocutionary* acts, in which the speaker, by speaking, does something to someone else, i.e., angers, consoles, persuades someone (*I'm sorry; Don't worry; Go ahead, tell me everything*, etc.) *has an affect on the other person*
Peter, have you vac yet!

The speaker's intentions are conveyed by the force that is given to the speech act. To be successfully interpreted, however, the words used must be appropriate, sincere, consistent with the speaker's general beliefs and conduct, and recognizable as meaningful by the hearer.

In sum, the type of meaning we get from a sign depends on type of referent encoded, situation, usage, and the pragmatics of communication. In effect, it is a product of an interaction between *langue* and *parole*.

TYPES OF MEANING

[handwritten margin note: cat ⇒ ⚥ denotative = secret/cool = connotative]

The meanings of *cat* in (1) and (2) are termed, as mentioned on pages 100 and 101, respectively as denotative and connotative. Denotation is the meaning that a sign is designed to encode initially. The referent to which it alludes is not something specific in the world, although it can be (*a cat in general* vs. *my aunt's orange cat*), but rather a prototypical exemplar of a *category*. The word *cat* refers to the *category* of animal that we recognize as having the quality "catness." The denotative meaning of *cat* is, therefore, really "a creature exemplifying catness." Catness can be specified in terms of a set of distinctive *semantic features* such as [+mammal], [+retractile claws], [+long tail], etc. This composite mental picture allows us to determine if a specific real or imaginary animal under consideration will fall within the category (= [+mammal], [+retractile claws], etc.). Similarly, the word *square* does not denote a specific "square," but rather "squareness," which has the semantic features [+four equal straight lines] and [+meeting at right angles]. It is irrelevant if the lines are thick, dotted, 2 meters long, 80 feet long, or whatever. As long as the figure can be seen to have the distinctive features [+four equal straight lines] and [+meeting at right angles], it is identifiable denotatively as a *square*.

Now, the meaning of a sign can be extended to encompass other kinds of referents that appear, by inference or analogy, to have something in common with the original referent. This extensional process is known as *connotation*. The meaning of *cat* as a jazz musician in (2) above is an example of how connotation works—the jazz musician is perceived to move slowly, sleekly, and rhythmically to slow jazz music, like the mammal called a *cat*.

As another example, consider the word *house*. This word denotes, more or less, "any (free-standing) structure intended for human habitation." This meaning can be seen in utterances such as *I bought a new house yesterday*, *House prices are continually going up in this city*, *We repainted our house the other day*, and so on. Now, note that the same word can be extended connotatively as follows:

(1) The *house* is in session = "legislative assembly, quorum"
(2) The *house* roared with laughter = "audience in a theater"
(3) They sleep at one of the *houses* at Harvard University = "dormitory"

However, such extensions of the word are hardly random or disconnected to the semantic features that make up the initial meaning of *house*—[+structure], [+human], [+habitation]. These are implicit in the above extensional uses; i.e.,

a legislative assembly, a theater audience, and a dormitory do indeed imply
"structures" of special kinds that "humans" can be said to "inhabit" (occupy)
in some specific way. Any connotative use of the word *house* is constrained
by the distinctive features of its meaning; i.e., *house* can be applied to refer to
anything that involves or implicates humans (or beings) coming together for
some specific reason. More formally, connotation can be defined as the mapping
of the semantic features of a sign onto a new referent if it is perceived to entail
these features by inference or analogy.

There is a special type of connotation that is worth mentioning here. It is
called *emotive*. The word *yes*, for example, can have various emotive
connotations, depending on the tone of voice with which it is uttered (as we
discussed briefly in chapter 3). If one says it with a normal tone of voice, it
will be understood as a sign of affirmation. If, however, one says it with a
raised tone, as in a question, *Yes?*, then it would imply doubt or incredulity.
Such "added meanings" to the word *yes* are examples of emotive connotation.

Connotation is yet another manifestation of Zipf's Law. To cover the
connotative meanings of *cat* and *house* above, at least six new words would
have to be coined. This would require much more effort in terms of memory,
lexical choice, and so on. Generally speaking, therefore, through connotation
Zipf's Law ensures that we will make use of a finite set of linguistic resources
to encompass an infinitude of meanings, thus decreasing cognitive effort in
matters of reference.

The distinction between denotative and connotative meanings is the key
principle used in the making of dictionaries—known as the science of
lexicography. The primary task in lexicography is to unravel the semantic
features that govern a word's meaning and from which all potential uses can
be derived.

At this point, it should be mentioned that there is a caveat in the use of the
concept of "semantic feature." As it turns out, specifying what features are
relevant in the meaning of a sign is not a straightforward matter. Consider the
word sets below:

(1) father, mother, son, daughter
(2) bull, cow, calf (male), heifer
(3) dog (male), dog (female), pup (male), pup (female)

If we contrast the items in these sets with words such as *bread, milk,
sword, car,* etc., we can easily see that they all share the property of animacy.
Hence, the feature [±animate] would appear to be a basic one in establishing

caveat = warning or caution

animate = having life

the meaning of the items in all three sets. Now, comparing the items in set (1) with those in (2) and (3) it is easy to see that they are kept distinct by the feature [±human]; and comparing the items in (2) and (3) it is obvious that the distinctions [±bovine] and [±canine] are needed. Within each set, what keeps the first two items separate from the second two is the feature [±adult]. Finally, [±male] and [±female] are needed to ensure that all items contrast by at least one feature.

This type of analysis is parallel to the <u>distinctive-feature approach</u> used in phonological analysis (chapter 3). We can draw up a similar type of chart to the one we drew up in chapter 3 to show which distinctive semantic features are possessed by each word as follows:

	animate	human	bovine	canine	adult	male	female
father	+	+	-	-	+	+	-
mother	+	+	-	-	+	-	+
son	+	+	-	-	-	+	-
daughter	+	+	-	-	-	-	+
bull	+	-	+	-	+	+	-
cow	+	-	+	-	+	-	+
calf (male)	+	-	+	-	-	+	-
heifer	+	-	+	-	-	-	+
dog (male)	+	-	-	+	+	+	-
dog (female)	+	-	-	+	+	-	+
pup (male)	+	-	-	+	-	+	-
pup (female)	+	-	-	+	-	-	+

This type of chart makes it possible to show what differentiates, say, *mother* from *daughter* or *heifer* from *dog (female)* in a precise manner:

father ~ mother
[+male] ~ [+female]

father ~ son
[+adult] ~ [-adult]

heifer ~ dog (female)
[+bovine] ~ [-bovine]

or
[-canine] ~ [+canine]
dog (male) ~ pup (female)

[+adult] ~ [-adult]
and
[+male] ~ [+female]

As in the case of phonetic distinctive features, there are also some predictable processes in the assignment of semantic features. Here are two of them:

(1) If an item possesses the feature [+human], then it also possesses [+animate], and vice versa.
(2) If an item possesses the feature [+male], then it possesses of course the feature [-female], and vice versa, if it possesses the feature [+female] it also possesses the feature [-male].

anomalous = deviation from the norm

Although this is a useful way of establishing the meaning of lexical items in relative terms, it can produce anomalous results. The opposition above between *heifer* and *dog (female)* can be given as either [+bovine] ~ [-bovine] or [-canine] ~ [+canine]. There really is no way to establish which one is, conceptually, the actual trigger in the opposition. Moreover, when certain words are defined in terms of features, it becomes obvious that to keep them distinct one will need quite a vast array of semantic features. The whole exercise would thus become artificial and convoluted. One might need as many features as words! Notice, as well, that not all distinctions are given word status. Although the term *bitch* does exist in English to refer denotatively to a female dog, it is rarely if ever used any longer because of the connotations it has taken on in the human domain. This simple example shows that denotative meaning can hardly ever, in the abstract, be determined without reference to connotation and other processes.

It is also to be noted that in studying languages of different cultures, different semantic feature arrays may have to be drawn up, since distinctions as to what is meaningful will vary. Nevertheless, as in phonological analysis, the technique of semantic distinctive feature analysis can be used simply as an organizing grid to understand the data collected at "face value." It is a starting point in fieldwork analysis. Obviously, the larger "meaning picture" will subsequently become dominant in refining the overall analysis of meaning.

One way to avoid the problem of deciding which features are relevant is to group words that share one or more features together into what are known as *lexical fields*. For example, one such field is that of colors, which all share the feature [+chromatic]. Now, distinguishing between individual color terms will depend on what wavelength a specific word denotes. The opposition is thus no longer one that involves feature differentiation, but rather degree. The topic of color terminology will be discussed in more detail in chapter 8. In essence, lexical fields are characterized by distinctive semantic features that differentiate the individual lexemes in the field from one another, and also by features shared by all the lexemes in the field. For example, items that have the feature [+seat] (i.e., "something on which to sit"), such as *chair, sofa, bench*, obviously belong to the same lexical field. Within the field they can be distinguished from one another according to how many people are accommodated, whether a back support is included, and so on.

Research on identifying a universal set of semantic features is ongoing, but it has yet to yield a manageable set of features. The theoretical problem that it poses has proven to be quite intractable. Unlike phonological systems, which are closed, semantic systems are open-ended and constantly changing to meet new social needs. This makes it virtually impossible to develop a core set of features for describing them.

Moreover, the technique is limited to determining literal meaning. It is virtually useless in helping the fieldworker unravel figurative meanings, such as those associated with *cat* in example (3) on page 100—*He let the cat out of the bag*. In traditional semantic approaches, this type of meaning, also called *metaphorical*, was considered to be a matter of ornamental style, rather than a feature of predictable semantic structure. It was thus largely ignored by linguists. However, since the late 1970s this view has changed radically. Many semanticists now see figurative meaning, not only as systematic and regular, but also as central to language.

Defining metaphor poses an interesting dilemma. In the metaphor *The professor is a snake,* there are two referents, not one, that are related to each other as follows:

- There is the primary referent, *the professor*, which is known as the *topic* of the metaphor.
- Then there is another referent, *the snake*, which is known as the *vehicle* of the metaphor.
- Their correlation creates a new meaning, called the *ground*, which is not the simple sum of the meanings of the two referents.

In the process of associating the two referents it is, obviously, not the denotative meaning of the vehicle that is transferred to the topic, but rather its

Connotative meaning of snake (vehicle referent) that is transferred to the topic

connotations, namely the culture-specific characteristics perceived in snakes—"slyness," "danger," "slipperiness," etc. It is this complex of connotations that produces the ground.

Metaphor reveals a basic tendency of the human mind to think of certain referents in terms of others. The question now becomes: Is there any psychological motivation for this? In the case of *The professor is a snake* the probable reason for correlating two semantically unrelated referents seems to be the *de facto* perception that humans and animals are interconnected in the *de facto* natural scheme of things—a phenomenon that appears to be universal (as will be discussed further in chapter 8).

The Americans George Lakoff and Mark Johnson were the first modern-day linguists to show, in their groundbreaking book of 1980, *Metaphors We Live By,* how metaphorical meanings constitute an integral part of semantic systems, not just the products of poetics and oratory. First, Lakoff and Johnson assert what the Greek philosopher Aristotle (384–322 BC)—the one who coined the term *metaphor* (from *meta* "across" + *pherein* "to bear")—claimed two millennia before, namely that there are two types of concepts—concrete and abstract. But the two scholars add a remarkable twist to the Aristotelian distinction, namely that abstract concepts are linked systematically to concrete ones via metaphor. They refer to the result of the linkage as a *conceptual metaphor.* For example, the expression *The professor is a snake* is really a token of something more general, namely, the conceptual metaphor [people are animals]. This is why we can replace *the professor* with *John, Mary* or any other person, and *snake* with any other animal—*dog, bird,* and so on. Each specific replacement (*John is a snake, Mary is a bird,* etc.) is not an isolated example of poetic fancy. It is really a manifestation of a more general metaphorical idea—people are animals.

people = target
animals = source of meaning

Each of the two parts of the conceptual metaphor is called a *domain*: [people] is called the *target domain* because it is the abstract concept itself (the "target" of the conceptual metaphor); and [animals] is called the *source domain* because it encompasses the class of vehicles that deliver the intended meanings (the "source" of the meaning in the conceptual metaphor). So, when we hear people talking, for instance, of *ideas* in terms of *geometrical figures and relations*—"Those ideas are *diametrically* opposite to mine"; "Our ideas are *parallel*"; etc.—we can now easily identify the two domains as [ideas] (= target domain) and [geometrical figures/relations] (= source domain) and, therefore, the conceptual metaphor as: [ideas are geometrical figures/relations].

Lakoff and Johnson trace the psychological source of conceptual metaphors to *image schemas.* These are the "figural outlines" in the mind that convert the experiences of concrete things (like perceived animal behaviors) into cognitive

people = target domain + Animals = Source (of ideas) domain

ideas = target + objects = source (fig domain)

de facto adj – exercising power or serv. a function w/o being legally or officially estab. (eg. a de facto gov't) – not formally recognized

templates for understanding abstractions (like human personality). These not only permit us to recognize patterns, but also to anticipate new patterns and to make inferences and deductions about them.

Lakoff and Johnson identify three basic types of image schemas. The first one involves *orientation*—thinking in its basic outline form—e.g., *up vs. down, back vs. front, near vs. far*, etc. This underlies conceptual metaphors such as [happiness is up] ("Today my spirits are *up*"; "My joy reaches the *sky*"). The second type involves *ontological* thinking. This undergirds conceptual metaphors in which activities, emotions, ideas, etc., are portrayed as entities and substances, again in basic outline form: e.g., [the mind is a container] ("My mind is *full* of good memories"). The third type of schema involves an association between entities that is culture-specific, as exemplified by the conceptual metaphor [time is a quantity] ("My time will *cost* you a lot"). Here is just a sampling of how image schemas underlie various conceptual metaphors:

[happiness is up/sadness is down]

(1) I'm feeling *up* today.
(2) They're feeling *down*.

[knowledge is light/ignorance is darkness]

(3) That idea is very *clear*.
(4) That's an *obscure* theory.

[ideas are food]

(5) That statement left a *bitter taste* in my mouth.
(6) It's impossible to *digest* all that knowledge.

[ideas are people]

(7) Those old ideas somehow *live* on.
(8) Cognitive psychology is in its *infancy*.

[ideas are fashion]

(9) Those ideas are old *fashioned*.
(10) That theory is in *style*.

We do not detect the presence of image schemas in such common expressions because of repeated usage. However, we obviously do see easily if required. The last relevant point made by Lakoff and Johnson in their truly fascinating book is that cultural groupthink is built (at least in some part) on conceptual metaphors. This is accomplished by a kind of "higher order" associative thinking. As target domains are associated with many kinds of source domains, the concepts become increasingly more complex, leading to what Lakoff and Johnson call *idealized cognitive models* (ICMs). To see what this means, consider the target domain of *sport talk*. The following source domains, among many others, shape a large portion of talk about sports: *ICM*

[fortune]

(1) That team is *lucky*.
(2) *Fortune* is on the side of the Yankees.

[war]

(3) That team knows how to use the *blitz*.
(4) That team has a great *attack* plan.

[chess]

(5) That player has great *moves*.
(6) That team is now in a *checkmate* situation.

[money]

(7) That team *cashed* in on the opportunity given to them.
(8) He *paid* dearly for that play.

[eating]

(9) They're *hungry* for a win.
(10) That team is *eating* up all their opponents.

[measurement]

(11) He made an *accurate* pass.
(12) They can go a *long* way with their defense alone.

[thought system]

(13) Their overall *theory* is to win with defense.
(14) That team has a winning *philosophy*,
     placing 2 or more things side by side

The constant <u>juxtaposition</u> of such source domains in common discourse produces, cumulatively, an ICM of sports. The diagram below can be used to show how these source domains converge to form the ICM:

lecture

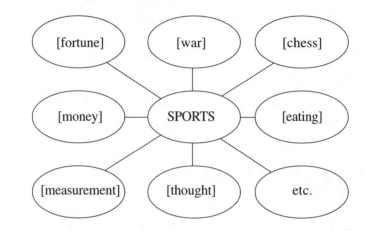

There are other source domains, of course, that make up the ICM of sports talk. The task of semantic analysis is to determine which are the most productive ones. Research on ICMs has shown that source domains overlap, intersect, and constantly piggyback on each other in the production of ICMs. The [eating] source domain, for instance, is used also to deliver the ICM of [ideas] ("I couldn't *swallow* that idea"), [emotional states] ("She had to *eat* her words"), among many others. Culture, from this standpoint, appears as a network of source domains that crisscross constantly in the construction of communal meanings.

The notion of ICM raises a host of interesting questions: Which ICMs are more or less productive in a culture? Is the concept of *love* more or less productive than, say, *ideas*? That is to say, does the concept of *love* surface more often in texts, in discourse, and in social rituals than does the concept of *ideas*? Which concepts are more or less productive cross-culturally?

By simply counting the number of source domains used to construct an ICM of some concept, we can get an idea of the productivity of that concept with relation to others. For example, as we saw above, in English [ideas/

thinking] was rendered by such source domains as [food], [people], and [fashion]. Other source domains can be added to the ICM: [buildings] ("Those ideas are *well-constructed*"), [plants] ("That idea has deep *roots*"), [commodities] ("Those ideas won't *sell*"), [vision] ("There's more to it than meets the *eye*"), [geometry] ("Those ideas are *parallel*"), among others. How many more are there? I was able to find at least 89 source domains by myself. On the other hand, I was able to come up with only 36 source domains for the ICM of [love]. Common ones are [physics] ("There were *sparks* between the two actors"), [health and disease] ("Their relationship has become *sick*"), [insane symptoms] ("He's gone *mad* over her"), [magic] ("She has *bewitched* her lover"), among others. My estimates suggest that [love] is a less productive concept than [thinking] is in English. Needless to say, my estimates were rough ones based primarily on introspection. Readers may come up with more source domains in both cases. It is unlikely, however, that they will find many more than I have (as I myself discovered by giving this very task as an assignment to several of my linguistics and semiotics classes a few years ago).

What does this imply? It suggests, arguably, that in English culture [thinking] is a concept that is given much more cognitive and representational salience than [love] is. This does not mean that the latter is not important, but simply that there are fewer ways to talk about it and, thus, to think about it. When I compared the English ICMs to Italian ones (my other language), I found that most of the source domains used to deliver the concept of [thinking] were identical—92 in total. However, I came up with 99 source domains for the Italian ICM of [love], suggesting that it is probably a more productive concept in Italian culture.

Before Lakoff and Johnson's trend-setting work, the study of metaphor fell within the field of *rhetoric*, where it was viewed as one of various *tropes* (figures of speech). But since the early 1980s the practice has been to consider most tropes as particular kinds of metaphor. Within this new tradition, *personification* ("My cat speaks Italian") would be seen as a particular kind of metaphor, one in which the target domain is an [animal] or [inanimate object] and the source domain a set of vehicles that are normally associated with [human beings].

But there are two tropes that are regularly considered separately from metaphor—metonymy and irony. *Metonymy* entails the use of a conceptual entity within a domain to represent the entire domain:

Metonymy uses conceptual entity

(1) She loves *Dostoyevsky* (= the writings of Dostoyevsky).
(2) There are so many new *faces* around here (= people).
(3) My dad doesn't like *nose rings* (= people with nose rings).
(4) They bought a *Fiat* (= car named Fiat).
(5) The *buses* are on strike (= bus drivers).
(6) The *Church* does not condone infidelity (= Catholic theologians, priests, etc.).
(7) The *White House* made another announcement today (= the president, the American government).

The use of the part to represent the whole, or vice versa, is known more traditionally as _synecdoche:_   *part rep. the whole*

(1) The *automobile* is destroying our health (= automobiles collectively).
(2) We need a couple of *strong bodies* for our teams (= strong people).
(3) I've got a new *set of wheels* (= car).
(4) We need *new blood* in this organization (= new people).

In parallelism with the notion of *conceptual metaphor*, the term *conceptual metonym* can be used to refer to generalized metonymical concepts such as [the face is the person]:   *conceptual metonym*

face = person

(1) He's just another pretty *face*.
(2) There are an awful lot of *faces* in the audience.
(3) We need some new *faces* around here.
(4) You must take her on *face* to *face*.

Conceptual metonyms are interconnected to other domains of meaning-making in a culture. The distribution of the concept [the face is the person] throughout the meaning pathways of a culture is the reason why portraits, in painting and photography, focus on the face. The face is, in effect, a symbol for personality.   *face = the person*

Here are some other examples of conceptual metonyms:

[the part for the whole]

(1) Get your *butt* over here!
(2) The Blue Jays need a *stronger arm* in left field.

(3)   We don't hire *crew cuts*.

[the producer (brand) for the product]

(4)   I'll have a *Heineken*.
(5)   We bought a *Ford*.
(6)   He's got a *Rembrandt* in his office.

[the object used for the user]

(7)   My *piano* is sick today.
(8)   The *meat and potatoes* is a lousy tipper.
(9)   The *buses* are on strike.

[the institution for the people in it]

(10) *Shell* has raised its prices again.
(11) The *Church* thinks that promiscuity is immoral.
(12) I don't approve of *government's* actions.

Irony constitutes a semantic strategy based on the use of words to convey a meaning contrary to their literal sense—e.g., "I love being tortured" uttered by someone in excruciating pain. It is, more formally, a cognitive strategy by which a concept is highlighted through opposition, antithesis, or antonymy. In this case, the interaction between *langue* and *parole* becomes rather conspicuous. If the sentence "I love being tortured" is uttered by a masochist, then it would hardly have an ironic meaning!

It is interesting to note that irony emerges late in verbal development (Winner 1988). Such ironic works as Woody Allen's (1935–) movies would hardly be understood or certainly appreciated by children before the age of puberty. Allen's films are ironic depictions of neurotic urban characters preoccupied with love and death. Movies such as *Bananas* (1971), *Everything You Always Wanted to Know About Sex* (1972), *Annie Hall* (1977), *Bullets over Broadway* (1994), and *Mighty Aphrodite* (1995) are based on irony as a means of criticizing human habits, ideas, and vacuous rituals.

WORD MEANING

[handwritten annotation: Estab word meaning by comparison)
1. synonymy   3. homonymy
2. antonymy   4. hyponymy]

The main technique for establishing word meaning is by comparison, since words can be seen to relate to each other in several specific ways. One such way is *synonymy*. Synonyms are words having the same or nearly the same meaning in one or more of their uses: e.g., *near-close, far-distant*, etc. However, by itself synonymy is not completely reliable, because the uses of the two words rarely overlap completely. Consider, *near* and *close*. Ignoring nuances of meaning for the sake of argument, in the following sentences, the two appear to be interpretable as essentially synonymous:

(1) My house is *near* the mall.
(2) My house is *close* to the mall.

However, the use of *near* in the following sentences as a synonym for *close* produces semantic anomalies (shown with an asterisk *).

(3) Mary and I have been *close* emotionally for years.
(4) * Mary and I have been *near* emotionally for years.
(5) I want to get *close* emotionally to Mary, but she won't let me.
(6) * I want to get *near* emotionally to Mary, but she won't let me.

The substitution of *near* for *close* is anomalous because only *closeness* is used in English as a vehicle to deliver the metaphorical concept of "emotional bonding."

Another way to determine word meaning is by *antonymy*. Antonyms are words that are felt to be opposite in meaning—*night-day, sad-happy, hot-cold, good-bad*, etc. But antonymy, like synonymy, is not completely reliable. Consider the use of *evil* as an antonym for *good*:

(1) Mac is an *evil* person.
(2) Sarah is a *good* person.
(3) He's more *evil* than you think.

To flesh out the conceptual differences between the two, it is useful to use them in specific statements and compare the appropriateness of the statements:

lecture

Evil	Good	Appropriate?
an evil tyrant	a good tyrant	?
the evil effects of a poor diet	the good effects of a poor diet X	no
evil omens	good omens	yes
an evil temper	a good temper	yes
evil news	good news	yes
an evil exterior paint X	a good exterior paint	?
an evil joke	a good joke	yes
an evil drink X	a good drink	?
evil taste	good taste	?
an evil table X	a good table	?

Contextualized meaning theory

As the above examples show, the two concepts do not always relate to each other antonymically—*a good table* means "a bountiful table," whereas *an evil table* implies that "evil people are at the table." Some expressions— such as *Good Heavens! Good grief!, the common good, the evil eye*, etc.—have frozen the meanings of each word, thus excluding any antonymic analysis of the pair.

Another way to determine word meaning is through *homonymy*. Homonyms are words with the same pronunciation and/or spelling, but with different meanings. If the homonymy is purely phonetic then the items are known as *homophones* (e.g., *aunt* vs. [as pronounced in American English] and *bore* vs. *boar*). If the homonymy is orthographic, then the words are known as *homographs* (*play* as in *Shakespeare's play* vs. *play* as in *He likes to play*). It is not the case that all homographs are homophones: e.g., the form *learned* has two pronunciations in (1) *He learned to play the violin* vs. (2) *He is a learned man*. Homonyms force us to focus on what each item means by comparison and contrast and, thus, what makes each one unique.

A fourth type of relation that words have with each other is known as *hyponymy*, the process by which the meaning of one sign is included in that of another: e.g., the meaning of *scarlet* is included in the meaning of *red*, the meaning of *tulip* is included in that of *flower*, etc. This allows us to relate word meanings to the overall meaning of lexical fields and, thus, to focus on those specific features that keep words within the field distinct.

F All Homographs are homographs
play / play

aunt x 2
boar bore

learned / learnéd

UTTERANCE MEANING

As we have seen a number of times already, the crucial aspect in determining the meaning of an utterance is *context*. This is the real-world condition or situation that constrains what an utterance means. Consider a sentence such as *The pig is ready to eat*. In this utterance the word *pig* has at least three meanings according to the social context in which it is used:

(1) If uttered by a farmer during feeding time, then the utterance has literal meaning: "There is an animal called a pig who is ready to eat."

(2) If uttered by a cook who is announcing the fact that he or she has finished cooking pork meat which is available for consumption, then the utterance has a different meaning: "The cooked pig is ready for people to eat."

(3) If uttered critically by a person to describe someone who appears to be gluttonous and to have a ravenous appetite, then the utterance has metaphorical meaning: "The person who appears to have the manners and appetite of a pig is ready to eat."

As work on communicative competence has shown since the 1970s, it is virtually impossible to separate purely linguistic competence (knowledge of phonology, morphology, syntax, and semantics) from knowledge of how to make words and sentences bear meanings in specific situations.

Utterance meaning can also be determined from nonverbal cues. Take, for instance, the gestures used during speech. Some can have quite specific meanings, such as those for saying goodbye or for asking someone to approach. In 1979, anthropologist Desmond Morris, together with several of his associates at Oxford University, examined 20 gestures in 40 different areas of Europe. They discovered that many of the gestures had several meanings, depending on culture: e.g., a tap on the side of the head can indicate completely opposite things—"stupidity" or "intelligence"—according to cultural context; the head gestures for "yes" and "no" used in the Balkans seem inverted to other Europeans, and so on.

In the performance of utterances, it is virtually impossible to stop the hands from gesturing. And, as the linguist David McNeill (1992) has shown, the accompanying gestures are hardly random; rather, they unconsciously reinforce the meanings in utterances. After videotaping a large sample of people as they spoke, McNeill found that the gestures that accompany speech, which

Gesticulants
1. iconic - bend like tree
2. metaphoric (cartoon)
3 beat/sequential
4 cohesive/globality
5 deictic
6

he called *gesticulants*, exhibit imagery that cannot be shown overtly in speech, as well as imagery of what the speaker is thinking about. This suggested to him that vocal utterances and gesture constitute a single integrated communication system that allows a speaker to get the message across effectively.

McNeill classified gesticulants into five main categories. First, there are *iconic* gesticulants, which, as their name suggests, bear a close resemblance to the referent or referential domain of an utterance: e.g., when describing a scene from a story in which a character bends a tree to the ground, a speaker observed by McNeill appeared to grip something and pull it back. His gesture was, in effect, a manual depiction of the action talked about, revealing both his memory image and his point of view (he could have taken the part of the tree instead).   *iconic*

Second, there are *metaphoric* gesticulants. These are also pictorial, but their content is abstract, rather than purely pictorial. For example, McNeill observed a male speaker announcing that what he had just seen was a cartoon, simultaneously raising up his hands as if offering his listener a kind of object. He was obviously not referring to the cartoon itself, but to the genre of the cartoon. His gesture represented this genre as if it were an object, placing it into an act of offering to the listener. This type of gesticulant typically accompanies utterances that contain metaphorical expressions such as *presenting an idea, putting forth an idea, offering advice*, and so on.   *metaphoric*

Third, there are *beat* gesticulants. These resemble the beating of musical tempo. The speaker's hand moves along with the rhythmic pulsation of speech, in the form of a simple flick of the hand or fingers up and down, or back and forth. Beats basically mark the introduction of new characters and themes in an utterance.   *beat*

Fourth, there are *cohesive* gesticulants. These serve to show how separate parts of an utterance are supposed to hold together. Beats emphasize sequentiality, cohesives globality. Cohesives can take iconic, metaphoric, or beat form. They unfold through a repetition of the same gesticulant. It is the repetition itself that is meant to convey cohesiveness.   *cohesive*

Fifth, there are *deictic* gesticulants. Deixis is the term used by linguists to designate all kinds of pointing signs. Deictic gesticulants are aimed not at an existing physical place, but at an abstract concept that had occurred earlier in the conversation. These reveal that we perceive concepts as having a physical location in space.   *deictic*

McNeill's work gives us a good idea of how the gestural mode of representation intersects with the vocal one in normal discourse. Gestures also relay emotional meaning (e.g., the typical hand movements and facial expressions that accompany happiness, surprise, fear, anger, sadness, contempt, disgust, etc.); help monitor, maintain, or control the speech of someone else (as, for example, the hand movements indicating *Keep going*, *Slow down*, *What else happened?* etc.); and convey some need or mental state (e.g., scratching one's head when puzzled, rubbing one's forehead when worried, etc.).

Linguists have also discovered languages where the two modalities—gesture and vocal speech—are complementary codes. One of the best-known examples is the gesture language developed by the Plains peoples of North America as a means of communication between tribes with different vocal languages. For example, the sign for a white person is made by drawing the fingers across the forehead, indicating a hat. The sensation of cold is indicated by a shivering motion of the hands in front of the body; and the same sign is used for winter and for year, because the Plains peoples count years in terms of winters. Slowly turning the hand, relaxed at the wrist, means vacillation, doubt, or possibility; a modification of this sign, with quicker movement, is the question sign. This sign language is so elaborate that a detailed conversation is possible using the gestures alone (Mallery 1972).

sources

NAMES

The semantic system of a language is both an "inward" and "outward" branching system. By inward I mean simply that it has structural roots "within" the overall linguistic system; by outward I mean that it links a language to the outside world of reality.

As a practical example of the latter, consider the phenomenon of *names*. The study of names falls under the branch of linguistics called *onomastics* (from Greek *onoma* "name"). A name identifies a person in relation to other persons; it is a product of historical forces and thus tied to cultural reality. Across cultures, a neonate is not considered a full-fledged member of society until he or she is given a name. In Inuit cultures, an individual is perceived to have a body, a soul, and a name; a person is not seen as complete without all three. The act of naming a newborn infant is, in effect, his or her first rite of passage in society. If a person is not given a name by his or her family, then society will step in to do so. A person taken into a family, by marriage, adoption, or for some other reason, is also typically assigned the family's name.

In Western culture, name-giving is a largely unregulated process. But even in the West, it is shaped by several customs and trends. Most of the common

Handwritten notes at top:

Sources of names.
1. Hebrew, (biblical) = John, Mary (Phil - loves horses)
2. Latin/Greek - abstract qualities
3. Place - Woods
4. Family name - Chinese (Fam, Gen, Given christian)
5 Event
6 Descriptive
Tall

given names come from Hebrew, Greek, Latin, or Teutonic languages. Hebrew names have traditionally provided the most important source of names—*John* ("gracious gift of God"), *Mary* ("wished for"), *Michael* ("who is like God"), *David* ("beloved"), *Elizabeth* ("oath of God"), *James* ("may God protect," "one who takes the place of another"), *Joseph* ("the Lord shall add"), *Hannah* ("God has favored me"), and *Samuel* ("God has heard"). Greek and Latin names often refer to abstract qualities—*Alexander* ("helper of humanity"), *Barbara* ("stranger"), *George* ("farmer"), *Helen* ("light"), *Margaret* ("pearl"), *Philip* ("lover of horses"), *Stephen* ("crown or garland"), *Clarence* ("famous"), *Emily* ("flattering"), *Patricia* ("of noble birth"), *Victor* ("conqueror"), and *Virginia* ("maidenly"). Teutonic names usually consist of two elements joined together. For example, *William* is composed of *Wille* ("will," "resolution") and *helm* ("helmet"). Some of these name elements may be found at the beginning, such as *ead* ("rich") in *Edwin* and *Edmund*, or at the end, such as *weard* ("guardian") in *Howard* and *Edward*.

Until the late Middle Ages, one personal name was generally sufficient as an identifier. Duplications, however, began to occur so often that additional identification became necessary. Hence, *surnames* were given to individuals (literally "names on top of a name"). These were designed to provide identification on the basis of such features as place (where the individual was *please* from), parentage (to which family or kinship group the individual belonged), or occupation. For example, in England a person living near or at a place where apple trees grew might be called "John where-the-apples-grow," hence, *John Appleby*. Such place names (known as *toponyms*) constitute a large number of surnames—*Wood* or *Woods*, *Moore*, *Church*, or *Hill*. Descendant surnames, or names indicating parentage, were constructed typically with prefixes and suffixes—*McMichael* ("of Michael"), *Johnson* ("son of John"), *Maryson* ("son of Mary"). Surnames reflecting medieval life and occupations include *Smith*, *Farmer*, *Carpenter*, *Tailor*, and *Weaver*.

The Chinese were the first known people to use more than one name. The Emperor Fuxi is said to have decreed the use of family names, or surnames, about 2852 BC. The Chinese customarily have three names. The family name, placed first, comes from one of the 438 words in the Chinese sacred poem *Baijia Xing* (also spelled *Po-Chia Hsing*). It is followed by a generation name, taken from a poem of 20 to 30 characters adopted by each family, and a given name corresponding to a Christian name. The Romans had at first only one name, but later they also started using three names: (1) the *praenomen* stood first as the person's given name; (2) next came the *nomen*, which indicated the *gens*, or clan, to which the person belonged; (3) finally came the *cognomen*, which designated the family. For example, Caesar's full name was *Gaius Julius Caesar*. A person sometimes added a fourth name, the *agnomen*, to commemorate an illustrious action or remarkable event. Family names became confused by the fall of the Roman Empire, and single names once again became customary.

Family names came into some use again in northern Italy in the latter part of the tenth century, becoming common by the thirteenth. Nobles first adopted family names to set themselves apart from common people. The nobles made these family names hereditary, passing them on from father to children. As a consequence, the use of a family name became the mark of a well-bred person, and this is why common people began to adopt the practice too. The Crusaders carried the custom of family names from Italy to the other countries of Western Europe. Throughout Europe, wealthy and noble families adopted the practice of using family names. At first, these were not hereditary, but merely described one person. For example, the "son of Robert" might be known as *Henry Robertson*, or *Henry, son of Robert*. At times, someone might be given a descriptive surname for some reason. Someone named *Robert* might be called *Robert, the small*, because of his height, shortened eventually to *Robert Small*. In such cases the "nickname" became the surname. Many surnames were formed in this way—names like *Reid*, *Reed*, and *Read*, for instance, are early spellings of "red" and refer to a man with red hair.

CONCLUDING REMARKS

The study of how meanings are built into words, phrases, sentences, utterances, and names is a central focus of AL. A fieldworker who does not know the meaning of a particular word may look for clues in the data collected, relating the word to other information or material by comparison or contrast, as has been shown in this chapter. The linguist might also turn to nonverbal clues for insight. Of these, gestures are the most important.

Discourse and Variation

You can stroke people with words.

F. Scott Fitzgerald (1896–1940)

PRELIMINARY REMARKS

In the previous four chapters the focus has been mainly on the internal workings of language, that is, on how the bits and pieces cohere together to produce forms and structures that bear meanings. In a word, the emphasis has been on *langue*.

However, the scientific analysis of language would not be complete if we stopped at this point. Language is a highly adaptive and context-sensitive instrument that is shaped by forces that are largely external to it. Its forms and rules are not only intertwined with each other, but are also highly susceptible to the subtle influences that discourse situations have on them. In a phrase, the internal structures of language are pliable entities that are responsive to social situations. *Langue* and *parole* are really two sides of the same coin, rather than separate dimensions. The focus in this chapter shifts to *parole*.

CONVERSATIONAL DEVICES

Consider the following snippets of dialogue, each of which shows how a 17-year-old high school student would say good-bye:

Good-bye to his English teacher:	Good-bye, sir!
Good-bye to his mother:	See ya' later, ma!
Good-bye to a peer:	I gotta split, man!

Clearly, the expressions used in each case are not interchangeable—the adolescent would not say "I gotta split, man!" to a teacher, and vice versa, he would not say, "Good-bye, sir!" to a peer. This simple, yet instructive, example shows that the choice of words and the types of structures that are utilized in specific discourse situations will vary predictably. This kind of practical knowledge is clearly different from the knowledge of word formation or sentence structure in themselves. As mentioned in previous chapters, it constitutes a pragmatic form of knowledge known as *communicative competence.*

The study of communicative competence now falls under the rubric of *pragmatics*, the branch of linguistics that deals with those aspects of form and meaning that vary according to situational and social variables. It deals with who says what to whom in specific conversational settings.

Conversations of all kinds are constructed with *devices* that are intended to maintain the smooth flow of communication and, as Zipf's Law would have it, to maximize its "economy." Consider, for instance, the following two texts, which tell the same story in different ways:

(1)
Mary went to the store yesterday. Mary ran into a friend at the store. Mary and the friend greeted each other. Mary hadn't seen the friend in a while.

(2)
Mary went to the store yesterday. She ran into a friend there. They greeted each other. Mary hadn't seen her friend in a while.

The first text appears stilted and odd, even though each sentence in it is well formed. The second text reads more like ordinary conversation because in English, as in other languages, repetition is discouraged in normal style. For this reason, the language makes available several devices that allow for the same information to be conveyed without the repetition. Devices that refer back to some word or syntactic category are called *anaphoric*. In (2) above, *she* refers back to *Mary*, *there* to *the store*, and *they* to *Mary and the friend*. Anaphora can thus be seen to be a "repetition-eliminating" strategy. The opposite of an anaphoric device is a *cataphoric* one. This is a word or particle that anticipates some other word. For example, in the sentence *Even though he will deny it, I tell you that Mark did it,* the pronoun *he* refers ahead to *Mark*. Subject and object pronouns, locative particles, demonstratives, adverbs, and

Sentences are parts of larger discourses.
Sentences are not constructed as units
autonomous structures

DISCOURSE AND VARIATION   123

other kinds of words, often function as anaphoric and cataphoric particles in conversations.

The foregoing discussion highlights the fact that sentences are not constructed as autonomous structures, but rather as parts of larger discourse units. In this view of sentence composition, it is obvious that sentence grammar tells only a small part of the story. Personal pronouns, for instance, are chosen typically to function as anaphoric or cataphoric devices serving conversational needs.

There are many kinds of such devices in conversation. Their function is to keep the conversation flowing smoothly with minimal effort. Another such device is known as a *gambit.* A gambit is a word or phrase used to open a conversation, to keep it going, to make it smooth, to repair any anomaly within it, and thus to maximize its economy. The following are common English gambits:

(1) Uh huh…yeah…hmm…aha… *ack. listening*
(2) You agree with me, don't you? *tag Q*
(3) May I ask you a question? *opening gambit*
(4) He arrived Monday; sorry, I meant Tuesday. *– repair gambit*

The grunt-like expressions uttered in (1) are part of a strategy for acknowledging that one is listening to an interlocutor, especially on the phone. Total silence is not an appropriate gambit in English, although it may be in other languages. The gambit in (2) is called a *tag question*—it is a questioning strategy that is designed to seek approval, agreement, consent, not an answer. Utterance (3) is an opening gambit for starting, taking a turn, or entering into a conversation. In English, expressions such as *May I? Sorry, but could you tell me…? Excuse me?* are all opening gambits. Utterance (4) is a gambit known as a *repair*. When there is a minor breakdown in a conversation, or something is not explained properly, then repairs allow the speaker to solve the problem.

DISCOURSE

In the previous chapter, the notion of *speech act* was introduced. A speech act is an utterance that aims to bring about, modify, curtail, or inhibit some real action. The utterance *Be careful!*, for instance, would have the same effect as putting a hand in front of someone to block him or her from crossing the road carelessly. The statement *I sentence you to life imprisonment* uttered by a judge has the same effect as marching the accused directly to prison and locking him or her up. The interesting thing about speech acts is that they influence the composition and structure of sentences, showing one more time that linguistic and communicative competence intersect constantly in the form and content of discourse.

There are various versions of speech act theory. The central idea in all of these is that grammatical and lexical structures are sensitive to situational variables, including the social status of the speakers, their ages, the intent of each one, the goal of the conversation, and so on and so forth. Speech acts allow people to carry out social functions. Think of the kind of grammar and words that you would need to carry out the following functions, and you will quickly understand how linguistic forms are adapted to fit a situation:

- initiating contact
- ending contact
- thanking
- congratulating
- showing satisfaction
- approving
- disapproving
- showing surprise
- offering to do something
- renouncing
- suggesting
- warning
- begging
- exchanging facts
- reporting
- comparing
- narrating
- asking for opinions
- remembering
- forgetting
- keeping track of time
- expressing spatial relations
- expressing notions of entity
- expressing notions of quantity
- self-portrayal

- explicating family relations
- explicating social relations
- understanding
- getting angry
- arguing
- reacting to statements
- ordering
- demanding

Although there is much leeway in the grammatical and lexical choices that can be made to carry out any one of the above functions in specific social situations, these are not completely subject to personal whims. Indeed, the choices made are governed largely by conventional and stylistic conventions. For example, the utterances below convey the same kind of anger, but in different ways:

(1) Don't do that, stupid!

(2) It is best that you not do that!

interlocutor—
someone who takes part in a conversation

Clearly, (1) would be uttered only by someone who is on close or intimate terms with an interlocutor; whereas (2) would be uttered by someone who is on formal terms with an interlocutor. This can be deduced, above all else, by the emotivity of the two sentences—(1) is abrasive and emotionally charged; (2) is evasive and emotionally neutral. Note also that the choice of verb tense is synchronized with the style or register—the verb in (1) is in the imperative (which is a tense commonly used to express anger to intimates), but the verb *do* in (2) is in the subjunctive (which is a tense that reflects formal style).

register

Research on discourse suggests that many situations are so typical that the speech forms used tend to be highly formulaic. For example, ordering from a menu at a restaurant tends to unfold in a script-like manner (*Can I take your order? What do you recommend?* etc.). Such implicit scripts characterize many social situations, making discourse effortless and predictable (once again corroborating Zipf's Law): e.g., asking for services (at a bank, at a post office), negotiating a transaction at a gas station, at a store, and so on.

As the foregoing discussion suggests, the rules of *langue* are intertwined with the rules of *parole*. In his classic study of communicative competence, Dell Hymes (1971) identified eight basic variables that shape the *langue-parole* interface in discourse. He cleverly named each variable so that its initial letter would be a letter in the word *speaking:*

[handwritten note in left margin: "del Hymes"]

S   = *setting* and *scene*: the time, place, and psychological setting
P   = *participants*: the speaker, listener, audience involved in a speech act
E   = *ends*: the desired or expected outcome
A   = *act sequence:* how form and content are delivered
K   = *key:* the mood or spirit (serious, ironic, jocular, etc.) of the speech act
I   = *instrumentalities:* the dialect or linguistic variety used by the speech community
N   = *norms:* conventions or expectations about volume, tone, rate of delivery, etc.
G   = *genres:* different types of performance (joke, formal speech, sermon, etc.)

[handwritten: phatic = social not dictionary; phatic communion eg howare you (not about health)]

One particularly important type of speech act is what the British anthropologist Bronislaw Malinowski (1922) termed *phatic communion.* He defined it as the exchange of words and phrases that are important less for their dictionary meanings than for their social functions. When we greet someone with *How are you?* we hardly expect a medical report, as would a doctor. The function of that statement is simply to make contact. Malinowski also showed that the type of language used in phatic communion could be used by the linguist to determine various social aspects of the speakers: i.e., if the speakers are adults or children, if there is a difference in status between the speakers, if they are well acquainted with each other, and so on.

Phatic communication is norm-based behavior. So is speech intended to convey politeness. This involves knowledge of how to communicate tact, generosity, approbation, modesty, agreement, and empathy with words, phrases, and tone of voice. For example, in English a tactful way of interrupting a conversation would be a statement such as "Could I interrupt you for just half a second?"

It should be mentioned at this point that, long before the fascination with discourse within mainstream linguistics, the Moscow-born linguist and semiotician who carried out most of his work in the United States, Roman Jakobson (1896–1982), gave a comprehensive model of the interaction between discourse and language in the late 1950s that is still useful today for conducting fieldwork. He posited, for instance, that there are six "constituents" that characterize all speech acts:

(1) an *addresser* who initiates a communication
(2) a *message* that he or she wishes to communicate
(3) an *addressee* who is the intended receiver of the message

(4) a *context* that permits the addressee to decipher the intent of the message and thus to extract an appropriate meaning from it

(5) a mode of *contact* between the addresser and addressee that shapes the nature of the interaction (as formal, friendly, etc.)

(6) a *code* providing the linguistic resources for constructing and deciphering the message

Jakobson then pointed out that the main kinds of messages are as follows:

(1) *emotive* = the addresser's intentions, emotions, attitudes, social status, etc., as they manifest themselves in the form and contents of the message

(2) *conative* = the intended effect (physical, psychological, social, etc.) that the message is expected to have on the addressee

(3) *referential* = a message constructed to convey information

(4) *poetic* = a message constructed to deliver meanings in a way similar to poetry

(5) *phatic* = a message designed to establish social contact

(6) *metalingual* = a message designed to refer to the code used *(The word noun is a noun)*

As Jakobson's analysis suggests, discourse is a form of acting, of presenting the Self through language. And it is intended to produce some effect, not only convey information.

Discourse also serves broad cultural functions, being the basis of most social rituals. Religious rites, sermons, prep rallies, political debates, and other ceremonial gatherings are anchored in discourse genres (as Hymes called them), either traditionally worded or specifically composed for the occasion. The use of language in ritual is not to create new meanings, but to assert communal sense-making and to ensure cultural cohesion. People typically love to hear the same speeches, songs, and stories at specific times during the year (at Christmas, at Passover, etc.) in order to feel united with the other members of the group.

Words in their origin were probably perceived as sacred forms. Those who possessed knowledge of words also possessed supernatural or magical powers. In many early cultures, just knowing the name of a deity was purported to give the knower great power—e.g., in Egyptian mythology, the sorceress Isis tricked the sun god, Ra, into revealing his name and, thus, gained power over him and all other gods. In most cultures, ancestral names given to children are perceived to weave a sort of magical protective aura on the child. In some traditional Inuit tribes, an individual will not pronounce his or her ancestral name, fearing that this senseless act could break the magical spell of protection that it brings with it.

Belief in the magical powers of language is not limited to oral tribal cultures. It abounds even in modern technological cultures. "Speak of the devil," we say in common parlance, and "he will appear." When someone sneezes, uttering "Bless you" is meant to ward off sickness. As Ann Gill (1994: 106) puts it, language, ritual, and magic are intrinsically intertwined:

> By portraying experience in a particular way, words work their unconscious magic on humans, making them see, for example, products as necessary for success or creating distinctions between better or worse—be it body shape, hair style, or brand of blue jeans. Words create belief in religions, governments, and art forms; they create allegiances to football teams, politicians, movie stars, and certain brands of beer. Words are the windows of our own souls and to the world beyond our fingertips. Their essential persuasive efficacy works its magic on every person in every society.

The other side of sacredness is *taboo*. This word comes from the Tongan language where it means "holy, untouchable." Taboos exist in all cultures. These are generally related to sexuality, the supernatural, excretion, death, and various aspects of social life. In our own culture, so-called four-letter words are generally considered obscene, but they are perceived as taboo if uttered in sacred places like churches and sanctuaries.

T Taboos exist in all cultures

VARIATION

Languages vary constantly. If the variable forms are used consistently by specific groups of people in a speech community, they are said to coalesce into a *social dialect* or *sociolect*. Social dialects develop over time as a consequence of divisions within a society, such as those related to economic class and religion. For example, the inhabitants of Martha's Vineyard, in Massachusetts, have adopted particular vowel pronunciations to distinguish themselves from people vacationing on the island. And, as mentioned in the opening chapter, in Java the aristocrats, the townsfolk, and the farmers have a distinct style of speech. The most formal style is used by aristocrats who do not know one another very well, but also by a member of the townsfolk if he or she happens to be addressing a high government official. The middle style is used by townsfolk who are not friends, and by peasants when addressing their social superiors. The low style is used by peasants, or by an aristocrat or town person talking to a peasant, and among friends on any social level. The latter is also the form of language used to speak to children.

Social dialects are characterized above all else by a type of vocabulary called *slang*, which is designed to create and reinforce a specific group's identity. A slang expression may be a new word, such as *glitzy* (gaudy) or *hype* (advertising that relies on gimmicks or tricks). Or it may be an old word with a new meaning, such as *fly* (stylish) or *cool* (sophisticated). People use slang more often in speaking than in writing, and more often with friends than with strangers. Slang thus resembles colloquialisms, which are expressions *slang* used in everyday conversation but not considered appropriate for formal speech ✳ or writing. Unlike colloquialisms, which may be understood by most people, many slang expressions are only used by a certain segment of society or by people in a specific occupation. In a hospital, a physician may be called to the emergency room *stat* (quickly) because a patient has *flatlined* (lost all heart functions). Young people often use slang to differentiate themselves from the adult world.

The type of slang used by specific occupational groups is known as *jargon*. Sometimes, the jargon will spread to society at large. Expressions such as *ham it up* (to overact) and *turkey* (failure), for instance, come from theater jargon. The increasing popularity of the Internet has spread into society at large a great deal of the jargon employed by computer users, including *cyber-* (dealing with computers and the Internet), *snail mail* (written messages delivered by the postal service), *hacker* (an expert computer programmer perhaps involved in illegal activities), *flaming* (a hostile response from a user), and *spamming* (sending numerous unsolicited messages to users).

People are highly sensitive to all kinds of linguistic variation. A classic study that brings this out is the one by American linguist William Labov (1967). Labov made tape recordings of conversations of New York City residents of different ethnic backgrounds and social classes. One of the features he was particularly interested in was the occurrence of /r/ after vowels in words such as *bird, tired, beer,* and *car*. An "/r/-less" pronunciation of such words constituted a prestigious innovation in the 1800s, modeled after British English. However, after World War I the prestige declined, quickly becoming perceived as old-fashioned—a trend confirmed by Labov's study, which found the highest occurrence of the pronunciation of /r/ in young people, aged 8 to 19. In a subsequent study (1972), Labov linked the pronunciation of /r/ in New York

City to social mobility—people aspiring to move from a lower class to a higher one attached prestige to pronouncing the /r/.

Another interesting study was conducted by John Fischer in 1958. As he interviewed a group of elementary school children, Fischer noticed that the children often alternated between two pronunciations of the present participle verb suffix -ing: /-ing/ vs. /-in/ (reading vs. readin'). The choice, Fischer realized, was related to the gender, social class, personality, and mood of the speakers. If they were girls, if they came from families with an above average income, if they had dominating or assertive personalities, and if they were tense, the children tended to use /-ing/. As the interviews progressed, the children became more relaxed and were thus more likely to use /-in/, no matter what their sex, social class, or personality—a finding that suggests that mood plays a greater role than other variables in speech.

Variation along the gender axis is a common aspect of speech communities. In certain languages, there are formal gender differences built directly into male and female speech codes. This is the case in Koasati, an aboriginal language (Haas 1944). The verb endings in that language must be chosen according to the sex of the speaker:

English Gloss	Women say...	Men say...
"he is saying"	/ka/	/kas/
"don't sing"	/taèilawan/	/taèilawas/
"lift it"	/lakaw^{h}ol/	/lakaw^{h}os/
"he is building a fire"	/ot/	/oè/

A similar pattern is found in the language spoken on the Island of Carib in the West Indies (Taylor 1977), where a large number of prescribed doublets (pairs of words with the same meaning) are gender-coded:

English Gloss	Women say...	Men say...
"rain"	/kuyu/	/kunobu/
"sun"	/kaèi/	/hueyu/
"canoe"	/kuriala/	/ukuni/
"manioc (cassava)"	/kawai/	/kiere/

Gender-coded differences exist in English as well. Psychologist Cheris Kramer (1974), for instance, noted that the speech of American women in the 1970s was characterized by a softer tone, fewer profanities, and a profusion of tag questions ("Don't you think?" "Isn't it?" etc.). Kramer showed the captions of cartoons taken from a number of magazines to a group of college students (25 men, 25 women), asking them to guess the sex of the speaker in the (unshown) cartoon. All classified the captions according to male and female speech characteristics, as instructed to do, with no hesitation. As expected, tags were assigned to the female gender more often than not, profanities to men, and so on. Although the situation has changed since then, gender differences continue to be encoded in English (in different ways), as they are in all other languages.

Dialects can also crystallize as a result of geographically based variation, not just as a result of social conditions. For example, in France the language spoken in Paris is considered the standard form of French. People who do not speak Parisian French are said to speak a dialect or regional variant, with all the social implications that this carries with it to speakers of French. The reasons why Parisian French achieved that status have a long social and cultural history behind them. They have nothing to do with any perception of Parisian French as more "aesthetically pleasing" or "cultured" than any other form of the language. This is true as well in the case of Italian. The emergence of Tuscan as the basis for the standard language was the consequence of factors that had nothing to do with verbal aesthetics. The Tuscan vernacular became the basis for the Italian language not because of the "quality" of any of its sounds or words, but because it was the particular language of great writers such as Dante, Petrarch, and Boccaccio. People from all over Italy simply wanted to read their works.

It is interesting to note that the first "dialectologist" may have been the great medieval poet Dante Alighieri (1265–1321) himself, since it was he who first described the complex Italian linguistic situation in his famous *De vulgari eloquentiae* ("Of Vulgar Tongues"). The *questione della lingua* ("the question of language"), as it came to be called, was never really resolved until a late nineteenth-century scholar, named Graziadio Isaia Ascoli (1882), took it upon himself to classify the Italian dialects comparatively on the basis of the phonetic and lexical similarities and differences that existed among them. Ascoli is also responsible for coming up with the concept of *substratum* influence, or the notion that an unexpected reflex in a language imposed on a population resulted from a structural or lexical tendency in the language spoken by the conquered people. For example, the aspiration of initial /f/ in Castilian Spanish—*facere*

sub stratum influence

conquerors
↓ influence
(reflex in lang) *conq people*

("to do") > *hacer* rather than *facer*—is attributed to the influence of the Iberian language that was spoken before the invasion of the Romans. That language did not have an /f/ in initial position.

In the US, there are three major regional dialects: (1) Northern, also called Eastern or New England; (2) Southern; and (3) Midland, also known as Western or Midwestern. Many local dialects exist within these main ones. The Northern dialect is spoken mainly in New York and New England. Some characteristics of Northern pronunciation include dropping the /r/ sound (*car* pronounced / kah/)), and using the short /o/ instead of the open /ɔ/ (*fog* = /fɔg/). The Southern dialect is spoken mainly in the Southern States. Some of its features include the loss of the /r/ sound, the use of the broad /a/ (*time* = /ta^{h}m/), and the use of a short /ɨ/ for /e/ before a nasal sound (*pen* = /pɨ^{h}n/). The Midland dialect is spoken in Pennsylvania, West Virginia, and most states west of the Appalachian Mountains. This dialect is sometimes considered the standard form of American English because it is spoken over the largest geographic region. Pronunciation characteristics of the Midland dialect include the use of the /r/ sound in all word positions, the use of the open /ɔ/ for short /o/, and the use of a long /ay/ in the word *time*.

To study dialects, a number of specific tools have been developed. One of the first to be fashioned is the so-called *dialect atlas*. This is, as its name indicates, a collection of maps of specific regions. Each map shows the actual form that a word or phrase takes on in the regions or areas surveyed. The first to construct such a map was a German school teacher named Georg Wenker in 1876. Wenker sent a list of sentences written in Standard German to other school teachers in northern Germany, asking them to return the list transcribed into the local dialect. By the end of the project, he had compiled over 45,000 questionnaires. Each questionnaire contained 40 sentences. Wenker then produced two sets of maps, highlighting different features. The maps were bound together under the title *Sprachatlas des Deutschen Reichs*.

The questionnaire method established by Wenker remains the basis for conducting dialect surveys to this day, although the procedure for gathering the data has, of course, changed. Dialectologists now send trained observers into the designated region(s) to conduct and record interviews. This fieldwork approach started with the Swiss linguist Jules Gilliéron in the last decade of the nineteenth century. Gilliéron devised a questionnaire for eliciting 1,500 common vocabulary items. He then chose a fieldworker, named Edmond Edmont, to compile the relevant data in the designated parts of France. From 1896 to 1900, Edmont recorded 700 interviews at 639 sites. Known as the *Atlas linguistique de la France*, publication of the atlas got under way in 1902 and was completed in 1910.

Today, in addition to questionnaire techniques, fieldwork, and the compilation of linguistic atlases, dialectologists have at their disposal a wide array of tools, including computer programs that allow them to analyze large amounts of data quickly and to produce linguistic maps with a great degree of accuracy.

BORROWING

To conclude the discussion on variation, a few comments on the notion *borrowing* are in order. Simply put, this is the adoption of words from another language. On almost every page of a dictionary of the English language one can find evidence of borrowing. Indeed, if one were to remove all the words borrowed from Latin and its descendants (Italian, French, Spanish, etc.) from the English lexicon everyday speech would become rather impoverished. One cannot handle an object, talk about some abstract concept, or praise the personality of another person without recourse to some Latin word or expression: e.g., *compact discs* trace their etymological origin to the Latin word *discus* (itself derived from the Greek *diskos*); abstract ideas expressed by nouns ending in *-tion* (*attention, education, nation*, etc.) have their roots in the Latin lexicon, as do most of the nouns ending in *-ty* (*morality, sobriety, triviality*, etc.), and the list could go on and on. How did this come about? And why did it?

[margin note: discs = Grk.]
[margin note: tion = Latin]
[margin note: ty = Latin]

About 1,500 years ago three closely related tribes (the Angles, the Saxons, and the Jutes) lived beside each other on the north shore of what is now northern Germany and southern Denmark. They spoke a language that was similar to the West German dialects. Known as "Old English," it allowed the tribes to establish cultural autonomy from their Germanic ancestry. Old English had inflections that resemble those of modern German, and it formed the new words it needed largely by rearranging and recombining those present in its lexical stock. It borrowed infrequently from other languages.

However, the situation changed drastically after the invasion and conquest of England by the Normans from northwestern France in 1066. Although they were originally of Viking extraction, by the middle of the eleventh century the Normans had adopted French as their language. Naturally they imposed their French-speaking ways upon the Anglo-Saxons. As a consequence, English vocabulary usage became saturated with Latin-based words, which have survived in common speech to this day. Their French origin is no longer

[margin note: Normans from Fr. invade Eng 1066]

consciously recognized because of the fact that they have become completely Anglicized in pronunciation and spelling.

In many instances, English came to adopt Latin-based synonyms even when they were not imposed by the Normans. There are several reasons for this, but perhaps the most important was that Latin was the language of prestige in the Medieval world. To borrow its words was perceived as a means of enriching the lexicon of any emerging vernacular. This is, in fact, one of the reasons for the coexistence of such synonymous pairs in English as *clap* and *applaud*, *fair* and *candid*, *wedding* and *matrimony*, etc., of which the latter item is of Latin descent.

The story behind many borrowings constitutes a fascinating record of human ingenuity. Take the word *rivals*. These can be competitors in business, love, and other affairs. But why should the word to describe such people derive from the Latin word for stream (*rivus*)? In Ancient Rome, when two people lived near a stream they invariably had to share it. And, of course, when two persons are in constant contact, it is easy for discord and dispute to result between them. Hence, the Latin word for *stream* has become by extension the word for *rivalry* in business, sports, love, and war. Examples such as this abound. The word *salary* (from *salarium*) makes reference to the fact that Roman soldiers usually received part of their wages in salt. The word *attention* comes from *attentio*, "a stretching of the mind towards something."

Borrowed words that gain general currency are typically adapted to the pronunciation habits of the borrowers—a process referred to as *nativization*. Among the words that English has nativized from Italian, one can mention, for instance, *alarm, bandit, bankrupt, carnival, gazette, piano, sonnet, stucco, studio, umbrella*, and *volcano*. The French words *naive* and *cliché*, the Italian words *gusto* and *bravo*, and the Spanish words *aficionado* and *macho* are examples of words that have had a fairly recent entry into the language, explaining why they have not been completely nativized.

Borrowing is characteristic of immigrant speech communities. A case-in-point is the Italian language spoken in North America. After World War II, Italian constituted the code with which Italian immigrants carried out daily communication within the family and within their own communities. But being constantly exposed to the English language, the Italian spoken by the immigrants came to be characterized by a large infusion of nativized words borrowed from English. Such words are known as *loanwords*. Predictably, borrowed nouns are assigned a gender through the addition of final vowels, and verbs are rendered as first conjugation verbs (ending in /-are/)—that being the most regular and the most frequent one in the Italian verb system:

English Loanword	Nativized Form	Standard Italian Form
garbage	*garbiccio*	immondizia, rifiuti
mortgage	*morgheggio*	mutuo, ipoteca
switch	*suiccia*	interruttore
fence	*fenza*	recinto
to push	*pusciare*	spingere
~~to smash~~	*~~smacciare~~*	~~frantumare~~
to squeeze	*squisare*	spremere

In addition to loanwords, the Italian of ethnic communities is replete with
calques. *Calques* are phrases that have been translated literally:

loan translation

calque = phrases translated literally

English Loanword	Nativized Form	Standard Italian Form
downtown	*bassa città*	centro
it looks good	*guarda bene*	sta bene
to make a call	*fare il telefono*	telefonare

perros calientes hot dogs

The primary reason why loanwords and calques are so plentiful in immigrant
community languages is need. They are forms that people require in order to
refer to the objects and ideas in the new physical and social environment with
facility. Lacking an appropriate dialectal word for *mortgage*, for instance, the
Italian immigrant was forced to adopt the English word and make it his or her
own linguistically. Once again, we can see the operation of Zipf's Law even in
this domain of linguistic phenomena.

CONCLUDING REMARKS

The study of discourse, variation, speech communities, and dialects is a crucial
part of AL. The artificial separation of *langue* and *parole* introduced into
linguistics by Saussure has allowed linguists to make great strides in
understanding language systems in themselves, but it has also made linguists

underestimate (until recently) the crucial social forces at work constantly in language. By focusing on the relation between *langue* and *parole* the linguist will be in a better position to understand the phenomenon of language on a more abstract level where he or she can observe the interplay between form and use.

X

Language and Reality

All objects, all phases of culture are alive. They have voices.
They speak of their history and interrelatedness. And they are all
talking at once!

Camille Paglia (1947–)

PRELIMINARY REMARKS

In his study of American aboriginal languages, Franz Boas discovered many
things that suggested to him that languages served people, above all else, as
classificatory devices for coming to grips with their particular environmental
and social realities. For example, he noted that the Eskimo language had devised
various terms for the animal we call a *seal*: one is the general term for "seal";
another renders the idea of "seal basking in the sun"; a third of "seal floating
on a piece of ice"; and so on. While English uses only one word to refer to all
these "realities," the Eskimo language uses a larger specialized vocabulary
because of the important role played by seals in Eskimo life.

Specialized vocabularies serve classificatory functions across the world,
encoding realities that are perceived to be critical within particular cultures.
This chapter will take a look at some of the ways in which language and reality
are interlinked—a topic that generally falls under the rubric of the Whorfian
Hypothesis (WH), as mentioned briefly in chapter 1, even though versions of
the WH can be found before Whorf, especially in the writings of Romantic
German scholars such as Johann Herder (1744–1803) and Wilhelm von
Humboldt (1762–1835). Essentially, the WH posits that language structures
predispose native speakers to attend to certain concepts as being necessary.
This does not imply, however, that people cannot understand each other. The

WH = concepts are necessary!

paraphrases used above to convey the various meanings of the terms used by the Eskimo to refer to seals show that there are ways in which the resources of any language can be used to communicate cross-culturally.

THE WHORFIAN HYPOTHESIS

The seeds of the WH were planted by Boas and his students at Columbia University in the 1920s, among whom Edward Sapir in particular devoted his career to determining the extent to which the language of a culture shaped the thought patterns of its users. Sapir was fascinated by the fact that every culture developed its own particular lexical and grammatical categories that largely determined the ways in which individuals in the culture came to view the world:

> Human beings do not live in the object world alone, nor alone in the world of social activity as ordinarily understood, but are very much at the mercy of the particular language system which has become the medium of expression for their society. It is quite an illusion to imagine that one adjusts to reality essentially without the use of language and that language is merely an incidental means of solving specific problems of communication or reflection. The fact of the matter is that the "real world" is to a large extent unconsciously built up on the language habits of the group (Sapir 1921: 75).

The idea that language shapes reality, incidentally, caught the attention of the Gestalt psychologists in the 1930s. Carmichael, Hogan, and Walter, for instance, conducted a truly remarkable experiment to test the idea in 1932. The researchers found that when they showed subjects a picture and then asked them later to reproduce it, the reproductions were influenced by the verbal label assigned to the picture. The drawing of two circles joined by a straight line, for instance (figure 1 on page 139), was generally reproduced as something resembling "eyeglasses" (figure 2 on page 139) by those subjects who were shown the *eyeglasses* label. On the other hand, those who were shown the *dumbbells* label tended to reproduce it as something resembling "dumbbells" (figure 3 on page 139):

1. 2. 3.

Clearly, the name given to figure (1) influenced recall of the figure. There is no other way to explain the results, other than to claim that language labels shape the way we see things.

Whorf was Sapir's student. For this reason, the WH is sometimes called the Sapir–Whorf hypothesis, acknowledging the common views of teacher and pupil. Like Boas, Whorf suggested that the function of language was to allow people to classify experience and, thus, that it was an organizing grid through which humans come to perceive and understand the world around them. For example, Whorf noted that "empty" gasoline drums were treated in his day carelessly, apparently because they were labeled as *empty* (despite the explosive vapor they still contained).

The language with which he became fascinated was Hopi, an American aboriginal language spoken in the southwest region of the US (Whorf 1956). Two things in particular about that language caught Whorf's attention (SAE = Standard Average European):

(1) *Plurality and Numeration.* SAE languages form both real and imaginary plurals—"4 people," "ten days." The latter is considered to be imaginary because it cannot be objectively experienced as an aggregate. Clearly, SAE tends to objectify time, treating it as a measurable object ("two days, four months," etc.). Hopi, on the other hand, does not have imaginary plurals, since only objective aggregates can be counted. Moreover, it treats units of time as cyclic events, not as measurable ones.

(2) *Verb Tense.* SAE languages have three basic tense categories that force speakers to view time sequences as occurring in the present, in the past, and in the future. Hopi verbs, on the other hand, are marked by *validity forms*, which indicate whether the speaker reports, anticipates, or speaks from previous experience, and by *aspectual forms*, which indicate duration and other characteristics of an action.

Here is Whorf's portrayal of what he saw as the critical differences between Hopi and SAE (Whorf 1956):

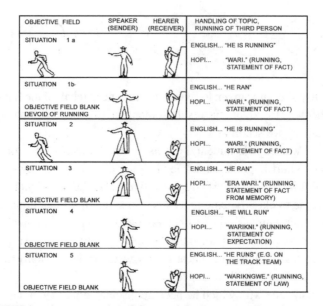

OBJECTIVE FIELD	SPEAKER (SENDER)	HEARER (RECEIVER)	HANDLING OF TOPIC, RUNNING OF THIRD PERSON
SITUATION 1a			ENGLISH... "HE IS RUNNING"
			HOPI... "WARI." (RUNNING, STATEMENT OF FACT)
SITUATION 1b OBJECTIVE FIELD BLANK DEVOID OF RUNNING			ENGLISH... "HE RAN"
			HOPI... "WARI." (RUNNING, STATEMENT OF FACT)
SITUATION 2			ENGLISH... "HE IS RUNNING"
			HOPI... "WARI." (RUNNING, STATEMENT OF FACT)
SITUATION 3 OBJECTIVE FIELD BLANK			ENGLISH... "HE RAN"
			HOPI... "ERA WARI." (RUNNING, STATEMENT OF FACT FROM MEMORY)
SITUATION 4 OBJECTIVE FIELD BLANK			ENGLISH... "HE WILL RUN"
			HOPI... "WARIKNI." (RUNNING, STATEMENT OF EXPECTATION)
SITUATION 5 OBJECTIVE FIELD BLANK			ENGLISH... "HE RUNS" (E.G. ON THE TRACK TEAM)
			HOPI... "WARIKNGWE." (RUNNING, STATEMENT OF LAW)

The WH has been a topic of fierce debate among linguists, ever since Whorf articulated it in the 1940s. Those opposed to the WH allege that it leads to the conclusion that we are prisoners of the languages we speak. But the WH makes no such strong claim. It simply states that language and cognition interact. And it certainly does not claim that the realities of others cannot be learned. This happens every time someone learns a foreign language, as a recent study of Navajo children shows (Kramsch 1998: 13–14). Navajo children speak a language that encodes the actions of "picking up a round object," such as a ball, and "picking up a long, thin flexible object," such as a rope, as obligatory categories. When presented with a blue rope, a yellow rope, and a blue stick, and asked to choose which object goes best with blue rope, Navajo children tend to choose the yellow rope, associating the objects on the basis of their shapes, whereas English-speaking children almost always choose the blue stick, associating the objects on the basis of color, even though both groups of children are perfectly able to distinguish colors and shapes. The experiment shows that speakers tend to sort out and distinguish things according to the categories provided by their languages. However, Navajo children who had studied English chose the blue stick and yellow rope in a fairly equal way.

SPECIALIZED VOCABULARIES

Specialized vocabularies lend themselves particularly well as litmus tests of the WH. Take, for instance, kinship terms. In English, the primary kinship relations are encoded by the words *mother, father, brother, sister, grandmother, grandfather, grandson, granddaughter, niece, nephew, mother-in-law, father-in-law, sister-in-law,* and *brother-in-law.* English vocabulary also distinguishes between *first* and *second cousins* and *great-aunts, great-uncles,* etc. However, it does not distinguish lexically between younger and older siblings. Moreover, English distinguishes a *nephew/niece* from a *grandchild.* But the latter distinction is not encoded in other languages. In Italian, for example, *nipote* refers to both "nephew/niece" and "grandchild."

What do kinship terms reveal? Above all else, they indicate how the family is structured in a given culture, what relationships are considered to be especially important, and what attitudes towards kin may exist. They thus give substance to the WH. Essentially, kinship terms sort similar and different kinds of persons into specific categories, influencing how they are perceived. Take, for instance, the Hawaiian kinship system, where all relatives of the same generation and sex are referred to with the same term—in one's parents' generation, the term used to refer to the father is used as well for the father's brother and the mother's brother. Similarly, one's mother, her sister, and one's father's sister are all lumped together under a single term. Essentially, kinship reckoning in Hawaiian culture involves putting all relatives of the same sex and age into the same category. On the other side of the kinship spectrum is the Sudanese system. In it, the mother's brother is distinguished from the father's brother/ mother's brother, who is distinguished from the father. The mother's sister is distinguished from the mother, as well as from the father's sister. Each cousin is distinguished from all others, as well as from siblings. This system is one of the most precise ones in existence. In few societies are all aunts, uncles, cousins, and siblings named and treated as equals in the kinship line.

One specialized vocabulary that has been used for decades to litmus-test the WH is color terminology. Experts estimate that we can distinguish perhaps as many as 10 million colors. Our names for colors are, thus, far too inexact to describe accurately all the colors we actually see. As a result, people often have difficulty trying to describe or match a certain color. If one were to put a finger at any point on the spectrum, there would be only a negligible difference in gradation in the colors immediately adjacent to the finger at either side. Yet, a speaker of English describing the spectrum will list the gradations as falling under the categories *purple, blue, green, yellow, orange,* and *red.* This is because that speaker has been conditioned by the English language to classify the content of the spectrum in specific ways. There is nothing inherently "natural" about our color scheme; it is a reflex of English vocabulary, not of Nature. What is a shade of color in one language is a distinct color in another.

Shona = 4 categories   Bassa = 2

Speakers of <u>Shona</u>, an indigenous <u>African language</u>, for instance, divide the spectrum up into *cipswuka, citema, cicena,* and *cipswuka* (again), and speakers of Bassa, a language of Liberia, segment it into just two categories, *hui* and *ziza.* The relative hues encoded by these terms vis-à-vis the hues encoded by English words can be shown graphically as follows:

6 *English* →	purple	blue	green	yellow	orange	red
4 *Shona* →	cipswuka	citema	cicena		cipswuka	
2 *Bassa* →	hui			ziza		
Potential Number of Categories	←——————→ 10 million ←——————→					

So, when an English speaker refers to, say, a ball as *blue,* a Shona speaker might refer to it as either *cipswuka* or *citema,* and a Bassa speaker as *hui.* What a Shona speaker would consider as shades of cicena, the English speaker would see two distinct colors, *green* and *yellow.* But such differences do not stop speakers of the above languages from relating their perceptions to those of the other two languages. This is, indeed, what a teacher of English does when he or she imparts the new color system to students with Shona and Bassa backgrounds. Moreover, in all languages there exist verbal resources for referring to more specific gradations on the spectrum if the situation should require it. In English, the words *crimson, scarlet, vermilion,* for instance, make it possible to refer to <u>types of *red.*</u> But these are still felt by speakers to be <u>*subcategories* or</u> shades of red, not distinct color categories on their own. Similar kinds of resources exist in Shona and Bassa.

A classic study of color terminology is the 1953 one by linguist <u>Verne Ray.</u> Ray interviewed the speakers of 60 different languages spoken in the southwestern part of the US. He showed them colored cards under uniform conditions of lighting, asking the speakers to name them. The colors denoted by *black, white* and *gray* were not included in the study. The following chart shows the results of Ray's study for nine of the 60 languages:

Ray = colour study

	Wave length	English	Salish	Sahaptin	Chinook	Salish	Athapaskan	Eskimo	Athapaskan	Takelma	Kalapuya
		Northwest U.S.	Sanpoil	Tenino	Wishram	Songish	Chilcotin	Atka	Chetco R.	Rogue R.	Santiam
Violet-red	comp 5600	X	X	lut'sa'	X	nɛsɛ̴'q'u	X	X	tsi'k	alčị'l	saʔkwala
Red	6571	red	qu'l		datbá'l						utsɛ·'lə
Orange-red	6340			mɛ̴kc		lɛlɛ̴č		u'lu·'ðax			t'sɪ·'lɪlɔ·
Red-orange	6230				dagá'c		rɪdrɛ'l		xa'ðəgi		
Orange	6085	orange				lɛlɛ̴čalts				ba'u̴x	ba'lamɪ
Yellow-orange	5870		kuya'i	pa'a'x				ču·mnu'χɪx			
Orange-yellow	5793				qa'naptsu	nɛkwa'i	rɛltso'·		tsu'	ɢwa'camt	tskɪ'lˀkwu
Yellow	5710	yellow									
Green-yellow	5390		qwi'n			čí'ʔalts		čɪ'ðɣɪx			
Yellow-green	5164				daptsá'x	sqwa'iux	rɪ'ɪ̆ča'n			tɢicɛ̴mt	
Green	5050	green		lɛ̴mt		nɛkwa'l			xa'dətsu'		pčí'x
Blue-green	4985		qwa'i							kiyɛ̴'x	
Green-blue	4695	blue				kwi'ɛmɛl					
Blue	4455			pu'u'x							
Blue-violet	4350		xɛ'n		iyaquitsabɛl			X	X	X	X
Violet	4210	violet		X							
Red-violet	comp 4990										
Violet-red	comp 5600										

The chart shows how languages overlap, contrast, and coincide with each other. In Tenino and Chilcotin, for example, a part of the range of English *green* is covered by a term that includes *yellow*. In Wishram and Takelma, on the other hand, there are as many terms as in English, but the boundaries are different. In still other cases, there are more distinctions than in English. Ray concludes as follows (1953): "Color systems serve to bring the world of color sensation into order so that perception may be relatively simple and behavioral response, particularly verbal response and communication, may be meaningful."

Shortly after, in 1955, Harold Conklin examined the four-term color system of the Hanunoo of the Philippines. He found that the four categories into which the Hanunoo grouped colors were interconnected with light and the plant world (the prefix *ma-* means "having" or "exhibiting"):

ma-biru ("darkness, blackness")
ma-lagti ("lightness, whiteness")
ma-rara ("redness, presence of red")
ma-latuy ("greenness, presence of green")

The *ma-biru* category implies absence of light, and thus includes not only *black* but also many deep shades—*dark blue, violet, green, gray*, etc. The *ma-lagti* category implies the presence of light, and thus includes *white* and many lightly pigmented shades. The other two terms derive from an opposition of freshness and dryness in plants— *ma-rara* includes *red, orange,* and yellow, and *ma-latuy* includes *light green* and *brown*. The Hanunoo language can, of course, refer to color gradations more specifically than this if the need should arise. But its basic system encodes a reality that is specific to the Hanunoo's environment.

In 1969 American anthropological linguists Brent Berlin and Paul Kay decided to study the relation between color systems and perception more extensively than had ever been done in the past. Their study has become a point of reference in discussing the WH ever since, because it apparently shows that differences in color terms are only superficial matters that conceal universal principles of color perception.

On the basis of the judgments of the native speakers of twenty widely divergent languages, Berlin and Kay came to the conclusion that there were "focal points" in basic (single-term) color vocabularies, which clustered in certain predictable ways. They identified eleven universal focal points, corresponding to the English words *black, white, red, yellow, green, blue, brown, purple, pink, orange,* and *gray.* Not all the languages they investigated had separate words for each of these colors, but there emerged a pattern that suggested to them a fixed sequence of naming across cultures. If a language had two colors, then the names were equivalents of English *black* and *white.* If it had three color terms, then the third one corresponded to *red.* A four-term system had a term for either *yellow* or *green,* but not both; while a five-term system had terms for both of these. A six-term system included a term for *blue;* a seven-term system had a term for *brown.* Finally, terms for *purple, pink, orange,* and *gray* were found to occur in any combination in languages that had the previous focal terms. Berlin and Kay found that languages with, say, a four-term system consisting of *black, white, red,* and *brown* did not exist. Berlin and Kay's universal color system is shown below:

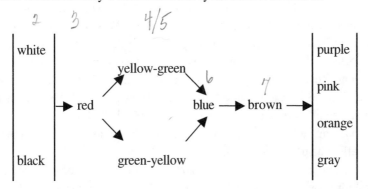

Kay revised the sequence in 1975 in order to account for the fact that certain languages, such as Japanese, encode a color category that does not exist in English, and which can only be rendered in that language as "green-blue." This category, which Kay labeled GRUE, may occur before or after *yellow* in the original sequence:

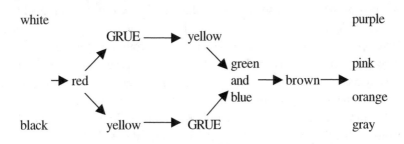

Since then it has been found that the sequence needs to be either modified, expanded, or even discarded. For example, Russian and Italian do not have a single color term for "blue," but rather distinguish "light blue" and "dark blue" as distinct focal colors.

Despite such gaps in the sequence, the Berlin–Kay study has had profound implications on several counts. First, it shows that the contrast between light and dark is the basic distinction made by human beings across the world. Second, it suggests that languages go through stages in the production of the other color terms and, thus, that color vocabularies are a product of human perception, not language traditions. Cultures provide the contexts in which the sequence develops—but the sequence remains universal.

Many linguists, anthropologists, and psychologists pursued the intriguing implications of the Berlin–Kay study vigorously in the 1970s. Eleanor Rosch, for instance, demonstrated that the Dani people of West Irian, who have a two-color system similar to the Bassa system described above, were able to discriminate easily eight focal points (Rosch 1975). Using a recognition-memory experiment, Rosch found that the Dani recognized focal colors better than non-focal ones. She also found that they learned new colors more easily when the color names were paired with focal colors. Such findings suggested to Rosch that languages provided a guide to the interpretation of color, but they did not affect its perception in any way.

But many problems remain to this day with the conclusions reached by such color researchers. For one thing, many of the terms Berlin and Kay listed turn out to be borrowings, which greatly undermines their theory. More importantly, the fact that the eleven focal colors posited by Berlin and Kay correspond to the color terms of their own language (English) colors the outcome (no pun intended) of the study. Could the researchers have been predisposed by their own language to gloss all other terms according to the English categories? The many exceptions to their universal sequence that have accrued over the years seem to bear this out. Moreover, as anthropologist Roger Wescott (1980) has amply documented, color vocabularies seem to have originated from specific experiences, not from the operation of innate perceptual mechanisms. In Hittite, for instance, words for colors initially designated plant and tree names such as *poplar, elm, cherry, oak,* etc.; in Hebrew, the name of the first man, *Adam,* meant "red" and "alive," and still today, in languages of the Slavic family *red* signifies "living" and "beautiful." In effect, the Berlin–Kay work has hardly refuted the WH. On the contrary, it seems to have kindled even more interest in it, as the continued proliferation of work on color terminologies today attests.

METAPHOR

The discussion of the WH leads to a further consideration of the role of metaphor in language and culture. As discussed in chapter 6, metaphor is a tool of groupthink that manifests itself in language in systematic ways. Above all else, it constitutes a cognitive strategy that allows people to portray and understand abstract concepts in terms of concrete experiences. This is why, for example, feelings across the world's languages are said to be *warm, hot, cool*; or why people are seen to be *dull* or *bright*. Ideas and feelings are experienced as if they were sensations and are named as such. As psycholinguist Roger Brown (1958a: 154) aptly puts it:

> The quality is first detected in one sense modality and is named at that stage. Afterward the quality is detected in many other phenomena that register with other senses. The original name tends to be extended to any experience manifesting the criterial quality (Brown 1958a: 154).

In his ground breaking 1936 book, *The Philosophy of Rhetoric*, the literary scholar I. A. Richards (1893–1979) argued that metaphor shapes reality because it springs from our experience of reality. In the domain of metaphor, therefore, the WH is a fact, not a theory. Consider the expression *John is a monkey*. The topic in this case is a person named *John* and the vehicle the animal known as a *monkey*. Portraying *John* as a *monkey* forces us to imagine a human person in simian terms. If one were to call *John* a *snake*, a *pig*, or a *puppy*, then our image of *John* would change in kind with each new vehicle—he would become serpentine, swine-like, and puppy-like to our mind's eye. Like Franz Kafka's (1883–1924) horrifying short story *Metamorphosis*, where the main character awakes one morning from a troubled dream to find himself changed to some kind of monstrous vermin, our perception of people (and of ourselves) is altered (probably permanently) the instant we paint a picture of their personality in animal terms. Like the spell put on people by shamans, people become what our metaphors say they are.

As we saw in chapter 6, *John* belongs to the domain of [people] and *monkey* to the domain of [animals]. The linkage of the two domains, [people are animals], produces a concept which suggests that we sense some intrinsic existential link between the two domains. And it has cultural consequences. It shows up, for example, in the use of animal surnames (*Fox, Bear,* etc.), in animal narratives told to children where animals represent people, in totemic practices, in naming sports teams *(Detroit Tigers, Chicago Bears,* etc.), in heraldic practices, and the list could go on and on.

Metaphors based on words for sensation and perception are called *root metaphors.* These suggest that we conceptualize an abstract phenomenon such as [thinking] as an extension of sensation. The number of root metaphorical constructions (idioms, phrases, etc.) in vocabularies throughout the world is immeasurable. Here is a handful in English based on vision:

flash of insight
spark of genius
a *bright* mind
a *brilliant* idea
a *flicker* of intelligence
a *luminous* achievement
a *shining* mind
a *bright* fire in his eyes
sparking interest in a subject
words *glowing* with meaning
flickering ideas

But vision is not the only sensory modality people use to name [thinking] processes. The etymology of common words for such processes in English reveals that vision is used alongside touch and grasping as root source domains:

apprehend (from Latin "to seize, lay hold of")
comprehend (from Latin *prehendere* "to grasp")
discern (from Latin *dis* + *cerno* "to separate")
examine (from Latin *ex* + *agmen-* "to pull out from a row")
idea (from Greek *ideein* "to see")
intelligence (from Latin *intellegere* "to pick, choose")
perceive (from Latin *-cipio* "to seize")
prospect (from Latin *pro* + *spectus* "looking ahead")
scrutinize (from Latin *scrutari* "to pick through trash")
speculate (from Latin *speculari* "to look at")
theory (from Greek *theoria* "view")
think (from Old English *thincean* "to take, handle")
understand (from Old English *ongietan* "to see, feel")

A sampling of various unrelated languages reveals that this kind of metaphorical modeling is universal:

- In Modern Hebrew *litpos* "to grasp" means "to understand."
- In Maori *kura* "seeing" refers to "knowledge in general," and *kia marama te titiro* "to see clearly" refers to "understanding."
- In Japanese *yoin* "reverberating sound" designates "human feelings."
- In Chinese *takuan* "to have seen through life" is used to refer to the ability "to understand that some things cannot be understood."
- In Sanskrit *maya* "to measure with the eye" refers to the danger inherent in relying upon one's mind to think about the world.

Not all words for the mind are, of course, root metaphors. The word *contemplate*, for instance, derives from Latin *templum* "temple"—the temple being the place where one "contemplates" (Wescott 1978: 27). But by and large, our concepts for the mind are root metaphors. They are no longer recognized as such because they have become conventionalized through protracted usage. Edie (1976: 165) offers the following relevant observation:

> A word which primarily designates a perceptual phenomenon—
> for example the perception of light—once constituted is available
> for a new purpose and can be used with a new intention—for
> example to denote the process of intellectual understanding, and
> we speak of (mental) illumination. Once established, the
> metaphorical use of the original word is no longer noticed; its
> essential ambiguity tends to fall below the level of awareness
> from the moment that it is taken as designating another, now
> distinguishable, experience.

In languages across the world, the human body is also a productive source domain for naming all kinds of things that are perceived to be like the body. This is why we refer to the *bowels* of the earth, to its *heart*, and so on. Here are some other examples in English of body metaphors:

a *body* of people
a *body* of water
the *body* of a work
the *eye* of a storm
the *eye* of the needle
the *face* of a clock
the *foot* of a mountain

the *head* of a table
the *head* of an organization
the *head* of the household
a *leg* of a race
? *holding* a meeting *arms*
taking things at *face* value
nosing around
mouthing lyrics
shouldering a burden
knuckling under
going *belly up*
toeing the line

The presence of similar body metaphors in vocabularies across the world suggests that the human mind perceives the things in the cosmos as being interconnected to each other anthropomorphically. *Shell for body* As a protective shell for the body, the home in particular is viewed cross-culturally in metaphorical terms. Take, for example, the language spoken by the Batammaliba people who live in the border region between the West African states of Togo and the Benin Republic. These people name all the parts of their house with body terms, as shown below (Tilley 1999: 41–49):

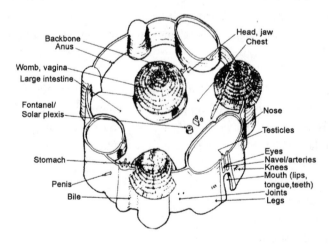

It should come as no surprise to find that automobiles too are named in a similar way. Take, for instance, the Western Apache language of east-central

Arizona. All the parts of the automobile are named in that language as if they were body parts, as shown below (Basso 1990: 15–24):

Apache Term	English Meaning	Auto Part
łik∂	*fat*	grease
dɔ	*chin and jaw*	front bumper
wos	*shoulder*	front fender
g∂n	*hand and arm*	front wheel
kai	*thigh and buttock*	rear fender
zɛ	*mouth*	gas pipe opening
ke	*foot*	rear wheel
y∂n	*back*	bed of truck
indá	*eye*	headlight
ni	*face*	area from top of windshield to bumper
či	*nose*	hood
ta	*forehead*	top, front of cab
ɛbiyí	*entrails*	machinery under hood
ts3s	*vein*	electrical wiring
zik	*liver*	battery
pit	*stomach*	gas tank
či	*intestine*	radiator hose
ji	*heart*	distributor
jisolɛ	*lung*	radiator

Basso explains the use of such body metaphors in two ways. First, there is the fact that cars have replaced horses in Apache life and, thus, the terms used to describe the horse have been reapplied to describe the car. Second, since vehicles can generate and sustain locomotion by themselves, they are likely to be perceived as extensions of bodily locomotion.

Root metaphors and anthropomorphic metaphors have, as mentioned above, "cultural consequences." Take, for instance, the [love is a sweet taste] conceptual metaphor in English, which can be seen in such common expressions as "She's my *sweetheart*," "They went on a *honeymoon*," etc. The fact that sweets are given to a loved one on St. Valentine's day, that matrimonial love is symbolized at a wedding ceremony by the eating of a cake, that we sweeten our breath with candy before kissing our loved ones, etc., are all "consequences" of this conceptual metaphor. Incidentally, in Chagga, a

Reification – regarding something abstract as a material thing or 2. rep. human being as a physical thing deprived of personal qual

Bantu language of Tanzania, similar cultural practices exist because the language possesses the same [love is a sweet taste] concept. In Chagga the man is perceived to be the eater and the woman his *sweet food*, as can be detected in expressions that mean, in translated form, "Does she taste sweet?" "She tastes sweet as sugar honey" (Emantian 1995: 168). This type of reification of something imagined metaphorically into something real is extensive across cultures. Take, as another example, the symbolism associated with [justice] in our culture: (1) the [justice is blind] conceptual metaphor is rendered palpable, for example, in the practice of sculpting statues of "Justice" with blindfolds; (2) the [the scales of justice] conceptual metaphor is commonly symbolized by corresponding sculptures of scales near or inside justice buildings.

reification = universal

Metaphor is also at the root of a culture's storehouse of proverbial wisdom. A common expression like *He has fallen from grace* would have been recognized instantly in a previous era as referring to the Adam and Eve story in the Bible. Today we continue to use it with only a dim awareness (if any) of its Biblical origins. Expressions that portray life as a journey—"I'm still a *long way* from my goal," "There is no *end* in sight," etc.—are similarly rooted in Biblical narrative. As the literary critic Northrop Frye (1981) pointed out, one cannot penetrate such expressions without having been exposed, directly or indirectly, to the original Biblical stories. These are the source domains for many of the conceptual metaphors we use today for judging human actions and offering advice, bestowing upon everyday life an unconscious metaphysical meaning and value. When we say *An eye for an eye and a tooth for a tooth* we are invoking imagery that reverberates with religious meaning in a largely unconscious way.

proverbial

Every culture has similar proverbs, aphorisms, and sayings. They constitute a remarkable code of ethics and of practical knowledge that anthropologists call "folk wisdom." Indeed, the very concept of *wisdom* implies the ability to apply proverbial language insightfully to a situation.

Scientific reasoning too is largely based on metaphorical imagery. Science often involves things that cannot be seen—atoms, waves, gravitational forces, magnetic fields, etc. So, scientists use their metaphorical know-how to envision this hidden matter. That is why waves are said to *undulate* through empty space, atoms to *leap* from one quantum state to another, electrons to *travel in circles* around an atomic nucleus, and so on. Metaphors are evidence of the human ability to see the universe as a coherent structure. As physicist Robert Jones (1982: 4) aptly puts it, for the scientist metaphor serves as "an evocation of the inner connection among things." When a metaphor is accepted as fact,

metaphor = fact

it enters human life, taking on an independent conceptual existence in the real world, suggesting ways to bring about changes in and to the world. Even the nature of experimentation can be seen in this light. Experimentation is a search for connections, linkages, associations of some sort or other. As Rom Harré (1981: 23) has pointed out, most experiments involve "the attempt to relate the structure of things, discovered in an exploratory study, to the organization this imposes on the processes going on in that structure." The physicist K. C. Cole (1984: 156) similarly puts it as follows:

> The words we use are metaphors; they are models fashioned from familiar ingredients and nurtured with the help of fertile imaginations. "When a physicist says an electron is like a particle," writes physics professor Douglas Giancoli, "he is making a metaphorical comparison like the poet who says "love is like a rose." In both images a concrete object, a rose or a particle, is used to illuminate an abstract idea, love or electron.

WRITING

The relation between language, reality, and culture can also be sought in the nature and function of writing systems. Before the advent of alphabets, people communicated and passed on their knowledge through the spoken word. But even in early "oral cultures," tools had been invented for recording and preserving ideas in pictographic form. So "instinctive" is pictography that it comes as little surprise to find that it has not disappeared from our own modern world, even though most of our written communication is based on the alphabet. The figures designating *male* and *female* on washrooms and the *no-smoking* signs found in public buildings, to mention but two common examples, are modern-day pictographs.

The earliest pictographs so far discovered were unearthed in western Asia from the Neolithic era. They are elemental shapes on clay tokens that were probably used as image-making forms or moulds (Schmandt-Besserat 1978, 1992). One of the first civilizations to institutionalize pictographic writing as a means of recording ideas, keeping track of business transactions, and transmitting knowledge was the ancient Chinese one. According to some archeological estimates, Chinese pictography may date as far as back the fifteenth century BC. Here are some examples of early Chinese pictographs:

Chinese
pictographs

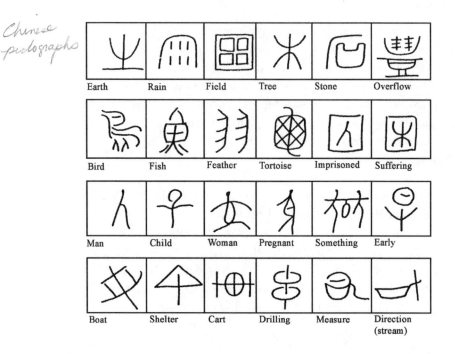

Earth	Rain	Field	Tree	Stone	Overflow

Bird	Fish	Feather	Tortoise	Imprisoned	Suffering

Man	Child	Woman	Pregnant	Something	Early

Boat	Shelter	Cart	Drilling	Measure	Direction (stream)

Pictographs   As can be seen, pictographs are images of objects, people, or events.
Ideo-
graphs   More abstract pictographic signs are called *ideographs*. These also bear
resemblance to their referents, but assume much more of a conventional
knowledge of the relation between form and referent on the part of the user.
International symbols for such things as public telephones and washrooms
today are examples of ideographs. Even more abstract pictographs are known
logo-
graphs   as *logographs*, which combine elements of basic pictography and ideography.
For example, the Chinese logograph for *east* is a combination of the pictographs
for *sun* and *tree*.

A pictographic system was also used by the ancient Sumerian culture that
emerged nearly 5,000 years ago. Called *cuneiform*, because it consisted of
wedge-shaped picture symbols, the Sumerians recorded their representations
on clay tablets, making it a very expensive and impracticable means of
communication. For this reason, cuneiform was developed, learned, and used
primarily by rulers and clerics. Below are some examples of early Sumerian
cuneiform script:

Pictographs - images of objects, people or events
Ideographs (more abstract) - bear resemblance to
their referents, but assume conventional knowledge.
ie intl: public wash or pub telephone
logographs (even more abstract) - combine pict + ideo

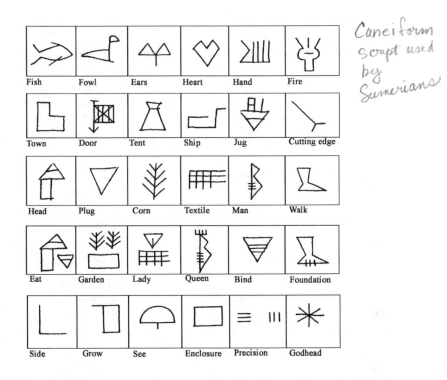

Cuneiform script used by Sumerians

From about 2700 to 2500 BC another type of pictographic script, called *hieroglyphic,* was invented in Egypt. This was very similar in style to the Sumerian one, as can be seen below:

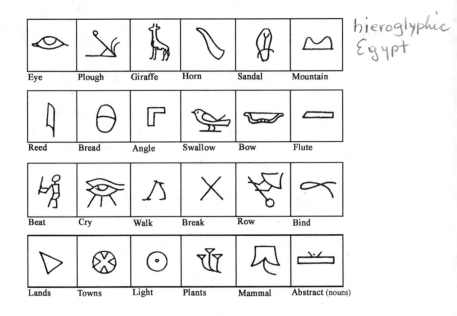

hieroglyphic Egypt

The Egyptians used papyrus (a type of early paper made from reeds) to record their hymns and prayers, the names and titles of individuals and deities, and various community activities—*hieroglyphic* derives from Greek *hieros* "holy" and *glyphein* "to carve." Indeed, in their origins most scripts were deemed to have sacred or divine power, and the myths of many cultures confirm this by attributing the origin of writing to deities—the Cretans to Zeus, the Sumerians to Nabu, the Egyptians to Toth, the Greeks to Hermes, and so on. The hieroglyphic system eventually developed *phonographic* elements within it—*phonographs* are forms standing for parts of words, such as syllables or individual sounds. The first true *syllabaries*—systems of signs for representing syllables—were developed by the Semitic peoples of Palestine and Syria from the Egyptian hieroglyphs during the last half of the second millennium BC. Syllabaries are still used in some cultures. Japanese, for example, is still written with two complete syllabaries—the *hiragana* and the *katakana*—devised to supplement the characters originally taken over from Chinese.

A phonographic system for representing single sounds is called *alphabetic*. The first alphabetic system emerged in the Middle East, and was transported by the Phoenicians (a people from a territory on the eastern coast of the Mediterranean, located largely in modern-day Lebanon) to Greece. It contained symbols for consonant sounds only. When it reached Greece, symbols for vowel sounds were added to it, making the Greek system the first full-fledged alphabetic one.

The transition from pictorial to sound representation came about to make writing rapid and efficient. It reflects, therefore, the operation of Zipf's Law in linguistic matters. Take, for example, the development of the alphabet character **A**. It started out as a pictograph of the head of an ox. The full head of the ox came to be drawn soon after in its bare outline. This came eventually to stand for the word for ox (*aleph* in Hebrew). The Phoenician scribes, who wrote from right to left, drew the ox figure sideways (probably because it was quicker for them to do so). This slanted figure came to stand just for the first sound in the word (*a* for *aleph*). The Greeks, who wrote from left to right, turned the Phoenician figure around the other way. Around 500 BC, as alphabetic writing became more standardized and letters stopped changing directions, the **A** assumed the upright position it has today—the ox had finally settled on its horns! The five-stage evolution of **A**, from pictograph to alphabet character (in Phoenician then Greek and finally Latin) can be shown as follows:

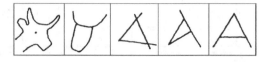

The Greeks started the practice of naming each symbol by such words as *alpha, beta, gamma,* etc., which were imitations of Phoenician words: *aleph* "ox," *beth* "house," *gimel* "camel," etc. The idea of an "alphabetic order" was derived from the fact that the sequence of letters from **A** to **Z** was used to count the numbers in order—**A** stood for 1, **B** for 2, **C** for 3, and so on. The earliest record of alphabetic order is Psalm thirty-seven where verses follow the Hebraic sequence.

Pictography did not alter the basic oral nature of daily communication, nor did it alter the oral mode of transmitting knowledge of early societies. That occurred after the invention of alphabetic writing around 1000 BC—an event that brought about the first true radical change in the world's social structure. The move away from pictographic to alphabetic writing was, to use philosopher Thomas Kuhn's (1922–1996) appropriate term, the first great "paradigm shift" of human history, since it constituted the initial step towards the establishment of a worldwide civilization. The second step was taken in the fifteenth century after the development of movable type technology—an event that made it possible to print and duplicate books cheaply. As a result, more books became available and more people gained literacy. With literacy came exposure to new ideas and independent thinking. And with independent thinking came many revolutions of a religious, political, social, and scientific nature. Moreover, since cheaply printed books could be sent all over the world, scientists, philosophers, artists, educators, historians, poets, and story writers read and translated each other's books. Ideas started crossing borders and vast spaces, uniting the world more and more. Standardized ways of doing things in the scientific and business domains emerged. In a phrase, the invention of the printing press was the technological event that paved the way to the establishment of a true global civilization.

The third step towards the founding of a worldwide civilization was taken at the start of the twentieth century, with advancements in electronics and the advent of the mass media for communicating information to larger and larger numbers of people. Since electronic signals can cross borders virtually unimpeded, Marshall McLuhan (1911–1980) characterized the world that was being united by electronic media as the "global village." Near the end of the twentieth century, the fourth step towards establishing a worldwide civilization was taken after computers became widely available and the Internet emerged as a truly global medium.

Alphabetic writing has become the norm in the global village, although pictography has not disappeared. We even use letters themselves in a pictographic or ideographic way. Take, for example, the *onomatope*, which is the graphic counterpart to onomatopoeia, as a technique for representing sounds in letters. Here are some examples:

onomatopoe (handwritten margin note)

Braaannnngggg! (graphic form for the noise of an alarm)
Aaaahhhhh! (graphic form for the sound of gulping for air or a cry of
    terror)
Hehheheh (graphic form for the belly sound associated with laughter)
Booooo! (graphic form for a sound made to evoke fear)

Certain signs are also used to simulate various aspects of regular conversation. For example, spaces between words indicate separation or identity of basic verbal units (such as words). Punctuation marks are also used to indicate such articulatory features as interrogatiion (?), exclamation (!), pause (period), and so on.

WH (handwritten margin note)

The use of scripts to represent things and ideas indirectly supports the WH. Writing from right to left or left to right, for instance, is bound to influence how we perceive certain things. For example, those who write from left to right perceive past time as a "left-oriented" phenomenon and future time as a "right-oriented" one. To grasp what this means, look at the line below, which has a point on it labeled "Now":

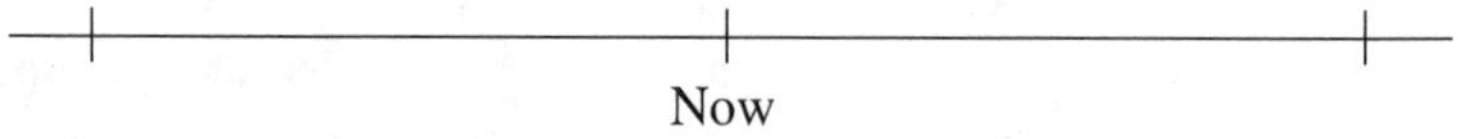

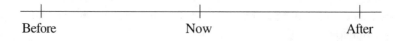

Now

Now, where would you put the labels "Before" and "After" on that line? If you are used to writing from left to right, you will put "Before" to the left and "After" to the right. Why? Because you have become accustomed to seeing what is written to the left on a page as something that has been written "before", and what will be written to the right as something that will be written "after":

Before   Now   After

Those who are accustomed to writing from right to left will reverse the labels for the same reason. It is interesting to note, as a final comment on writing, that in his book *Historia*, the Greek historian Herodotus made the remark that Egyptians "thought differently from Greeks" because "they wrote from right to left!"

CONCLUDING REMARKS

The Whorfian Hypothesis, and more generally the view that language and reality are two sides of the same coin, is not a theory of mind; it simply acknowledges that there is a dynamic interaction between language and cognition. But this does not mean that one "determines" the other. The philosopher Giambattista Vico (1688–1744) explained the emergence of language as a product of what he called the *fantasia* and the *ingegno*. The former is the capacity that allows human beings to imagine literally anything they desire freely and independently of biological or cultural processes; it is the creative force behind new thoughts, new ideas, art, science, and so on. The latter is the capacity that allows human beings to convert their new thoughts and ideas into expressive representational structures—words, metaphors, stories, works of art, scientific theories, etc. So, although human beings are indeed shaped in large part by their particular biology and by the cultural system in which they are reared, they are also endowed with creative faculties that are well beyond the capacities of the current sciences of biology and psychology to explain. The human being is, indeed, a true enigma among living species.

Through fieldwork and a comparison of languages, the anthropological linguist can gain insight into this enigma. My final comment is, however, cautionary. No matter how scientific or theoretically sound a linguist's account of the connection between language and reality might appear or might be purported to be, no science can ever truly account for the remarkable phenomenon that we call language. We might be able to describe what the bits and pieces are like and how they mesh together; but we will never be able to put into a theory or model all there is to know about language.

In a sense, linguistic analysis is comparable to solving a jigsaw puzzle. The goal of the puzzle-solver is to figure out how the pieces of the puzzle fit together to produce the hidden picture that they conceal as disconnected pieces. But solving the jigsaw puzzle tells the solver nothing about why he or she is fascinated by such puzzles in the first place, nor what relevance they have to human life. Analogously, the linguist seeks to figure out how the bits and pieces (phonemes, morphemes, etc.) cohere into the organism of language. But having described the anatomy and physiology of this organism, he or she is still left with the dilemma of why such an organism came into being in the first place.

Activities and
Topics for Discussion

CHAPTER 1

1. Explain the following terms and notions in your own words.
    (a) linguistics
    (b) comparative method
    (c) diachronic analysis
    (d) synchronic analysis
    (e) phonology
    (f) morphology
    (g) syntax
    (h) semantics
    (i) variation
    (j) structuralism
    (k) langue
    (l) parole
    (m) grammar
    (n) linguistic competence
    (o) communicative competence
    (p) speech act
    (q) register
    (r) Zipf's Law
    (s) protolanguage
    (t) PIE

2. How would you characterize linguistic method after having read this chapter?

3. Give the importance of the following people in the history of linguistics.
    (a) Panini
    (b) Dionysius Thrax
    (c) Jacob Grimm
    (d) the neogrammarians
    (e) Ferdinand de Saussure
    (f) Franz Boas
    (g) Edward Sapir
    (h) Leonard Bloomfield
    (i) Noam Chomsky
    (j) Dell Hymes

4. Explain the difference between *langue* and *parole* in your own words.

5. What is the difference between theoretical and applied linguistics?

6. Determine what aspects of English the following violate.
    (a) pfind
    (b) churchs (churches)
    (c) ilregular (irregular)
    (d) Goes to school Sarah every day.
    (e) What Alexander is doing?

7. Point out the semantic differences between the words in the following pairs.
    (a) blue – celeste
    (b) table – desk
    (c) chair – sofa
    (d) cat – dog

8. Identify what is anomalous *irregular* in each statement.
    (a) Madam, I gotta split!
    (b) Mary, I wish to inform you that I am in love with you.
    (c) Little child, could you indicate to me what your name is?

9. Can you find any examples of the operation of Zipf's Law in English or any other language you know?

10. Give a summary of language development in childhood.

CHAPTER 2

1. Define the following terms and notions in your own words.
    (a) assimilation
    (b) palatalization
    (c) vocalization
    (d) Nostratic
    (e) reconstruction
    (f) core vocabulary
    (g) voicing
    (h) cognate
    (i) diversification
    (j) borrowing
    (k) glottochronology
    (l) sound symbolism
    (m) lexicostatistics
    (n) Principle of Economic Change
    (o) Principle of the Historical Cycle

2. Paraphrase the five main language origin theories, giving examples of your own to illustrate each one.

3. Devise your own "universal core vocabulary" of 25 terms, explaining why you chose each one.

4. Use Robert Lees's formula to estimate time depth between two related languages of your choice.

5. Utilize Hockett's typology to assess other animal communication systems that you may know.

6. What kinds of evidence are used to reconstruct a protolanguage?

7. Look up the following words in an etymological dictionary, indicating their source language. Explain the change from source language word to modern English form in your own words.
    (a) friend
    (b) truth
    (c) jazz

    (d) secular

    (e) name

    (f) foot

    (g) program

8. Can you give any examples of economically motivated changes in English?

9. Give examples of regular sound change from Old English to contemporary English.

10. Do you think that human language can ever be taught in its entirety to primates? Explain your answer.

CHAPTER 3

1. Define the following terms in your own words.

    (a) phonetics

    (b) point of articulation

    (c) manner of articulation

    (d) vowel

    (e) consonant

    (f) noncontinuant

    (g) continuant

    (h) obstruent

    (i) sonorant

    (j) syllable

    (k) stress

    (l) nucleus

    (m) contour

    (n) onset

    (o) coda

    (p) suprasegmental feature

    (q) intonation

    (r) slip of the tongue

    (s) phonology

    (t) phoneme

    (u) allophone

    (v) distinctive feature

(w) minimal pair

(x) complementary distribution

2. Into what areas does the study of sound systems fall?

3. What is the goal of phonetic description?

4. List the English vowel phones and define them in articulatory terms.

5. List the English consonant phones and define them in articulatory terms.

6. Transcribe phonetically the following words.
    (a) lip
    (b) pill
    (c) spill
    (d) kilt
    (e) easy
    (f) breezy
    (g) price

7. Using tree diagrams show the stress patterns of the following words.
    (a) tremor
    (b) correct
    (c) correction
    (d) error
    (e) interesting
    (f) lovingly
    (g) friendliness

8. Provide three minimal pairs to show that each of the following contrasts have phonemic status in English. Use distinctive features to pinpoint the nature of the contrast.
    (a) /p/ ~ /t/
    (b) /č/ ~ /k:/
    (c) /k/ ~ /g/
    (d) /s/ ~ /ʃ/
    (e) /r/ ~ /l/
    (f) /m/ ~ /n/

9. Identify words in which each of the following sounds or clusters is (probably) sound symbolic.
    (a) /ʃ/ (as in *shin*)
    (b) /pl/
    (c) /fl/
    (d) /kr/
    (g) /sw/
    (h) /k/
    (i) /m/
    (j) /r/
    (k) /w/

10. Give examples of slips of the tongue in English or any other language you know.

CHAPTER 4

1. Define the following notions in your own words.
    (a) morphology
    (b) morpheme
    (c) allomorph
    (d) lexeme
    (e) grammatical morpheme
    (f) segmentation
    (g) bound morpheme
    (h) free morpheme
    (i) inflectional morpheme
    (j) derivational morpheme
    (k) affix
    (l) prefix
    (m) suffix
    (n) infix
    (o) circumfix
    (p) unmarked category
    (q) marked category
    (r) isolating language
    (s) agglutinative language

2. What are some popular misconceptions about what a *word* is?

3. If you know another language, translate Sapir's sentence *He will give it to you*, and then compare your translation with the translations in the aboriginal languages.

4. Give your own examples of the operation of Zipf's Law in word formation.

5. Identify fully the morphemes in the following words.
    (a) friendliness ³
    (b) predictable ²
    (c) incomprehensible
    (d) truthfully
    (e) insincere
    (f) unlikely
    (g) survival
    (h) aforementioned
    (i) verisimilitude
    (j) speedy
    (k) speedier
    (l) dysfunctional
    (m) congruous
    (n) headmistress

6. Using tree diagrams, show the morphemic structure of the words above.

7. Identify the allomorphs in the set of oppositions below, writing an appropriate complementary distribution rule.
    (a) legitimate – illegitimate
    (b) regular – irregular
    (c) complete – incomplete
    (d) sure – unsure
    (e) clear – unclear
    (f) typical – untypical
    (g) friendly – unfriendly

8. Identify the affix in each word, if any, explaining its meaning or function.
    (a) deduce
    (b) induce

(c) produce
(d) reduce
(e) betterment
(f) enjoyment
(g) childish
(h) iffy
(i) mice
(j) lice

9. Discuss the differences between isolating and agglutinative languages. Can you give examples of language of both types?

10. Do you think that the concept of universal or artificial language is useful? Explain your answer. How would you design a universal language if requested to do so?

CHAPTER 5

1. Define the following terms and notions in your own words.
   (a) syntax
   (b) sentence
   (c) phrase structure
   (d) lexicon
   (e) subject
   (f) object
   (g) lexical insertion
   (h) universal grammar
   (i) subcategorization
   (j) grammar
   (k) subordination
   (l) coordination

2. Underline the actors and actions in the following text, relating them to each other in syntactic terms.

   My general theory since 1971 has been that the word is literally a virus, and that it has not been recognised as such because it has achieved a state of relatively stable symbiosis with its human host; that is to say, the word virus (the Other Half) has established

itself so firmly as an accepted part of the human organism that it
can now sneer at gangster viruses like smallpox and turn them in
to the Pasteur Institute.

William Burroughs (1914–)

3. Now identify the various kinds of coordination and subordination
    relationships in the following text:

I am a dreamer of words, of written words. I think I am reading;
a word stops me. I leave the page. The syllables of the word
begin to move around. Stressed accents begin to invert. The
word abandons its meaning like an overload which is too heavy
and prevents dreaming. Then words take on other meanings as if
they had the right to be young. And the words wander away,
looking in the nooks and crannies of vocabulary for new company,
bad company.

Gaston Bachelard (1884–1962)

4. Graph the sentence structure of the following sentences using tree diagrams.
    Identify any symbol (e.g., Adv = adverb) that you might need.
    (a) Jillian's mother is American.
    (b) She is an extremely intelligent girl.
    (c) Those friends always go to the movies together.
    (d) Everyone wants to go to France this year.
    (e) You also watch TV every night.
    (f) I call her every night.
    (g) This book is outstanding.
    (h) Her smile is attractive and it goes a long way.
    (i) His smile is as attractive as hers.

5. Discuss the validity of the notion of *universal grammar*.

6. Collect the editorials of two newspapers that are vastly different in style—
    e.g., a *Daily News/Sun* type and a *Times/Chronicle* type—over a month or
    two-month period. Then compare the sentence structures used and the
    average length of the sentences.

7. What implications can you derive from the above comparison?

8. Do you think you would get the same results in other areas of language
    use?

CHAPTER 6

1. Define the following terms and notions in your own words.
    (a) semantics
    (b) sign
    (c) referent
    (d) denotation
    (e) connotation
    (f) figurative meaning
    (g) metaphor
    (h) locutionary act
    (i) illocutionary act
    (j) perlocutionary act
    (k) lexicography
    (l) metonymy
    (m) irony
    (n) conceptual metaphor
    (o) source domain
    (p) target domain
    (q) topic
    (r) vehicle
    (s) ground
    (t) lexical field

2. Give synonyms, antonyms, hyponyms, and/or homonyms, if possible or relevant, for the following words.
    (a) table
    (b) man
    (c) woman
    (d) idea
    (e) love
    (f) coward
    (g) cagey
    (h) walk
    (i) take
    (j) gladly
    (k) well

3. Give connotative uses of the following words.
    (a) dog
    (b) tail
    (c) wing
    (d) foot
    (e) song

4. Identify each utterance as locutionary, illocutionary, or perlocutionary.
    (a) Really? *ill*
    (b) It's not true.
    (c) My friend lives in Italy. *Loc*
    (d) Tell me all that you know. *Loc*
    (e) Quiet! *Per*
    (f) What time is it?
    (g) My name is Alexander. *Loc*

5. Establish the least number of semantic features that will be needed to keep each set of words distinct.

    (a)
    mouth
    arm
    hair (on the head)
    neck
    body
    finger
    face
    forehead
    leg
    knee
    elbow
    cheek
    lip
    tongue
    hand
    nose
    eye
    ear
    chest

foot
shoulder
head
fingernail

(b)
mother
father
son
daughter
brother
sister
grandfather
grandmother
uncle
aunt
cousin (male)
cousin (female)

6. Indicate if the following pairs of items are synonyms, antonyms, homonyms, or hyponyms.
    (a) happy – content *syn*
    (b) ugly – beautiful *ant*
    (c) bull – animal *hyponym*
    (d) son **distribution**family
    (e) always – never *ant*
    (f) motorcycle – vehicle *hyponym*
    (g) in front – facing *syn*

7. Identify the source from which the following names are derived.
    (a) John
    (b) Mary
    (c) Alexander
    (d) Sarah
    (e) Sunny
    (f) Tiberius
    (g) Violet
    (h) Blanche

8. Identify the source of the following surnames.
    (a) Rivers
    (b) Singer
    (c) Cardinal
    (d) Green
    (e) Dickenson

9. In the following metaphorical utterances identify the topics and the vehicles. Then paraphrase the ground (meaning) of each utterance.
    (a) He's a lightning rod.
    (b) Mary's a real fox.
    (c) My house is a hole.
    (d) My computer is a treasure.
    (e) My life is a hell.

10. Give the conceptual metaphor that underlies each set of statements.

    (a)
    He has a few cogs missing from his mind.
    My mind isn't working.
    My memory system has broken down.

    (b)
    Ours is a deep friendship.
    Their friendship is hardly superficial.
    My friend and I have a profound relation.

11. Give potential source domains for delivering the following concepts, providing one or two examples for each.
    (a) love
    (b) hope
    (c) justice
    (d) time
    (e) wisdom
    (f) ideas
    (g) hate

12. Explain the difference among metaphor, metonymy, and irony. Give examples of the latter two.

13. Give examples of gesticulants that might be used to accompany the delivery of the concepts in 11 above. Identify the type of gesticulant used.

14. Draw up your own ICMs for [love] and [thinking], comparing the number you derived with the number given in this chapter for each. Then draw up ICMs for the two concepts in any other language you know. Compare the productivity of each concept with the corresponding English concept.

CHAPTER 7

1. Define the following terms and notions in your own words.
   (a) discourse
   (b) calque
   (c) pidgin
   (d) speech community
   (e) communicative competence
   (f) pragmatics
   (g) speech act
   (h) anaphoric device
   (i) cataphoric device
   (j) gambit
   (k) repair
   (l) addresser
   (m) addressee
   (n) message
   (o) code
   (p) context
   (q) contact
   (r) emotive function
   (s) conative function
   (t) poetic function
   (u) metalingual function
   (v) referential function
   (w) phatic function
   (x) borrowing

2. How would a 17-year-old say hello to the following today?
   (a) a peer
   (b) a teacher
   (c) his or her mother or father

3. What kind of social function or effect would the following utterances have?
   (a) Be quiet!
   (b) Wait here!
   (c) Where are you going?
   (d) Who's that person?
   (e) Hi, Paul!
   (f) Here are Laurie, Paul, Kate, and Mary!
   (g) Hi, all!

4. Provide a script for carrying out the following functions.
   (a) Asking a policeman directions to find a street
   (b) Answering the phone
   (c) Making an appointment with a doctor
   (d) Asking a bank teller to make a deposit

5. Identify the communicative function(s) of each utterance. Use Jakobson's typology.
   (a) Hi, Claudia. How are you?
   (b) I've got a headache!
   (c) See you tomorrow!
   (d) Good morning.
   (e) Good night.
   (f) I don't like opera.

6. Rewrite the following passage using appropriate anaphoric, cataphoric, and other kinds of conversational devices that would render it more cohesive and stylistically appropriate.

   Mack loves Julie. Yesterday Mack saw Julie, as Julie was walking on the street. Mack has known Julie for four years, and now Mack is in love with Julie. Mack called out to Julie, and then Mack gave Julie a kiss. Mack gave Julie a kiss because Mack loves Julie. But Julie doesn't love Mack, so Julie did not appreciate the kiss.

7. Underline and identify the anaphoric and cataphoric devices in each of the following.
    (a) Mary likes the CD I bought her yesterday.
    (b) I gave it to Sarah, that is, the cup.
    (c) Who ate the slice? I ate it.
    (d) When did you go to Venice? I went there five years ago.

8. Identify the type of gambit used in the following utterances, along with its function.
    (a) Yeah…yeah…
    (b) I get it, you know?
    (c) You agree, don't you?
    (d) Allow me…

9. Explain the role of phatic communion in a speech community. Give examples of words and phrases that are used in English discourse in a phatic way.

10. Do you know of any features in English, or any language you speak, that are markers of:
    (a) age?
    (b) ethnicity?
    (c) sex?
    (d) social class?

11. Define each one of the following, giving examples of each from any language you know.
    (a) calque
    (b) slang
    (c) jargon
    (d) loanword
    (e) nativization

CHAPTER 8

1. Do you agree with the Whorfian Hypothesis? Explain your answer.

2. Make a list of all the emotions designated by color terms in English or any language you speak, giving a probable reason why the terms and the emotions were linked in the first place.

3. Look up color terms in other languages. Compare them to English terms. What conclusions can you glean from the comparison?

4. Give examples of any symbolic or ritualistic practices, if any, that ensue from the following two conceptual metaphors.
   (a) [love is a plant]
   (b) [memory is a container]

5. Investigate the pictographic origin of the alphabet characters used in English.

6. Go through a dictionary of a non-Western language. Set up the following categories of vocabulary, translating them and thus comparing them to English. What patterns, if any, do you notice?
   (a) kinship
   (b) occupations
   (c) plants
   (d) animals
   (e) spatial terms

Glossary of Technical Terms

addressee	initiator of a verbal interaction.
addresser	intended receiver of a verbal interaction.
affix	morpheme that is added to another morpheme (e.g., the *ir-* in *irregular* and the *–al* in *national*).
agglutinative language	language characterized in general by words made up of more than one morpheme (one word = several morphemes).
allomorph	variant of a morpheme, i.e., the actual form that a morpheme takes in a phrase: e.g., *a* and *an* are allomorphs of the same indefinite article morpheme, with *a* used before forms beginning with a consonant *(a boy, a girl)* and *an* before forms beginning with a vowel *(an egg, an apple).*
allophone	variant of a phoneme i.e., the actual form that a phoneme takes in a word: e.g., the [l] and [ɫ] sounds are allophones of /l/: the latter occurs at the end of syllables and words *(will, bill),* the former occurs elsewhere *(love, life).*
alphabet	system of symbols, known as letters or characters, whereby each symbol stands for a sound (or sounds) in words.
analytic language	language that depends mainly on word-order to convey meaning.

anaphoric device	word or particle that refers back to a word uttered or written previously in a sentence or a discourse: e.g., the *he* in *Alex says that he likes baseball.*
antonym	word with the opposite meaning of another word: e.g., *night* vs. *day.*
argot	slang of specialized groups, especially criminal.
assimilation	process by which one sound in contact with another assumes one or all of its phonetic properties.

B

beat gesture	gesture accompanying speech by which the hand moves in such a way as to keep beat.
borrowing	process of adopting a word form another language, for general use: e.g., Italian has borrowed the word *sport* from English.
bound morpheme	morpheme that must be attached to another morpheme: e.g., the *un-* and *-ly* in *unlikely.*

C

calque	word-by-word translation of a foreign phrase or expression: e.g., the expression *The Brothers Karamazov* is a calque of the corresponding Russian phrase (the word order in English should be *The Karamazov Brothers*).
cataphoric device	word or particle that anticipates a word in a sentence or paragraph: e.g., the *he* in *Although he likes Italy, Alex is not going this year.*
circumfix	two affixes that are added simultaneously to a morpheme.
coda	end part of a syllable.
cognates	words in different languages that are derived from the same source: e.g., Latin *pater* and English *father*.

cohesive gesture
gesture accompanying speech that aims to tie the meanings in utterance together.

communicative competence
ability to use a language appropriately in social contexts.

commutation test
test comparing two forms that are alike in all respects except one, in order to see if a difference in meaning results: e.g., *pill* vs. *bill.*

comparative grammar
early school of the language sciences based on comparing forms in languages to see if they are related.

complementary distribution
process whereby allophones of the same phoneme occur in different environments: e.g., in English [pʰ] occurs in word-initial position followed by a vowel *(pin, pill)*, whereas [p] occurs in all other positions *(spin, spill, prize, cap).*

conative function
the effect a message has or is intended to have on its receiver.

conceptual metaphor
generalized metaphorical formula: e.g., [people are animals] underlies *He's a dog, She's a cat*, etc.

connotation
extensional meanings of a word.

consonant
sound produced with some obstruction to the airstream emanating from the lungs.

contact
the physical situation in which discourse occurs.

context
the psychological, social, and emotional relations people assume during discourse.

continuant
a sound produced by not blocking the airstream.

contour
the sound that can come before or after a nuclear vowel in a syllable.

contrast (opposition)
the minimal difference between two elements.

core vocabulary
the basic vocabulary of a language, containing items such as *mother, father, son, daughter*, etc.

cuneiform
wedge-shaped writing that makes it possible to inscribe symbols on hard materials (such as stone).

D

deep structure	level of sentence-formation where basic phrase structure is formed.
deictic gesture	gesture accompanying speech that shows ideas in the utterance as occurring before or after.
denotation	basic meaning of a word.
derivational morpheme	morpheme that is derived from some other morpheme: e.g., *cautiously* is derived from *cautious*.
diachronic analysis	analysis of change in language.
dialect	regional or social version of a language.
dialectology	study of dialects.
discourse	message constructed linguistically in a specific social context.
displacement	feature of language whereby a word evokes what it stands for even if it is not present for the senses to process.
distinctive feature	minimal trait in a form that serves to keep it distinct from other forms.
diversification	process of languages developing from a single language and thus becoming diverse from it.

E

emotive function	speaker's intent during discourse.
endocast	a reconstructed skull providing a model of the actual skull.

F

free morpheme	morpheme that can exist on its own: e.g., the *cautious* in *cautiously*.
free variation	existence of two variant forms: e.g., the pronunciation of the /o/ in *tomato* as either open or close.
function word	a word such as *the* or *and* that has a grammatical function.

G

---

gambit   verbal strategy for initiating or maintaining discourse flow.

generative grammar   analysis of language based on examining the types of rules and rule-making principles by which sentences are generated.

gesture   communication involving hand movement.

glottochronology   determination of time depth, or of the time frame when languages of the same family became separate.

grammar   system of rules for the formation of words and sentences.

ground   meaning of a metaphor.

H

---

hieroglyph   type of pictographic symbol used by the ancient Egyptians.

holophrase   one word utterance employed by children.

homograph   word that is spelled the same as another but with a different meaning: e.g., *port* as in *The ship arrived at the post* vs. *Portuguese port is excellent wine.*

homonym   word that is pronounced or spelled the same as another but with a different meaning.

homophone   word that is pronounced the same as another but with a different meaning: *aunt* vs. *ant.*

hyponym   a word that is inclusive of another: *flower* vs. *rose.*

I

---

iconic gesture   gesture accompanying discourse that aims to actually show the shape of something mentioned in the utterance.

**idealized cognitive model
(ICM)**   amalgam of source domains used to deliver a cultural concept.

ideograph	symbol that is partly pictographic and partly abstract.
illocutionary act	type of speech act that specifies a call to action: e.g., *Come here!*
infix	affix added internally in a morpheme: e.g., the *-li-* in *friendliness*.
inflection	change in the form of a word.
inflectional morpheme	morpheme that results from inflection.
intonation	pitch and tone in language.
irony	word or statement used in such a way that it means the opposite of what it denotes: *What a beautiful day!* uttered on a stormy day.
isolating language	language that forms its words primarily with single morphemes (one morpheme = one word).

J

jargon	slang of specialized groups (e.g., lawyers, doctors, etc.).

L

langue	theoretical knowledge of a language (its rules, its structure, etc.).
lexeme	morpheme with lexical meaning: e.g., the *logic* in *logical*.
lexical field	collection of lexemes that are interrelated thematically (e.g., sports vocabulary).
lexicography	dictionary-making.
lexicon	set of morphemes in a language.
lexicostatistics	mathematical study of time depth, the length of time since two related languages became separated.
linguistic competence	abstract knowledge of a language.
linguistic performance	knowledge of how to use a language.
loanword	word borrowed from another language: e.g., *cipher* was borrowed from the Arabic language.

locutionary act	speech act that entails a referential statement: *Her blouse is green.*
logograph	pictograph that stands for a word.

M

manner of articulation	how a sound is articulated.
marked category	form that is specific and not representative of the entire category.
message	information or intent of a communication.
metalingual function	referring to the forms of language used in discourse: *The word noun is a noun.*
metaphor	process by which something abstract is rendered understandable by reference to something concrete: *Love is sweet.*
metaphoric gesture	gesture accompanying speech that represents the vehicle (concrete part) of a metaphor used in the utterance.
metonymy	process whereby the part stands for the whole: *the White House* for "the American government."
minimal pair	pair like *pill ~ bill*, which differ by only one sound in the same position.
morpheme	minimal unit of meaning: e.g., in *cautiously* there are two morphemes *cautious* and *-ly*.
morphology	level of language where words are formed.
mutual intelligibility	the ability of speakers to understand each other.

N

name	word that identifies a person (and by extension animals, products, etc.).
nativization	process whereby a loanword is reshaped phonetically to become indistinguishable from a native word.
noncontinuant	consonant that is produced through complete blockage of the air stream, e.g., [p], [t].
nonsegmental feature	feature that is not vocalic or consonantal.

nucleus core of a syllable, usually a vowel.

O

obstruent sound produced with a degree of obstruction.
onomastics study of names.
onset part that precedes a nuclear vowel.

P

palatalization process by which a sound becomes a palatal, or more like a palatal.
parole knowledge of how to use a language.
perlocutionary act speech act that entails request for some action: e.g., *Can you call me?*
phatic function use of language to make or maintain social contact: e.g., *How's it going?*
phoneme minimal unit of sound that distinguishes meaning.
phonetics description of how sounds are articulated.
phonology sound system of a language.
phrase structure basic type of word arrangement in the construction of sentences.
pictography use of pictures to represent things, ideas, actions, etc.
poetic function language that aims to have an emotive effect.
point of articulation place in the mouth where a sound is articulated.
pragmatics study of discourse.
prefix affix that is added before another morpheme: e.g., the *il-* in *illogical.*
protolanguage an undocumented language that has been reconstructed.

R

referent what a word refers to.

referential function use of words to refer to something other than the words themselves.

register style of language used in social situations.

repair strategy for correcting a misused language form.

root morpheme morpheme with lexical meaning: the form *logic* in *logically*.

S

segmentation decomposing a form or a phrase into its minimal elements: e.g., the word *illogically* can be segmented into *il-*, *logic*, *-al*, and *-ly*.

semantics study of meaning in language.

sentence minimal syntactic unit.

sign something that stands for something other than itself.

slang socially based variant of a language used by specific groups.

slip of the tongue an error caused by anticipating some word, by preserving the pronunciation of a previous word, by blending parts of words, and so on.

sociolect social dialect.

sonorant voiced sound.

sound symbolism the tendency to use sounds to construct words in such a way that they resemble the sound properties of their referents or to bring out some sound-based perception of meaning.

source domain concrete part of a conceptual metaphor: e.g., the [sweet] in [love is sweet].

speech act specific use of language to imply an action.

speech community the group of speakers of a language.

stress degree of force used to pronounce a vowel.

structuralism *p5* *Saussure's approach* type of linguistic analysis aiming to study language as a system of structures.

subcategorization rule that classifies a lexeme according to its potential uses in syntax.

suffix affix added to the end of a morpheme: e.g., the *-ly* in *logically*.

suprasegmental feature	feature that is not vocalic or consonantal (e.g., stress, tone).
surface structure	the actual form that a sentence takes.
syllabary	list of symbols representing syllables.
syllable	minimal breath group in the pronunciation of words.
synchronic analysis	study of language at a particular point in time, usually the present.
synonym	word that has the same (approximate) meaning as another word: *happy – content.*
syntax	study of how sentences are organized.
synthetic language	highly inflectional language that does not depend on word order.

T

target domain	topic of a conceptual metaphor: e.g., the [love] in [love is sweet].
topic	what the metaphor is about: the *love* in *love is sweet.*
transformational rule	rule that transforms deep structure strings into surface structures.
typological classification	classifying languages according to the type of grammatical system they have.

U

universal grammar	set of rule-making principles that define the language faculty.
√ **unmarked category**	default form in a class of forms.

V

variation	process whereby forms vary according to geography, social class, etc.
vehicle	concrete part of a metaphor: the *sweet* in *love is sweet.*

vocalization	process by which a consonant is changed to a vowel.
voicing	process whereby a voiceless consonant is voiced.
vowel	sound produced with no obstruction.

W

Whorfian Hypothesis   theory which posits that a language predisposes its speakers to attend to certain aspects of reality as necessary.

Z

Zipf's Law   theory which claims that language forms are condensed, abbreviated, reduced, or eliminated to minimize the effort expended in producing and using them.

Cited Works and General Bibliography

The works listed here include both those cited directly in this book and those that have been used to glean information of various kinds (but are not cited directly). This list can thus be consulted as general bibliography for further reading in anthropological linguistics.

There is also a very useful website that readers can go to for more information:

http://anthropology.buffalo.edu/WEDA/

It contains an international directory of anthropologists and scholars in related professions. It also includes: (1) e-mail addresses for those who specialize in physical and social science, art history, ancient languages, and classical studies; and (2) the names and mailing addresses of anthropology museums, academic and research institutions, journals, and electronic databases as well.

A

Aitchison, J. (1983). *The Articulate Mammal: An Introduction to Psycholinguistics*. London: Hutchison.

Aitchison, J. (1996). *The Seeds of Speech: Language Origin and Evolution*. Cambridge: Cambridge University Press.

Allan, K. (1986). *Linguistic Meaning*. London: Routledge.

Allwood, J. and Gärdenfors, P. (1998) (eds.). *Cognitive Semantics: Meaning and Cognition*. Amsterdam: John Benjamins.

Alpher, B. (1987). Feminine as the Unmarked Grammatical Gender: Buffalo Girls Are No Fools. *Australian Journal of Linguistics* 7: 169–187.

Andersch, E. G., Staats, L. C., and Bostrom, R. C. (1969). *Communication in Everyday Use*. New York: Holt, Rinehart & Winston.

Andrews, E. (1990). *Markedness Theory*. Durham: Duke University Press.

Anttila, R. (1989). *Historical and Comparative Linguistics*, 2nd ed. Amsterdam: John Benjamins.

Appelbaum, D. (1990). *Voice*. Albany: State University of New York Press.

Aristotle. (1952a). *Rhetoric*. In: W. D. Ross (ed.), *The Works of Aristotle*, Vol. 11. Oxford: Clarendon Press.

Aristotle. (1952b). *Poetics*. In: W. D. Ross (ed.), *The Works of Aristotle*, Vol. 11. Oxford: Clarendon Press.

Armstrong, D. F., Stokoe, W. C., and Wilcox, S. E. (1995). *Gesture and the Nature of Language*. Cambridge: Cambridge University Press.

Arnheim, R. (1969). *Visual Thinking*. Berkeley: University of California Press.

Asch, S. (1950). On the Use of Metaphor in the Description of Persons. In: H. Werner (ed.), *On Expressive Language*, pp. 86–94. Worcester: Clark University Press.

Asch, S. (1958). The Metaphor: A Psychological Inquiry. In: R. Tagiuri and L. Petrullo (eds.), *Person Perception and Interpersonal Behavior*, pp. 28–42. Stanford: Stanford University Press.

Ascoli, G. I. (1882). Italia dialettale. *Archivio Glottologico Italiano* 8: 98–128.

Austin, J. L. (1962). *How to Do Things with Words*. Cambridge, Mass.: Harvard University Press.

B

Barbaud, P., Ducharme, C., and Valois, D. (1982). D'un usage particulier du genre en canadien-français: la féminisation des noms à initiale vocalique. *Canadian Journal of Linguistics* 27: 103–133.

Barbe, K. (1995). *Irony in Context*. Amsterdam: John Benjamins.

Barkow, J. H., Cosmides, L., and Tooby, J. (1992) (eds.). *The Adapted Mind: Evolutionary Psychology and the Generation of Culture*. Oxford: Oxford University Press.

Baron, D. (1986). *Grammar and Gender*. New Haven: Yale University Press.

Baron, N. (1992). *Growing Up with Language: How Children Learn to Talk*. Reading, Mass.: Addison-Wesley.

Barron, R. and Serzisko, F. (1982). Noun Classifiers in the Siouan languages. In: H. Seiler and F. J. Stachowiak (eds.), *Apprehension: Das sprachliche Erfassen von Gegenständenm Teil II: Die Techniken und ihr Zusammenhang in Einzelsprachen*, pp. 85–105. Tübingen: Gunter Narr.

Basso, K. H. (1976). *Meaning in Anthropology*. Albuquerque: University of New Mexico Press.

Basso, K. H. (1990). *Western Apache Language and Culture: Essays in Linguistic Anthropology*. Tucson: University of Arizona Press.

Battistella, E. L. (1990). *Markedness: The Evaluative Superstructure of Language*. Albany: State University of New York Press.

Bauer, L. (1988). *Introducing English Morphology*. Edinburgh: Edinburgh University Press.

Beaken, M. (1996). *The Making of Language*. Edinburgh: Edinburgh University Press.

Benedict, H. (1979). Early Lexical Development: Comprehension and Production. *Journal of Child Language* 6: 183–200.

Benedict, R. (1934). *Patterns of Culture.* New York: New American Library.

Bennett, T. J. A. (1988). *Aspects of English Colour Collocations and Idioms.* Heidelberg: Winter.

Bergen, J. (1980). The Semantics of Gender Contrasts in Spanish. *Hispania* 63: 48–57.

Bergin, T. G. and Fisch, M. (1984 [1948]). *The New Science of Giambattista Vico.* Ithaca: Cornell University Press.

Berlin, B. and Berlin, E. A. (1975). Aguarana Color Categories. *American Ethnologist* 2: 61–87.

Berlin, B. and Kay, P. (1969). *Basic Color Terms.* Berkeley: University of California Press.

Best, A. (1975). The Comedians' World: Three Methods of Structural Analysis for Free Association Data. *Southeastern Psychological Association Meeting*, Atlanta, March 1975.

Bickerton, D. (1969). Prolegomena to a Linguistic Theory of Metaphor. *Foundations of Language* 5: 34–52.

Bickerton, D. (1981). *The Roots of Language.* Ann Arbor: Karoma Publishers.

Bickerton, D. (1990). *Language and Species.* Chicago: University of Chicago Press.

Bickerton, D. (1995). *Language and Human Behavior.* Seattle: University of Washington Press.

Billeter, J. F. (1990). *The Chinese Art of Writing.* New York: Rizzoli.

Birren, F. (1997). *The Power of Color.* Secaucus: Citadel.

Black, M. (1962). *Models and Metaphors.* Ithaca: Cornell University Press.

Bloom, A. (1981). *The Linguistic Shaping of Thought: A Study in the Impact of Language on Thinking in China and the West.* Hillsdale: Lawrence Erlbaum Associates.

Bloomfield, L. (1933). *Language.* New York: Holt.

Boas, F. (1940). *Race, Language, and Culture.* New York: Free Press.

Bomhard, A. R. (1992). The Nostratic Macrofamily. *Word* 43: 61–84.

Bonner, J. T. (1980). *The Evolution of Culture in Animals.* Princeton: Princeton University Press.

Bonvillain, N. (2003). *Language, Culture, and Communication: The Meaning of Messages.* Upper Saddle River: Prentice-Hall.

Booth, W. (1979). Metaphor as Rhetoric: The Problem of Evaluation. In: S. Sacks (ed.), *On Metaphor*, pp. 47–70. Chicago: University of Chicago Press.

Borsley, R. D. (1991). *Syntactic Theory: A Unified Approach.* London: Edward Arnold.

Bosmajian, H. (1974). *The Language of Oppression.* Washington: Public Affairs Press.

Bosmajian, H. (1992). *Metaphor and Reason in Judicial Opinions.* Carbondale: Southern Illinois University Press.

Botha, R. P. (1989). *Challenging Chomsky: The Generative Garden Game.* London: Blackwell.

Boysson-Bardies, B. de and Vihman, M. M. (1991). Adaptation to Language: Evidence from Babbling and First Words in Four Languages. *Language* 67: 297–319.

Brakel, A. (1983). *Phonological Markedness and Distinctive Features*. Bloomington: Indiana University Press.

Bremer, J. and Roodenburg, H. (1991) (eds.). *A Cultural History of Gesture*. Ithaca: Cornell University Press.

Britton, J. (1970). *Language and Learning*. Harmondsworth: Penguin.

Brown, P. and Levinson, S. C. (1989). *Politeness: Some Universals in Language Usage*. Cambridge: Cambridge University Press.

Brown, R. L. (1967). *Wilhelm von Humboldt's Conception of Linguistic Relativity*. The Hague: Mouton.

Brown, R. W. (1958a). *Words and Things: An Introduction to Language*. New York: The Free Press.

Brown, R. W. (1958b). How Shall a Thing Be Called? *Psychological Review* 65: 14–21.

Brown, R. W. (1970). *Psycholinguistics*. New York: The Free Press.

Brown, R. W. (1973). *A First Language*. Cambridge, Mass.: Harvard University Press.

Brown, R. W. (1986). *Social Psychology*. New York: Free Press.

Brown, R. W., Leiter, R. A., and Hildum, D.C. (1957). Metaphors from Music Criticism. *Journal of Abnormal and Social Psychology* 54: 347–352.

Bruce, L. (1984). *The Alamblak Language of Papua New Guinea (East Sepik)*. Canberra: Australian National University.

Brugman, C. M. (1983). *Story of Over*. Bloomington: Indiana Linguistics Club.

Brusatin, M. (1991). *A History of Colors*. Boston: Shambhala.

Buck, C. D. (1949). *A Dictionary of Selected Synonyms in the Principal European Languages*. Chicago: University of Chicago Press.

Bühler, K. (1934). *Sprachtheorie: Die Darstellungsfunktion der Sprache*. Jena: Fischer.

Bühler, K. (1951 [1908]). On Thought Connection. In: D. Rapaport (ed.), *Organization and Pathology of Thought*, pp. 81–92. New York: Columbia University Press.

Bybee, J., Perkins, R., and Pagliuca, W. (1994) (eds.). *The Evolution of Grammar: Tense, Aspect, and Modality in the Languages of the World*. Chicago: University of Chicago Press.

C

Candland, D. K. (1993). *Feral Children and Clever Animals*. Oxford: Oxford University Press.

Carmichael, L., Hogan, H. P., and Walter, A. A. (1932). An Experimental Study of the Effect of Language on Visually Perceived Form. *Journal of Experimental Psychology* 15: 73–86.

Cartmill, M., Pilbeam, D., and Isaac, G. (1986). One Hundred Years of Paleoanthropology. *American Scientist* 74: 410–420.

Casad, E. H. (1996) (ed.). *Cognitive Linguistics in the Redwoods: The Expansion of a New Paradigm in Linguistics*. Berlin: Mouton de Gruyter.

Cassirer, E. A. (1946). *Language and Myth*. New York: Dover.

Casson, R. W. (1981). Folk Classification: Relativity and Universality. In: R. W. Casson (ed.), *Language, Culture, and Cognition*, pp. 75–89. New York: Macmillan.

Chafe, W. (1963). *Handbook of the Seneca Language*. Albany: State Museum.

Chambers, J. K. and Trudgill, P. (1998). *Dialectology*, 2nd ed. Cambridge: Cambridge University Press.

Cherry, C. (1957). *On Human Communication*. Cambridge, Mass.: MIT Press.

Cherwitz, R. and Hikins, J. (1986). *Communication and Knowledge: An Investigation in Rhetorical Epistemology*. Columbia: University of South Carolina Press.

Chomsky, N. (1957). *Syntactic Structures*. The Hague: Mouton.

Chomsky, N. (1965). *Aspects of the Theory of Syntax*. Cambridge, Mass.: MIT Press.

Chomsky, N. (1975). *Reflections on Language*. New York: Pantheon.

Chomsky, N. (1982). *Some Concepts and Consequences of the Theory of Government and Binding*. Cambridge, Mass.: MIT Press.

Chomsky, N. (1986). *Knowledge of Language: Its Nature, Origin, and Use*. New York: Praeger.

Chomsky, N. (1990). Language and Mind. In: D. H. Mellor (ed.), *Ways of Communicating*, pp. 56–80. Cambridge: Cambridge University Press.

Chomsky, N. (1995). *The Minimalist Program*. Cambridge, Mass.: MIT Press.

Chomsky, N. (2000). *New Horizons in the Study of Language and Mind*. Cambridge: Cambridge University Press.

Chomsky, N. (2002). *On Nature and Language*. Cambridge: Cambridge University Press.

Clark, E. V. (1993). *The Lexicon in Acquisition*. Cambridge: Cambridge University Press.

Cole, K. C. (1984). *Sympathetic Vibrations*. New York: Bantam.

Conklin, H. (1955). Hanonóo Color Categories. *Southwestern Journal of Anthropology* 11: 339–344.

Corbett, G. (1991). *Gender*. Cambridge: Cambridge University Press.

Coulmas, F. (1989). *The Writing Systems of the World*. Oxford: Blackwell.

Craig, C. (1986) (ed.). *Noun Classes and Categorization*. Amsterdam: John Benjamins.

Crawford, M. (1995). *Talking Difference: On Gender and Language*. Thousand Oaks: Sage.

Croft, W. (1991). *Syntactic Categories and Grammatical Relations*. Chicago: University of Chicago Press.

Croft, W. (1994). Semantic Universals in Classifier Systems. *Word* 45: 145–171.

Crystal, D. (1987). *The Cambridge Encyclopedia of Language*. Cambridge: Cambridge University Press.

Cumming, R. and Porter, T. (1990). *The Colour Eye*. London: BBC.

Curat, H. (1981). Psychosémiologie du genre des substantifs en français moderne. *Canadian Journal of Linguistics* 26: 171–178.

Curtis, S. (1977). *Genie: A Psycholinguistic Study of a Modern-day "Wild Child."* New York: Academic.

Cutting, J. (2002). *Pragmatics and Discourse*. London: Routledge.

D

D'Andrade, R. (1995). *The Development of Cognitive Anthropology.* Cambridge: Cambridge University Press.

D'Andrade, R. and Strauss, C. (1992) (eds.). *Human Motives and Cultural Models.* Cambridge: Cambridge University Press.

Dance, F. (1967). *Human Communication Theory.* New York: Holt, Rinehart & Winston.

Dane, J. A. (1991). *The Critical Mythology of Irony.* Athens: University of Georgia Press.

Danesi, M. (1987). *Robert A. Hall and American Structuralism.* Lake Bluff: Jupiter Press.

Danesi, M. (1993). *Vico, Metaphor, and the Origin of Language.* Bloomington: Indiana University Press.

Daniels, P. T. and Bright, W. (1995) (eds.). *The World's Writing Systems.* Oxford: Oxford University Press.

Davidoff, J. (1991). *Cognition through Color.* Cambridge, Mass.: MIT Press.

De Laguna, G. A. (1927). *Speech: Its Function and Development.* Bloomington: Indiana University Press.

Deacon, T. W. (1997). *The Symbolic Species: The Co-Evolution of Language and the Brain.* New York: Norton.

Deane, P. (1992). *Grammar in Mind and Brain: Explorations in Cognitive Syntax.* Berlin: Mouton de Gruyter.

Dennett, D. C. (1991). *Consciousness Explained.* Boston: Little, Brown.

Denny, J. P. and Creider, C. A. (1976). The Semantics of Noun Classes in Proto-Bantu. *Studies in African Linguistics* 7: 1–30.

Descartes, R. (1637). *Essaies philosophiques.* Leyden: L'imprimerie de Ian Maire.

Diamond, A. A. (1959). *The History and Origin of Language.* New York: Philosophical Library.

Dirven, R. and Verspoor, M. (1998). *Cognitive Exploration of Language and Linguistics.* Amsterdam: John Benjamins.

Dixon, R. M. (1982). *Where Have All the Adjectives Gone?* The Hague: Mouton.

Duchan, J. F., Bruder, G. A., and Hewitt, L. E. (1995) (eds.). *Deixis in Narrative: A Cognitive Science Perspective.* Hillsdale: Lawrence Erlbaum Associates.

Dunbar, R. (1997). *Grooming, Gossip, and the Evolution of Language.* Cambridge, Mass.: Harvard University Press.

Dundes, A. (1972). Seeing Is Believing. *Natural History* 81: 9–12.

E

Eckman, F. R. et al. (1983) (eds.). *Markedness.* New York: Plenum.

Edie, J. M. (1976). *Speaking and Meaning: The Phenomenology of Language.* Bloomington: Indiana University Press.

Edwards, D. (1997). *Discourse and Cognition.* London: Sage.

Elcock, D. (1960). *The Romance Languages*. London: Faber.

Ellis, R. and McClintock, A. (1990). *If You Take My Meaning: Theory into Practice in Human Communication*. London: Arnold.

Emantian, M. (1995). Metaphor and the Expression of Emotion: The Value of Cross-Cultural Perspectives. *Metaphor and Symbolic Activity* 10: 163–182.

Emmorey, K. and Reilly, J. (1995) (eds.). *Language, Gesture, and Space*. Hillsdale: Lawrence Erlbaum Associates.

Espes Brown, J. (1992). Becoming Part of It. In: D. M. Dooling and P. Jordan-Smith (eds.), *I Become Part of It: Sacred Dimensions in Native American Life*, pp. 1–15. New York: HarperCollins.

Everaert, M. et al. (1995). *Idioms: Structural and Psychological Perspectives*. Mahwah: Lawrence Erlbaum Associates.

F

Fairclough, N. (1995). *Critical Discourse Analysis: The Critical Study of Language*. London: Longman.

Farb, P. (1974). *Word Play*. New York: Bantam.

Fauconnier, G. (1985). *Mental Spaces*. Cambridge: Cambridge University Press.

Fauconnier, G. (1997). *Mappings in Thought and Language*. Cambridge: Cambridge University Press.

Fauconnier, G. and Sweetser, E. (eds.) (1996). *Spaces, Worlds, and Grammar*. Chicago: University of Chicago Press.

Fauconnier, G. and Turner, M. (2002). *The Way We Think: Conceptual Blending and the Mind's Hidden Complexities*. New York: Basic.

Ferguson, C. A. (1959). Diglossia. *Word* 15: 325–340.

Fernandez, J. W. (1991) (ed.). *Beyond Metaphor: The Theory of Tropes in Anthropology*. Stanford: Stanford University Press.

Firth, J. R. (1957). *Papers in Linguistics: 1934–1951*. Oxford: Oxford University Press.

Fischer, J. L. (1958). Social Influences in the Choice of a Linguistic Variant. *Word* 14: 47–57.

Fogelin, R. J. (1988). *Figuratively Speaking*. New Haven: Yale University Press.

Friedrich, P. (1970). Shape in Grammar. *Language* 46: 379–407.

Friedrich, P. (1986). *The Language Parallax: Linguistic Relativism and Poetic Indeterminacy*. Austin: University of Texas Press.

Frisch, K. von (1962). Dialects in the Language of Bees. *Scientific American* 207: 79–87.

Frisch, K. von (1967). *The Dance Language and Orientation of Bees*. Cambridge, Mass.: Harvard University Press.

Fromkin, V. A. (1973). Slips of the Tongue. *Scientific American* 229: 110–117.

Fromkin, V. and Rodman, R. (1998). *An Introduction to Language*, 6th ed. New York: Harcourt Brace.

Frye, N. (1981). *The Great Code: The Bible and Literature*. Toronto: Academic Press.

Frye, N. (1990). *Words with Power*. Harmondsworth: Penguin.

Fucilla, J. G. (1943). *Our Italian Surnames*. Evanston: Chandler's.

G

Gamkrelidze, T. V. and Ivanov, V. V. (1984). *Indo-European and the Indo-Europeans: A Reconstruction and Historical Typological Analysis of a Protolanguage and Proto-Culture.* Moscow: Tblisi State University.

Gamkrelidze, T. V. and Ivanov, V. V. (1990). The Early History of Indo-European Languages. *Scientific American* 262/3: 110–116.

Gans, E. (1981). *The Origin of Language: A Formal Theory of Representation.* Berkeley: University of California Press.

Gardner, B. T. and Gardner, R. A. (1975). Evidence for Sentence Constituents in the Early Utterances of Child and Chimpanzee. *Journal of Experimental Psychology* 104: 244–262.

Geertz, C. (1973). *The Interpretation of Cultures.* New York: Harper Torch.

Gelb, I. J. (1963). *A Study of Writing.* Chicago: University of Chicago Press.

Gentner, D. (1982). Are Scientific Analogies Metaphors? In: D. S. Miall (ed.), *Metaphor: Problems and Perspectives*, pp. 106–132. Atlantic Highlands: Humanities Press.

Gessinger, J. and Rahden, W. von (1988) (eds.). *Theorien vom Ursprung der Sprache.* Berlin: Mouton de Gruyter.

Gibbs, R. W. (1994). *The Poetics of Mind: Figurative Thought, Language, and Understanding.* Cambridge: Cambridge University Press.

Gibson, K. R. and Ingold, T. (1993) (eds.). *Tools, Language and Cognition in Human Evolution.* Cambridge: Cambridge University Press.

Gill, A. (1994). *Rhetoric and Human Understanding.* Prospect Heights: Waveland.

Gill, J. H. (1991). *Merleau-Ponty and Metaphor.* Atlantic Highlands: Humanities Press.

Givón, T. (2001). *Syntax*, 2 vols. Amsterdam: John Benjamins.

Glucksberg, S. (1988). Language and Thought. In: R. J. Sternberg and E. E. Smith (eds.), *The Psychology of Human Thought*, pp. 214–241. Cambridge: Cambridge University Press.

Glucksberg, S. and Danks, J. H. (1975). *Experimental Psycholinguistics: An Introduction.* New York: John Wiley and Sons.

Goatley, A. (1997). *The Language of Metaphors.* London: Routledge.

Goffman, E. (1978). Response Cries. *Language* 54: 787–815.

Goldberg, A. E. (1996) (ed.). *Conceptual Structure, Discourse and Language.* Stanford: Center for the Study of Language and Information.

Goldwasser, O. (1995). *From Icon to Metaphor: Studies in the Semiotics of the Hieroglyphs.* Freiburg: Universitätsverlag.

Goodwin, C. and Duranti, A. (1992). Rethinking Context: An Introduction. In: A. Duranti and C. Goodwin (eds.), *Rethinking Context: Language as an Interactive Phenomenon*, pp. 1–13. Cambridge: Cambridge University Press.

Goossens, L. et al. (1995). *By Word of Mouth: Metaphor, Metonymy and Linguistic Action in a Cognitive Perspective.* Berlin: Mouton de Gruyter.

Green, K. (1996) (ed.). *New Essays in Deixis, Discourse, Narrative, Literature.* Amsterdam: Rodopi.

Greenberg, J. H. (1966). *Language Universals*. The Hague: Mouton.

Greenberg, J. H. (1968). *Anthropological Linguistics*. New York: Random House.

Greenberg, J. H. (1987). *Language in the Americas*. Stanford: Stanford University Press.

Gregory, B. (1988). *Inventing Reality: Physics as Language*. New York: John Wiley and Sons.

Gregory, R. L. (1970). *The Intelligent Eye*. New York: McGraw-Hill.

Gregory, R. L. (1974). *Concepts and Mechanisms of Perception*. London: Duckworth.

Grice, H. P. (1975). Logic and Conversation. In: P. Cole and J. Morgan (eds.), *Syntax and Semantics*, Vol. 3, pp. 41–58. New York: Academic.

Griffin, D. R. (1981). *The Question of Animal Consciousness*. New York: Rockefeller University Press.

Griffin, D. R. (1992). *Animal Minds*. Chicago: University of Chicago Press.

Grolier, E. de (1983) (ed.). *Glossogenetics: The Origin and Evolution of Language*. Amsterdam: Harwood Academic Publishers.

Grossman, M. (1988). *Colori e lessico*. Tübingen: Narr.

Gumpel, L. (1984). *Metaphor Reexamined: A Non-Aristotelian Perspective*. Bloomington: Indiana University Press.

H

Haas, M. (1944). Men's and Women's Speech in Koasati. *Language* 20: 142–149.

Haegeman, L. (1991). *An Introduction to Government and Binding Theory*. Oxford: Blackwell, 1991.

Hall, K. and Bucholtz, M. (1996). *Gender Articulated: Language and the Socially Constructed Self*. London: Routledge.

Hall, M. B. (1992). *Color and Meaning*. Cambridge: Cambridge University Press.

Hall, R. A. (1971). *Le strutture dell'italiano*. Roma: Armando.

Haller, H. (1999). *The Other Italy: Literary Canon in Dialect*. Toronto: University of Toronto Press.

Halliday, M. A. K. (1975). *Learning How to Mean: Explorations in the Development of Language*. London: Arnold.

Halliday, M. A. K. (1985). *Introduction to Functional Grammar*. London: Arnold.

Hardin, C. L. (1986). *Color for Philosophers*. Indianapolis: Hackett Publishing Company.

Hardin, C. L. and Maffi, L. (1997) (eds.). *Color Categories in Thought and Language*. Cambridge: Cambridge University Press.

Harman, G. (1974) (ed.). *On Noam Chomsky: Critical Essays*. Garden City: Anchor.

Harnad, S. R., Steklis, H. B., and Lancaster, J. (1976) (eds.). *Origins and Evolution of Language and Speech*. New York: New York Academy of Sciences.

Harré, R. (1981). *Great Scientific Experiments*. Oxford: Phaidon Press.

Harris, R. (1986). *The Origin of Writing*. London: Duckworth.

Harris, R. (1993). *The Linguistics Wars*. Oxford: Oxford University Press.

Harris, R. and Talbot, T. J. (1989). *Landmarks in Linguistic Thought: The Western Tradition from Socrates to Saussure*. London: Routledge.

Harvey, K. and Shalom, C. (1997) (eds.). *Language and Desire: Encoding Sex, Romance, and Intimacy.* London: Routledge.

Hayakawa, S. I. (1991). *Language in Thought and Action*, 5th ed. New York: Harcourt Brace Jovanovich.

Heine, B. (1982). African Noun Class Systems. In: H. Seiler and F. J. Stachowiak (eds.), *Apprehension: Das sprachliche Erfassen von Gegenständenm Teil II: Die Techniken und ihr Zusammenhang in Einzelsprachen*, pp. 189–216. Tübingen: Gunter Narr.

Heine, B., Claudi, U. and Hünnemeyer, F. (1982). *Grammaticalization: A Conceptual Framework.* Chicago: University of Chicago Press.

Hewes, G. W. (1973). Primate Communication and the Gestural Origin of Language. *Current Anthropology* 14: 5–24.

Hewes, G. W. (1974). *Language Origins: A Bibliography.* The Hague: Mouton.

Hewes, G. W. (1976). The Current Status of the Gestural Theory of Language Origin. In: S. R. Harnad, H. D. Steklis, and J. Lancaster (eds.), *Origins and Evolution of Language and Speech*, pp. 482–504. New York: New York Academy of Sciences.

Hickerson, N. P. (1980). *Linguistic Anthropology.* New York: Holt, Rinehart and Winston.

Hilbert, D. R. (1987). *Color and Color Perception: A Study in Anthropocentric Realism.* Stanford: Center for the Study of Language and Information.

Hinton, J., Nichols, J. and Ohala, J. J. (1994) (eds.). *Sound Symbolism.* Cambridge: Cambridge University Press.

Hockett, C. F. (1960). The Origin of Speech. *Scientific American* 203: 88–96.

Hoek, K. van (1997). *Anaphora and Conceptual Structure.* Chicago: University of Chicago Press.

Holloway, R. L. (1974). The Casts of Fossil Hominid Brains. *Scientific American* 23: 106–115.

Holloway, R. L. and LaCoste-LeRaymondie, M. C. de (1982). Brain Endocast Asymmetry in Pongids and Hominids: Some Preliminary Findings on the Paleontology of Cerebral Dominance. *American Journal of Physical Anthropology* 58: 108–110.

Holm, J. A. (1989). *Pidgins and Creoles.* Cambridge: Cambridge University Press.

Huck, G. and Goldsmith, J. A. (1995). *Ideology and Linguistic Theory: Noam Chomsky and the Deep Structure Debates.* London: Routledge.

Hughes, G. (1991). *Swearing.* London: Blackwell.

Humboldt, W. von (1836 [1988]). *On Language: The Diversity of Human Language-Structure and Its Influence on the Mental Development of Mankind*, P. Heath (trans.). Cambridge: Cambridge University Press.

Hutcheon, L. (1995). *Irony's Edge: The Theory and Politics of Irony.* London: Routledge.

Hymes, D. (1971). *On Communicative Competence.* Philadelphia: University of Pennsylvania Press.

I

Ibrahim, M. H. (1973). *Grammatical Gender: Its Origin and Development.* The Hague: Mouton.

Indurkhya, B. (1992). *Metaphor and Cognition*. Dordrecht: Kluwer.

Ingham, P. (1996). *The Language of Gender and Class*. London: Routledge.

J

Jackendoff, R. (1994). *Patterns in the Mind: Language and Human Nature*. New York: Basic Books.

Jackendoff, R. (1997). *The Architecture of the Language Faculty*. Cambridge, Mass.: MIT Press.

Jakobson, R. (1978). *Six Lectures on Sound and Meaning*, John Mepham (trans.). Cambridge, Mass.: MIT Press.

Jakobson, R. (1985). *Selected Writings VII*, S. Rudy (ed.). Berlin: Mouton.

Janssen, T. and Redeker, G. (2000) (eds.). *Cognitive Linguistics: Foundations, Scope, and Methodology*. Berlin: Mouton de Gruyter.

Jarvella, R. J. and Klein, W. (1982) (eds.). *Speech, Place, and Action: Studies in Deixis and Related Topics*. New York: John Wiley and Sons.

Jaynes, J. (1976). *The Origin of Consciousness in the Breakdown of the Bicameral Mind*. Toronto: University of Toronto Press.

Jespersen, O. (1922). *Language: Its Nature, Development and Origin*. London: Allen and Unwin.

Johanson, D. and Edgar, B. (1995). *From Lucy to Language*. New York: Simon and Schuster.

Johnson, M. (1987). *The Body in the Mind: The Bodily Basis of Meaning, Imagination and Reason*. Chicago: University of Chicago Press.

Johnson, M. (1989). Image-Schematic Bases of Meaning. *Semiotic Inquiry* 9: 109–118.

Johnson, M. (1991). The Emergence of Meaning in Bodily Experience. In: B. den Ouden and M. Moen (eds.), *The Presence of Feeling in Thought*, pp. 153–167. New York: Peter Lang.

Jones, R. (1982). *Physics as Metaphor*. New York: New American Library.

Joos, M. (1967). *The Five Clocks*. New York: Harcourt, Brace and World.

K

Kakehi, H., Mito, Y., Hayase, M., Tsuzuki, M., and Young, R. (1981). *Nichi-ei taishô onomatope jiten*. Tokyo: Gaku-shobô.

Kaplan, J. and Bernays, A. (1996). *The Language of Names: What We Call Ourselves and Why It Matters*. New York: Simon and Schuster.

Katamba, F. (1989). *An Introduction to Phonology*. London: Longman.

Kay, P. (1975). Synchronic Variability and Diachronic Change in Basic Color Terms. *Language in Society* 4: 257–270.

Kay, P. (1997). *Words and the Grammar of Context*. Cambridge: Cambridge University Press.

Kay, P. and McDaniel, C. K. (1978). The Linguistic Significance of the Meanings of Basic Color Terms. *Language* 47: 866–887.

Kaye, J. (1989). *Phonology: A Cognitive View*. Hillsdale: Lawrence Erlbaum.

Kennedy, J. M. (1993). *Drawing and the Blind: Pictures to Touch*. New Haven: Yale University Press.

Kimura, D. (1987). The Origin of Human Communication. In: J. M. Robson (ed.), *Origin and Evolution of the Universe*, pp. 227–246. Montreal: McGill–Queen's University Press.

Kitcher, P. (1985). *Vaulting Ambition: Sociobiology and the Quest for Human Nature*. Cambridge, Mass.: MIT Press.

Kittay, E. F. (1987). *Metaphor: Its Cognitive Force and Linguistic Structure*. Oxford: Clarendon Press.

Kiyomi, S. (1992). Animateness and Shape in Classifiers. *Word* 43: 15–36.

Klein, W. (1994). *Time in Language*. London: Routledge.

Koch, W. A. (1989) (ed.). *Geneses of Language*. Bochum: Brockmeyer.

Köhler, W. (1925). *The Mentality of Apes*. London: Routledge and Kegan Paul.

Kövecses, Z. (1986). *Metaphors of Anger, Pride, and Love: A Lexical Approach to the Structure of Concepts*. Amsterdam: John Benjamins.

Kövecses, Z. (1988). *The Language of Love: The Semantics of Passion in Conversational English*. London: Associated University Presses.

Kövecses, Z. (1990). *Emotion Concepts*. New York: Springer.

Kramer, C. (1974). Folk Linguistics: Wishy-washy Mommy Talk. *Psychology Today* 8 (1): 82–85.

Kramsch, C. (1998). *Language and Culture*. Oxford: Oxford University Press.

Krantz, G. S. (1988). Laryngeal Descent in 40,000 Year Old Fossils. In: M. E. Landsberg (ed.), *The Genesis of Language*, pp. 173–180. Berlin: Mouton de Gruyter.

Kress, G. (1985). *Linguistic Processes in Sociocultural Practice*. Melbourne: Deakin University Press.

Kroeber, A. L. and Kluckholn, C. (1963). *Culture: A Critical Review of Concepts and Definitions*. New York: Vintage.

L

Labov, W. (1967). The Effect of Social Mobility on a Linguistic Variable. In: S. Lieberson (ed.), *Explorations in Sociolinguistics*, pp. 23–45. Bloomington: Indiana University Research Center in Anthropology, Linguistics and Folklore.

Labov, W. (1972). *Language in the Inner City*. Philadelphia: University of Pennsylvania Press.

Labov, W. (1973). The Boundaries of Words and Their Meanings. In: C. Bailey and R. Shuy (eds.), *New Ways of Analyzing Variation in English*, pp. 340–373. Washington: Georgetown University Press.

Ladefoged, P. A. (1982). *A Course in Phonetics*, 2nd ed. New York: Harcourt, Brace, Jovanovich.

Laitman, J. T. (1983). The Evolution of the Hominid Upper Respiratory System and Implications for the Origins of Speech. In: E. de Grolier (ed.), *Glossogenetics: The Origin and Evolution of Language*, pp. 63–90. Utrecht: Harwood.

Laitman, J. T. (1990). Tracing the Origins of Human Speech. In: P. Whitten and D. E. K. Hunter (eds.), *Anthropology: Contemporary Perspectives*, pp. 124–130. Glenview: Scott, Foresman and Company.

Lakoff, G. (1987). *Women, Fire, and Dangerous Things: What Categories Reveal about the Mind*. Chicago: University of Chicago Press.

Lakoff, G. and Johnson, M. (1980). *Metaphors We Live By*. Chicago: Chicago University Press.

Lakoff, G. and Johnson, M. (1999). *Philosophy in the Flesh: The Embodied Mind and Its Challenge to Western Thought*. New York: Basic.

Lakoff, G. and Turner, M. (1989). *More than Cool Reason: A Field Guide to Poetic Metaphor*. Chicago: University of Chicago Press.

Lakoff, R. (1975). *Language and Woman's Place*. New York: Harper and Row.

Lamb, T. and Bourriau, J. (1995) (eds.). *Colour: Art and Science.* Cambridge: Cambridge University Press.

Landesman, C. (1989). *Color and Consciousness: An Essay in Metaphysics*. Philadelphia: Temple University Press.

Landsberg, M. E. (1988) (ed.). *The Genesis of Language: A Different Judgement of Evidence.* Berlin: Mouton.

Langacker, R. W. (1987). *Foundations of Cognitive Grammar*. Stanford: Stanford University Press.

Langacker, R. W. (1990). *Concept, Image, and Symbol: The Cognitive Basis of Grammar*. Berlin: Mouton de Gruyter.

Langacker, R. W. (1999). *Grammar and Conceptualization*. Berlin: Mouton de Gruyter.

Leakey, R. E. and Lewin, R. (1978). *People of the Lake: Mankind and Its Beginnings.* New York: Avon.

Leatherdale, W. H. (1974). *The Role of Analogy, Model and Metaphor in Science*. New York: New Holland.

Lee, D. (2001). *Cognitive Linguistics: An Introduction.* Oxford: Oxford University Press.

Lee, P. (1996). *The Whorf Theory Complex: A Critical Reconstruction*. Amsterdam: John Benjamins.

Lees, R. (1953). The Basis of Glottochronology. *Language* 29: 113–127.

Leezenberg, M. (2001). *Contexts of Metaphor*. Amsterdam: Elsevier.

Lehman, W. P. (2002). *Pre-Indo-European*. Washington: Institute for the Study of Man.

Lemay, M. (1976). Morphological Cerebral Asymmetries of Modern Man, Fossil Man, and Nonhuman Primate. In: S. R. Harnad, H. D. Steklis, and J. Lancaster (eds.), *Origins and Evolution of Language*, pp. 349–366. New York: New York Academy of Sciences.

Lenneberg, E. (1967). *The Biological Foundations of Language.* New York: John Wiley.

Levelt, W. J. M. (1989). *Speaking: From Intention to Articulation.* Cambridge, Mass.: MIT Press.

Levin, S. R. (1988). *Metaphoric Worlds*. New Haven: Yale University Press.

Levine, R. (1997). *A Geography of Time: The Temporal Misadventures of a Social Psychologist or How Every Culture Keeps Time Just a Little Bit Differently.* New York: Basic.

Lévi-Strauss, C. (1958). *Structural Anthropology.* New York: Basic Books.

Libert, A. (2000). *A Priori Artificial Languages.* Münich: Lincom.

Lieberman, P. (1972). *The Speech of Primates.* The Hague: Mouton.

Lieberman, P. (1975). *On the Origins of Language.* New York: MacMillan.

Lieberman, P. (1984). *The Biology and Evolution of Language.* Cambridge, Mass.: Harvard University Press.

Lieberman, P. (1991). *Uniquely Human: The Evolution of Speech, Thought, and Selfless Behavior.* Cambridge, Mass.: Harvard University Press.

Lieberman, P. (2000). *Human Language and Our Reptilian Brain.* Cambridge, Mass.: Harvard University Press.

Linden, E. (1986). *Silent Partners: The Legacy of the Ape Language Experiments.* New York: Signet.

Lucy, J. A. (1992). *Language Diversity and Thought: A Reformulation of the Linguistic Relativity Hypothesis.* Cambridge: Cambridge University Press.

Lucy, J. A. (1994). *Grammatical Categories and Cognition: A Case Study of the Linguistic Relativity Hypothesis.* Cambridge: Cambridge University Press.

Lucy, J. A. and Schweder, R. A. (1979). Whorf and His Critics: Linguistic and Nonlinguistic Influences on Color Memory. *American Anthropologist* 81: 581–607.

Lumsden, C. J. and Wilson, E. O. (1983). *Promethean Fire: Reflections on the Origin of Mind.* Cambridge, Mass.: Harvard University Press.

Luria, A. R. (1970). *Traumatic Aphasia.* New York: Humanities Press.

Lyons, J. (1977). *Semantics.* Cambridge: Cambridge University Press.

Lyons, J. (1991). *Chomsky,* 2nd ed. London: Fontana.

M

MacCormac, E. (1976). *Metaphor and Myth in Science and Religion.* Durham: Duke University Press.

MacCormac, E. (1985). *A Cognitive Theory of Metaphor.* Cambridge, Mass.: MIT Press.

MacLaury, R. (1989). Zapotec Body-Part Locatives: Prototypes and Metaphoric Extensions. *International Journal of American Linguistics* 55: 119–154.

MacLaury, R. E. (1997). *Color and Cognition in Mesoamerica: Constructing Categories as Vantages.* Austin: University of Texas Press.

Maiden, M. and Parry, M. (1997) (eds.), *The Dialects of Italy.* London: Routledge.

Malinowski, B. (1922). *Argonauts of the Western Pacific.* New York: Dutton.

Malinowski, B. (1929). *The Sexual Life of Savages in North-Western Melanesia.* New York: Harcourt, Brace, and World.

Mallery, G. (1972). *Sign Language among North American Indians Compared with That among Other Peoples and Deaf-Mutes.* The Hague: Mouton.

Mallory, J. P. (1989). *In Search of the Indo-Europeans: Language, Archaeology and Myth.* London: Thames and Hudson.

Malotki, E. (1983). *Hopi Time: A Linguistic Analysis of the Temporal Concepts in the Hopi Language.* Berlin: Mouton de Gruyter.

Maratsos, M. (1979). Learning How and When to Use Pronouns and Determiners. In: P. Fletcher and M. Garman (eds.), *Language Acquisition*, pp. 225–240. Cambridge: Cambridge University Press.

Marks, L. E., Hammeal, R. J., and Bornstein, M. H. (1987). *Perceiving Similarity and Comprehending Metaphor.* Chicago: Monographs of the Society for Research in Child Development 215.

Martin, J. H. (1990). *A Computational Model of Metaphor Interpretation.* New York: Academic.

Martinet, A. (1955). *Économie des changements phonétiques.* Berne: Verlag.

Mathiot, M. (1979) (ed.). *Ethnolinguistics: Boas, Sapir and Whorf Revisited.* The Hague: Mouton.

Matthews, P. H. (1974). *Morphology: An Introduction to the Theory of Word-Structure.* Cambridge: Cambridge University Press.

McNeill, D. (1992). *Hand and Mind: What Gestures Reveal about Thought.* Chicago: University of Chicago Press.

Megarry, T. (1995). *Society in Prehistory: The Origins of Human Culture.* New York: New York University Press.

Miller, G. (1951). *Language and Communication.* New York: McGraw-Hill.

Miller, G. A. and Gildea, P. M. (1991). How Children Learn Words. In: W. S.-Y. Wang, (ed.),*The Emergence of Language: Development and Evolution*, pp. 150–158. New York: W. H. Freeman.

Miller, G. A. and Johnson-Laird, P. N. (1976). *Language and Perception.* Cambridge, Mass.: Harvard University Press.

Miller, R. L. (1968). *The Linguistic Relativity Principle and Humboldtian Ethnolinguistics: A History and Appraisal.* The Hague: Mouton.

Milroy, L. (1987). *Analyzing Linguistic Variation.* Oxford: Blackwell.

Morford, J. P., Singleton, J. L., and Goldin-Meadow, S. (1995). The Genesis of Language: How Much Time Is Needed to Generate Arbitrary Symbols in a Sign System? In: K. Emmorey and J. Reilly (eds.), *Language, Gesture, and Space*, pp. 313–332. Hillsdale: Lawrence Erlbaum Associates.

Morris, D. et al. (1979). *Gestures: Their Origins and Distributions.* London: Cape.

Mufwene, S. S. (2001). *The Ecology of Language Evolution.* Cambridge: Cambridge University Press.

Müller, F. M. (1861). *Lectures on the Science of Language.* London: Longmans, Green.

Myers, G. E. and Myers, M. T. (1985). *The Dynamics of Human Communication.* New York: McGraw-Hill.

Myers, R. E. (1976). Comparative Neurology of Vocalization and Speech: Proof of a Dichotomy. In: S. R. Harnad, H. D. Steklis, and J. Lancaster (eds.), *Origins and Evolution of Language and Speech*, pp. 745–757. New York: New York Academy of Sciences.

N

Nespoulous, J. L., Perron, P., and Lecours, A. R. (1986) (eds.). *The Biological Foundations of Gestures: Motor and Semiotic Aspects.* Hillsdale: Lawrence Erlbaum Associates.

Newmeyer, F. J. (1986). *Linguistic Theory in America.* Chicago: University of Chicago Press.

Noble, W. and Davidson, I. (1996). *Human Evolution, Language and Mind.* Cambridge: Cambridge University Press.

Noiré, L. (1917). *The Origin and Philosophy of Language.* Chicago: Open Court.

Nuessel, F. (1991). Metaphor and Cognition: A Survey of Recent Publications. *Journal of Literary Semantics* 20: 37–52.

Nuessel, F. (1992). *The Study of Names: A Guide to the Principles and Topics.* Westport: Greenwood.

Nuyts, J. (2001). *Epistemic Modality, Language, and Conceptualization: A Cognitive-Pragmatic Perspective.* Amsterdam: John Benjamins.

Nuyts, J. and Pederson, E. (1997) (eds.). *Language and Conceptualization.* Cambridge: Cambridge University Press.

O

Ochs, E. (1992). Indexing Gender. In: A. Duranti and C. Goodwin (eds.), *Rethinking Context: Language as an Interactive Phenomenon*, pp. 335–358. Cambridge: Cambridge University Press.

Ogden, C. K. and Richards, I. A. (1923). *The Meaning of Meaning.* London: Routledge and Kegan Paul.

Ong, W. J. (1977). *Interfaces of the Word: Studies in the Evolution of Consciousness and Culture.* Ithaca: Cornell University Press.

Opie, I. and Opie, P. (1959). *The Lore and Language of Schoolchildren.* Frogmore: Paladin.

Ortony, A. (1979) (ed.). *Metaphor and Thought.* Cambridge: Cambridge University Press.

Ortony, A., Clore, G. L., and Collins, A. (1988). *The Cognitive Structure of Emotions.* Cambridge: Cambridge University Press.

Osgood, C. E., Suci, G. J., and Tannenbaum, P. H. (1957). *The Measurement of Meaning.* Urbana: University of Illinois Press.

P

Paget, R. (1930). *Human Speech.* London: Kegan Paul.

Palmer, G. B. (1996). *Toward a Theory of Cultural Linguistics.* Austin: University of Texas Press.

Patterson, F. G. (1978). The Gestures of a Gorilla: Language Acquisition in Another Pongid. *Brain and Language* 5: 72–97.

Patterson, F. G. and Linden, E. (1981). *The Education of Koko*. New York: Holt, Rinehart and Winston.

Payne, D. (1986). Noun Classification in Yagua. In: Colette Craig (ed.), *Noun Classes and Categorization*, pp. 113–131. Amsterdam: John Benjamins.

Pearson, B. L. (1977). *Introduction to Linguistic Concepts*. New York: Alfred A. Knopf.

Pedersen, H. (1931). *The Discovery of Language*. Bloomington: Indiana University Press.

Pei, M. A. (1941). *The Italian Language*. New York: Columbia University Press.

Peirce, C. S. (1931–1958). *Collected Papers*. Cambridge, Mass.: Harvard University Press.

Penn, J. M. (1972). *Linguistic Relativity Versus Innate Ideas: The Origins of the Sapir-Whorf Hypothesis in German Thought*. The Hague: Mouton.

Perrine, L. (1971). Four Forms of Metaphor. *College English* 33: 125–138.

Piaget, J. and Inhelder, J. (1969). *The Psychology of the Child*. New York: Basic Books.

Piattelli-Palmarini, M. (1980) (ed.). *Language and Learning: The Debate between Jean Piaget and Noam Chomsky*. Cambridge, Mass.: Harvard University Press.

Pinker, S. (1994). *The Language Instinct: How the Mind Creates Language*. New York: William Morrow.

Pinker, S. (1997). *How the Mind Works*. New York: Norton.

Pollio, H. and Burns, B. (1977). The Anomaly of Anomaly. *Journal of Psycholinguistic Research* 6: 247–260.

Pollio, H., Barlow, J., Fine, H. and Pollio, M. (1977). *The Poetics of Growth: Figurative Language in Psychology, Psychotherapy, and Education*. Hillsdale: Lawrence Erlbaum Associates.

Pollio, H. and Smith, M. (1979). Sense and Nonsense in Thinking about Anomaly and Metaphor. *Bulletin of the Psychonomic Society* 13: 323–326.

Postal, P. (1964). Boas and the Development of Phonology: Comments Based on Iroquois. *International Journal of American Linguistics* 30: 269–280.

Premack, A. J. (1976). *Why Chimps Can Read*. New York: Harper and Row.

Premack, D. and Premack, A. J. (1983). *The Mind of an Ape*. New York: Norton.

Pretto, A. (1985). Il genere grammaticale. In: A. Franchi De Bellis and L. M. Savoia (eds.), *Sintassi e morfologia della lingua italiana d'uso. Teoria e applicazioni descrittive*, pp. 289–309. Roma: Bulzoni.

Pullum, G. and Laudusaw, W. A. (1986). *Phonetic Symbol Guide*. Chicago: University of Chicago Press.

Pütz, M. and Vespoor, M. H. (2000) (eds.) *Explorations in Linguistic Relativity*. Amsterdam: John Benjamins.

R

Raffler-Engel, W. von, Wind, J., and Jonker, A. (1989) (eds.). *Studies in Language Origins*. Amsterdam: John Benjamins.

Ray, V. (1953). Human Color Perception and Behavioral Response. *Transactions of the New York Academy of Sciences*, Volume 16.

Renfrew, C. (1988). *Archaeology and Language: The Puzzle of Indo-European Origins.* Cambridge: Cambridge University Press.

Révész, G. (1956). *The Origins and Prehistory of Language.* New York: Philosophical Library.

Robins, R. H. A. (1990). *A Short History of Linguistics*, 3rd ed. London: Longman.

Romaine, S. (1984). *The Language of Children and Adolescence.* Oxford: Blackwell.

Rosch, E. (1973). On the Internal Structure of Perceptual and Semantic Categories. In: T. E. Moore (ed.), *Cognitive Development and Acquisition of Language*, pp. 111–144. New York: Academic.

Rosch, E. (1975). Cognitive Reference Points. *Cognitive Psychology* 7: 532–547.

Rosch, E. (1981). Prototype Classification and Logical Classification: The Two Systems. In: E. Scholnick (ed.), *New Trends in Cognitive Representation: Challenges to Piaget's Theory*, pp. 73–86. Hillsdale: Lawrence Erlbaum Associates.

Rosch, E. and Mervis, C. (1975). Family Resemblances. *Cognitive Psychology* 7: 573–605.

Ross, P. E. (1991). Hard Words. *Scientific American* 264/4: 138–147.

Rousseau, J. J. (1966). *Essay on the Origin of Language*, J. H. Moran and A. Gode (trans.). Chicago: University of Chicago Press.

Ruhlen, M. (1994). *On the Origin of Languages: Studies in Linguistic Taxonomy.* Stanford: Stanford University Press.

Rumbaugh, D. M. (1977). *Language Learning by Chimpanzee: The Lana Project.* New York: Academic.

Ruwet, N. (1991). *Syntax and Human Experience.* Chicago: University of Chicago Press.

S

Sapir, E. (1921). *Language.* New York: Harcourt, Brace, and World.

Sapir, E. and Swadesh, M. (1946). American Indian Grammatical Categories. *Word* 2: 103–112.

Sappan, R. (1987). *The Rhetorical-Logical Classification of Semantic Changes.* Braunton: Merlin Books.

Saussure, F. de (1916). *Cours de linguistique générale.* Paris: Payot.

Savage-Rumbaugh, E. S. (1986). *Ape Language: From Conditioned Response to Symbol.* New York: Columbia University Press.

Savage-Rumbaugh, E. S., Rumbaugh, D. M., and Boysen, S. L. (1978). Symbolic Communication between Two Chimpanzees. *Science* 201: 641–644.

Saville-Troike, M. (1989). *The Ethnography of Communication: An Introduction,* 2nd ed. Oxford: Blackwell.

Schlegel, F. von (1849). *The Aesthetic and Miscellaneous Works of Friedrich von Schlegel.* London: Bohn.

Schmandt-Besserat, D. (1978). The Earliest Precursor of Writing. *Scientific American* 238: 50–59.

Schmandt-Besserat, D. (1992). *Before Writing*, 2 vols. Austin: University of Texas Press.

Schogt, H. (1988). *Linguistics, Literary Analysis, and Literary Translation.* Toronto: University of Toronto Press.

Searle, J. R. (1969). *Speech Acts: An Essay in the Philosophy of Language.* Cambridge: Cambridge University Press.

Shevoroshkin, V. (1989) (ed.). *Reconstructing Languages and Cultures.* Bochum: Brockmeyer.

Shevoroshkin, V. (1990). The Mother Tongue. *The Sciences* 30/3: 20–27.

Shields, K. (1979). Indo-European Basic Colour Terms. *Canadian Journal of Linguistics* 24: 142–146.

Skomale, S. N. and Polomé, E. C. (1987) (eds.). *Proto-Indo-European: The Archaeology of a Linguistic Problem: Studies in Honor of Marija Gimbutas.* Washington: University of Washington.

Skousen, R. (1989). *Analogical Modeling of Language.* Dordrecht: Kluwer.

Slagle, U. von (1974). *Language, Thought, and Perception.* The Hague: Mouton.

Smith, C. G. (1985). *Ancestral Voices: Language and the Evolution of Human Consciousness.* Englewood Cliffs: Prentice-Hall.

Smith, J. W. (1977). *The Behavior of Communicating: An Ethological Approach.* Cambridge, Mass.: Harvard University Press.

Smith, N. (1989). *The Twitter Machine: Reflections on Language.* Oxford: Blackwell.

Sontag, S. (1978). *Illness as Metaphor.* New York: Farrar, Straus & Giroux.

Sontag, S. (1989). *AIDS and Its Metaphors.* New York: Farrar, Straus & Giroux.

Spencer, A. (1991). *Morphological Theory.* Oxford: Blackwell.

Sperber, D. (1996). *Explaining Culture: A Naturalistic Approach.* Oxford: Blackwell.

Stam, J. (1976). *Inquiries in the Origin of Language: The Fate of a Question.* New York: Harper and Row.

Stam, J. H. (1980). An Historical Perspective on Linguistic Relativity. In: R. W. Reiber (ed.), *Psychology of Language and Thought*, pp. 239–262. New York: Plenum.

Stross, B. (1976). *The Origin and Evolution of Language.* Dubuque: W.C. Brown.

Surridge, M. E. (1984). Le genre grammatical des emprunts anglais en français: la perspective diachronique. *Canadian Journal of Linguistics* 29: 58–72.

Surridge, M. E. (1985). Le genre grammatical des composés en français. *Canadian Journal of Linguistics* 30, 247–271.

Surridge, M. E. (1986). Genre grammatical et dérivation lexical en français. *Canadian Journal of Linguistics* 31: 267–284.

Surridge, M. E. (1989). Le facteur sémantique dans l'attribution du genre aux inanimés en français. *Canadian Journal of Linguistics* 34: 19–44.

Surridge, M. E. and Lessard, G. (1984). Pour une prise de conscience du genre grammatical. *Canadian Modern Language Review* 41: 43–52.

Swadesh, M. (1951). Diffusional Cumulation and Archaic Residue as Historical Explanations. *Southwestern Journal of Anthropology* 7, 1–21.

Swadesh, M. (1959). Linguistics as an Instrument of Prehistory. *Southwestern Journal of Anthropology* 15: 20–35.

Swadesh, M. (1971). *The Origins and Diversification of Language.* Chicago: Aldine-Atherton.

Sweetser, E. (1990). *From Etymology to Pragmatics: The Mind-as-Body Metaphor in Semantic Structure and Semantic Change.* Cambridge: Cambridge University Press.

T

Tannen, D. (1989). *Talking Voices*. Cambridge: Cambridge University Press.

Tannen, D. (1994). *Gender and Discourse*. Oxford: Oxford University Press.

Taylor, D. M. (1977). *Languages of the West Indies*. Baltimore: Johns Hopkins.

Taylor, J. R. (1995). *Linguistic Categorization: Prototypes in Linguistic Theory*. Oxford: Oxford University Press.

Terrace, H. S. (1979). *Nim*. New York: Knopf.

Teschner, R. V. (1983). Spanish Gender Revisited: -*z* Words as Illustrating the Need for Expanded Phonological and Morphological Analysis. *Hispania* 66: 252–256.

Thomas, O. (1969). *Metaphors and Related Subjects*. New York: Random House.

Thompson, E. (1995). *Colour Vision: A Study in Cognitive Science and Philosophy of Science*. London: Routledge.

Tiersma, P. M. (1982). Local and General Markedness. *Language* 58: 832–849.

Tilley, C. (1999). *Metaphor and Material Culture*. Oxford: Blackwell.

Trabant, J. and Ward, S. (2001) (eds.). *New Essays on the Origin of Language*. Berlin: Mouton de Gruyter.

Trager, G. (1972). *Language and Languages*. San Francisco: Chandler.

Trubetzkoy, N. (1968). *Introduction to the Principles of Phonological Description*, L. A. Muny (trans.). The Hague: Martinus Nijhoff.

Turner, M. (1991). *Reading Minds: The Study of English in the Age of Cognitive Science*. Princeton: Princeton University Press.

Tylor, E. B. (1865). *Researches into the Early History of Mankind and the Development of Civilization*. London: John Murray.

Tylor, E. B. (1871). *Primitive Culture*. London: Murray.

U

Ungerer, F. and Schmid, H.-J. (1996). *An Introduction to Cognitive Linguistics*. Harlow: Longman.

Unterbeck, B., Rissanen, M., Nevelainen, T., and Saari, M. (1999). *Gender in Grammar and Cognition*. Berlin: Mouton de Gruyter.

V

Valentine, T., Brennen, T., and Brédart, S. (1996). *The Cognitive Psychology of Proper Names*. London: Routledge.

Van Dijk, T. (1997) (ed.). *Discourse as Social Interaction*. London: Sage.

Viberg, A. (1983). The Verbs of Perception: A Typological Study. *Linguistics* 21: 123–162.

Vihman, M. M. (1996). *Phonological Development: The Origins of Language in the Child*. London: Blackwell.

Vygotsky, L. S. (1962). *Thought and Language*. Cambridge, Mass.: MIT Press.
Vygotsky, L. S. (1984). *Vygotsky's Collected Works,* R. Rieber and A. Carton (eds. and trans.). Cambridge, Mass.: Harvard University Press.

W

Walker, C. B. F. (1987). *Cuneiform*. Berkeley: University of California Press.
Way, E. C. (1991). *Knowledge Representation and Metaphor.* Dordrecht: Kluwer.
Weinreich, U. (1954). Is a Structural Dialectology Possible? *Word* 10: 388–400.
Weissenborn, J. and Klein, W. (1982) (eds.). *Here and There: Cross-Linguistic Studies on Deixis and Demonstration.* Amsterdam: John Benjamins.
Werner, A. (1919). *Introductory Sketch of the Bantu Languages*. New York: Dutton.
Werner, H. and Kaplan, B. (1963). *Symbol Formation: An Organismic-Developmental Approach to the Psychology of Language and the Expression of Thought.* New York: John Wiley.
Wescott, R. W. (1974) (ed.). *Language Origins.* Silver Spring: Linstok Press.
Wescott, R. W. (1978). Visualizing Vision. In: B. Rhandawa and W. Coffman (eds.), *Visual Learning, Thinking, and Communication*, pp. 21–37. New York: Academic.
Wescott, R. W. (1980). *Sound and Sense*. Lake Bluff: Jupiter Press.
Westphal, J. (1987). *Color: Some Philosophical Problems from Wittgenstein.* Oxford: Basil Blackwell.
Wheelwright, P. (1954). *The Burning Fountain: A Study in the Language of Symbolism.* Bloomington: Indiana University Press.
Whorf, B. L. (1956). *Language, Thought, and Reality*, J. B. Carroll (ed.). Cambridge, Mass.: MIT Press.
Wierzbicka, A. (1990). The Meaning of Color Terms: Semantics, Culture, Cognition. *Cognitive Linguistics* 1: 99–150.
Wilson, F. R. (1998). *The Hand: How Its Use Shapes the Brain, Language, and Human Culture*. New York: Pantheon.
Winner, E. (1988). *The Point of Words: Children's Understanding of Metaphor and Irony.* Cambridge, Mass.: Harvard University Press.
Witkowski, S. R. and Brown, C. H. (1977). An Exploration of Color Nomenclature. *American Anthropologist* 79: 50–57.
Wundt, W. (1901). *Sprachgeschichte und Sprachpsychologie*. Leipzig: Eugelmann.
Wundt, W. (1973). *The Language of Gestures*. The Hague: Mouton.

Y

Yu, N. (1998). *The Contemporary Theory of Metaphor: A Perspective from Chinese.* Amsterdam: John Benjamins.

Z

Zipf, G.K. (1949). *Human Behavior and the Principle of Least Effort*. Cambridge: Addison-Wesley.

Index